12th Workshop on Natural Language Processing for Computer Assisted Language Learning (NLP4CALL 2023)

NEALT Proceedings Series Volume 53

Torshavn, Faroe Islands
22-24 May 2023

ISBN: 978-1-7138-9058-4

Printed from e-media with permission by:

Curran Associates, Inc.
57 Morehouse Lane
Red Hook, NY 12571

Some format issues inherent in the e-media version may also appear in this print version.

Printed with permission by Curran Associates, Inc. (2025)

For permission requests, please contact the Association for Computational Linguistics at the address below.

Association for Computational Linguistics
209 N. Eighth Street
Stroudsburg, Pennsylvania 18360

Phone: 1-570-476-8006
Fax: 1-570-476-0860

acl@aclweb.org

Additional copies of this publication are available from:

Curran Associates, Inc.
57 Morehouse Lane
Red Hook, NY 12571 USA
Phone: 845-758-0400
Fax: 845-758-2633
Email: curran@proceedings.com
Web: www.proceedings.com

Proceedings of the

12th Workshop on Natural Language Processing for Computer Assisted Langauge Learning (NLP4CALL 2023)

edited by
David Alfter, Elena Volodina, Thomas François, Arne Jönsson and Evelina Rennes

Preface

The workshop series on Natural Language Processing (NLP) for Computer-Assisted Language Learning (NLP4CALL) is a meeting place for researchers working on the integration of Natural Language Processing and Speech Technologies in CALL systems and exploring the theoretical and methodological issues arising in this connection. The latter includes, among others, the integration of insights from Second Language Acquisition (SLA) research, and the promotion of "Computational SLA" through setting up Second Language research infrastructures.

The intersection of Natural Language Processing (or Language Technology / Computational Linguistics) and Speech Technology with Computer-Assisted Language Learning (CALL) brings "understanding" of language to CALL tools, thus making CALL intelligent. This fact has given the name for this area of research –Intelligent CALL, or for short, ICALL. As the definition suggests, apart from having excellent knowledge of Natural Language Processing and/or Speech Technology, ICALL researchers need good insights into second language acquisition theories and practices, as well as knowledge of second language pedagogy and didactics. This workshop therefore invites a wide range of ICALL-relevant research, including studies where NLP-enriched tools are used for testing SLA and pedagogical theories, and vice versa, where SLA theories, pedagogical practices or empirical data and modeled in ICALL tools. The NLP4CALL workshop series is aimed at bringing together competences from these areas for sharing experiences and brainstorming around the future of the field.

We invited submissions:

- that describe research directly aimed at ICALL
- that demonstrate actual or discuss the potential use of existing Language and Speech Technologies or resources for language learning
- that describe the ongoing development of resources and tools with potential usage in ICALL, either directly in interactive applications, or indirectly in materials, application, or curriculum development, e.g. learning material generation, assessment of learner texts and responses, individualized learning solutions, provision of feedback
- that discuss challenges and/or research agenda for ICALL
- that describe empirical studies on language learner data

In this edition of the workshop a special focus is given to work done on error detection/ correction and feedback generation. We encouraged paper presentations and software demonstrations describing the above-mentioned themes primarily, but not exclusively, for the Nordic languages.

A special feature in this year's workshop was a shared task on grammatical error detection that was held in connection to the workshop: the MultiGED shared task on token-level error detection for L2 Czech, English, German, Italian and Swedish, organized by the Computational SLA working group. System descriptions from participating teams are included in these proceedings.

Invited speakers

This year, we had the pleasure to welcome two invited speakers: Marije Michel (University of Groningen) and Pierre Lison (Norwegian Computing Center).

Marije Michel is chair of Language Learning at Groningen University in the Netherlands. Her research and teaching focus on second language acquisition and processing with specific attention to task-based language pedagogy, digitally-mediated interaction and writing in a second language.

In her talk, *TELL: Tasks Engaging Language Learners*, she reviewed the most important principles of designing engaging learning tasks, highlighted examples of practice-induced L2 research using digital tools, and showcased some of her own work on task design for L2 learning during digitally mediated communication and L2 writing.

Pierre Lison is a senior researcher at the Norwegian Computing Center, a research institute located in Oslo and conducting research in computer science, statistical modelling and machine learning. Pierre's research interests include privacy-enhancing NLP, spoken dialogue systems, multilingual corpora and weak supervision. Pierre currently leads the CLEANUP project on data-driven models for text sanitization. He also holds a part-time position as associate professor at the University of Oslo.

In this talk, *Privacy-enhancing NLP: a primer*, he discussed the privacy concerns associated with personal data in text documents, particularly in the context of Computer-Assisted Language Learning. He highlighted the presence of lexical and grammatical errors that can inadvertently reveal the author's identity and discussed privacy-enhancing techniques to mitigate these risks. These techniques include text sanitization, text rewriting, and privacy-preserving training. He also presented their own research on data-driven text sanitization, which incorporates explicit measures of privacy risks. Furthermore, he introduced the Text Anonymization Benchmark (TAB) as a tool for evaluating such methods.

Previous workshops

This workshop follows a series of workshops on NLP4CALL organized by the NEALT Special Interest Group on Intelligent Computer-Assisted Language Learning (SIG-ICALL[1]). The workshop series has previously been financed by the Center for Language Technology at the University of Gothenburg, the SweLL project[2],the Swedish Research Council's conference grant, Språkbanken Text[3], L2 profiling project[4], itec[5] and the CENTAL[6].

Submissions to the twelve workshop editions have targeted a wide range of languages, ranging from well-resourced languages (Chinese, German, English, French, Portuguese, Russian, Spanish) to lesser-resourced languages (Erzya, Arabic, Estonian, Irish, Komi-Zyrian, Meadow Mari, Saami, Udmurt, Võro). Among these, several Nordic languages have been targeted, namely Danish, Estonian, Finnish, Icelandic, Norwegian, Saami, Swedish and Võro. The wide scope of the workshop is also evident in the affiliations of the participating authors as illustrated in Table 1.

The acceptance rate has varied between 50% and 77%, the average being 65% (see Table 2). Although the acceptance rate is rather high, the reviewing process has always been very rigorous with two to three double-blind reviews per submission. This indicates that submissions to the workshop have usually been of high quality.

[1] `https://spraakbanken.gu.se/en/research/themes/icall/sig-icall`
[2] `https://spraakbanken.gu.se/en/projects/swell`
[3] `https://spraakbanken.gu.se`
[4] `https://spraakbanken.gu.se/en/projects/l2profiles`
[5] `https://itec.kuleuven-kulak.be`
[6] `https://cental.uclouvain.be`

Country	Count	Country	Count
Algeria	1	Japan	7
Australia	2	Lithuania	1
Belgium	10	Netherlands	4
Canada	4	Norway	16
Cyprus	3	Portugal	6
Czech Republic	1	Romania	1
Denmark	5	Russia	10
Egypt	1	Slovakia	1
Estonia	3	Spain	4
Finland	15	Sweden	78
France	10	Switzerland	13
Germany	110	UK	18
Iceland	6	Uruguay	5
Ireland	2	US	8
Israel	1	Vietnam	3
Italy	11		

Table 1: NLP4CALL speakers' and co-authors' affiliations, 2012–2023

Workshop year	Submitted	Accepted	Acceptance rate
2012	12	8	67%
2013	8	4	50%
2014	13	13	77%
2015	9	6	67%
2016	14	10	72%
2017	13	7	54%
2018	16	11	69%
2019	16	10	63%
2020	7	4	57%
2021	11	6	54%
2022	23	13	56%
2023	18	12	67%

Table 2: Submissions and acceptance rates, 2012-2023

Program committee

We would like to thank our Program Committee for providing detailed feedback for the reviewed papers:

- David Alfter, University of Gothenburg, Sweden
- Serge Bibauw, Universidad Central del Ecuador, Ecuador
- Claudia Borg, University of Malta, Malta
- António Branco, Universidade de Lisboa, Portugal
- Andrew Caines, University of Cambridge, UK
- Xiaobin Chen, Universität Tübingen, Germany
- Frederik Cornillie, University of Leuven, Belgium
- Kordula de Kuthy, Universität Tübingen, Germany
- Piet Desmet, University of Leuven, Belgium
- Thomas François, Université catholique de Louvain, Belgium
- Thomas Gaillat, Université Rennes 2, France
- Johannes Graën, University of Zurich, Switzerland
- Andrea Horbach, FernUniversität Hagen, Germany
- Arne Jönsson, Linköping University, Sweden
- Ronja Laarmann-Quante, FernUniversität Hagen, Germany
- Herbert Lange, University of Hamburg, Germany
- Peter Ljunglöf, University of Gothenburg, Sweden and Chalmers Institute of Technology, Sweden
- Margot Mieskes, University of Applied Sciences Darmstadt, Germany
- Lionel Nicolas, EURAC research, Italy
- Ulrike Pado, Hochschule für Technik Stuttgart, Germany
- Magali Paquot, Université catholique de Louvain, Belgium
- Evelina Rennes, Linköping University, Sweden
- Egon Stemle, EURAC research, Italy
- Francis M. Tyers, Indiana University Bloomington, US
- Sowmya Vajjala, National Research Council, Canada
- Elena Volodina, University of Gothenburg, Sweden
- Zarah Weiss, Universität Tübingen, Germany

- Torsten Zesch, FernUniversität Hagen, Germany
- Ramon Ziai, Universität Tübingen, Germany
- Robert Östling, Stockholm University, Sweden

We intend to continue this workshop series, which so far has been the only ICALL-related recurring event based in the Nordic countries. Our intention is to co-locate the workshop series with the two major LT events in Scandinavia, the Swedish Language Technology Conference (SLTC) and the Nordic Conference on Computational Linguistics (NoDaLiDa), thus making this workshop an annual event. Through this workshop, we intend to profile ICALL research in Nordic countries as weell as beyond, and we aim at providing a dissemination venue for researchers active in this area.

Workshop website

`https://spraakbanken.gu.se/en/research/themes/icall/nlp4call-workshop-series/nlp4call2023`

Workshop organizers

- David Alfter, Gothenburg Research Infrastructure in Digital Humanities (GRIDH), University of Gothenburg, Sweden
- Elena Volodina, Språkbanken Text, University of Gothenburg, Sweden
- Thomas François, Cental, Université catholique de Louvain, Belgium
- Arne Jönsson, Department of Computer and Information Science, Linköping University, Sweden
- Evelina Rennes, Department of Computer and Information Science, Linköping University, Sweden

Acknowledgments

We gratefully acknowledge the financial support from the VR funded project *Grandma Karl is 27 years old: automatic pseudonymization of research data*[7], project id *2022-02311_VR.*
Elena Volodina has been supported by the Swedish Language Bank *Språkbanken Text*[8] and by *HumInfra*[9] through funding from the Swedish Research Council (contracts 2017-00626 and 2021-00176).

[7] `https://spraakbanken.gu.se/en/projects/mormor-karl`
[8] `https://spraakbanken.gu.se/`
[9] `https://www.huminfra.se/`

Content

MultiGED-2023 shared task at NLP4CALL: Multilingual Grammatical Error Detection

Elena Volodina[1], **Christopher Bryant**[2], **Andrew Caines**[2], **Orphée De Clercq**[3], **Jennifer-Carmen Frey**[4], **Elizaveta Ershova**[5], **Alexandr Rosen**[6], **Olga Vinogradova**[7]

[1]University of Gothenburg, Sweden, elena.volodina@svenska.gu.se
[2]ALTA Institute, University of Cambridge, UK, {cjb255,apc38}@cam.ac.uk
[3]LT3, Ghent University, Belgium, orphee.declercq@ugent.be
[4]EURAC Research, Italy, JenniferCarmen.Frey@eurac.edu
[5]JetBrains, Cyprus, elizaveta.ershova@jetbrains.com
[6]Charles University, Czech Republic, alexandr.rosen@ff.cuni.cz
[7]Independent researcher, Israel, olgavinogr@gmail.com

Abstract

This paper reports on the NLP4CALL shared task on Multilingual Grammatical Error Detection (MultiGED-2023), which included five languages: Czech, English, German, Italian and Swedish. It is the first shared task organized by the *Computational SLA*[1] working group, whose aim is to promote less represented languages in the fields of Grammatical Error Detection and Correction, and other related fields. The MultiGED datasets have been produced based on second language (L2) learner corpora for each particular language. In this paper we introduce the task as a whole, elaborate on the dataset generation process and the design choices made to obtain MultiGED datasets, provide details of the evaluation metrics and CodaLab setup. We further briefly describe the systems used by participants and report the results.

1 Introduction

Shared tasks are competitions that challenge researchers around the world to solve practical research problems in controlled conditions (e.g., Nissim et al., 2017; Parra Escartín et al., 2017). Within the field of (second) language acquisition and linguistic issues related to language learning, there have now been several shared tasks on various topics, including:

- argumentative essay analysis for feedback generation[2] (e.g., Picou et al., 2021), where the challenge was to classify text sections into argumentative discourse elements, such as claim, rebuttal, evidence, etc.;
- essay grading / proficiency level prediction (e.g., Ballier et al., 2020), where, given an essay, the major task was to assign a corresponding CEFR proficiency level (A1, A2, B1, B2, etc);
- second language acquisition modeling (e.g., Settles et al., 2018), where the challenge was to predict where a learner might make an error given their error history;

Most prominent, though, have been challenges on so-called grammatical error detection (GED) and correction (GEC), where the task has been to either detect tokens in need of correction, or to produce a correction. Note that the attribute *grammatical* is used traditionally rather than descriptively, since other types of errors (e.g. lexical, orthographical, syntactical) are also targeted. GEC and GED have complemented each other over the years, and the historical interest in the two tasks is visualized in Figure 1. In their comprehensive overview of approaches to GEC, Bryant et al.

[1]The acronym SLA stands for Second Language Acquisition. More information on the working group can be found here: https://spraakbanken.gu.se/en/compsla

[2]https://www.kaggle.com/competitions/feedback-prize-2021/

Elena Volodina, Christopher Bryant, Andrew Caines, Orphée De Clercq, Jennifer-Carmen Frey, Elizaveta Ershova, Alexandr Rosen and Olga Vinogradova. MultiGED-2023 shared task at NLP4CALL: Multilingual Grammatical Error Detection . *Proceedings of the 12th Workshop on Natural Language Processing for Computer Assisted Language Learning (NLP4CALL 2023).* Linköping Electronic Conference Proceedings 197: 1–16.

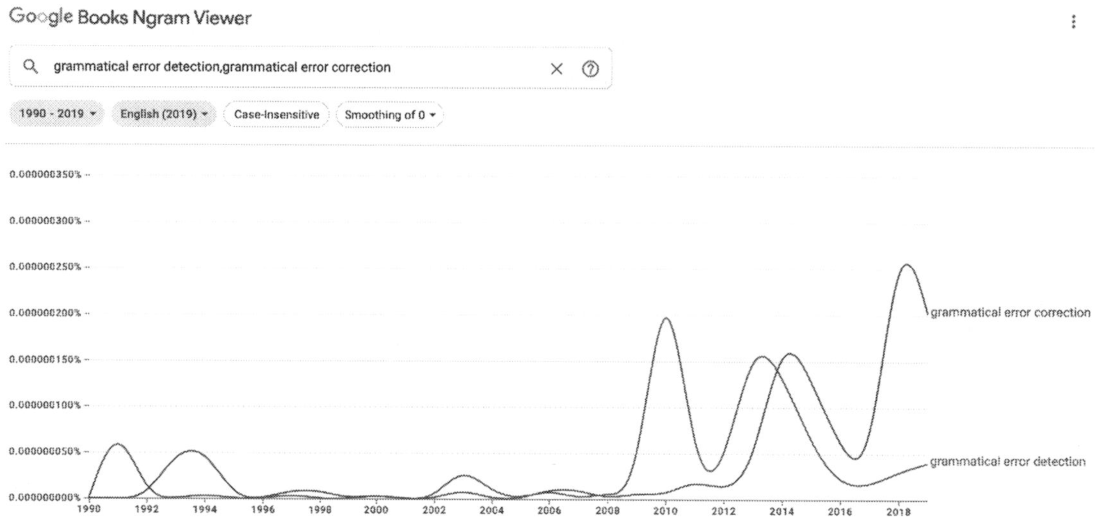

Figure 1: Terms *grammatical error detection* and *grammatical error correction* in Google N-grams (1990–2019)

(2023) observe that most GEC shared tasks have focused only on English, including HOO-2011/12 (Dale and Kilgarriff, 2011; Dale et al., 2012), CoNLL-2013/14 (Ng et al., 2013, 2014), AESW-2016 (Daudaravicius et al., 2016) and BEA-2019 (Bryant et al., 2019), with only a few exploring other languages, such as QALB-2014 and QALB-2015 for Arabic (Mohit et al., 2014; Rozovskaya et al., 2015) and NLPTEA 2014–2020 (Rao et al., 2020) and NLPCC-2018 (Zhao et al., 2018) for Mandarin Chinese.

Though datasets do exist for languages other than English – including for GEC and GED tasks – these rarely feature in shared tasks[3]. Examples of such GEC/GED initiatives are Náplava and Straka (2019) for Czech, Rozovskaya and Roth (2019) for Russian, Davidson et al. (2020) for Spanish, Syvokon and Nahorna (2022) for Ukranian, Cotet et al. (2020) for Romanian, Boyd (2018) for German, Östling and Kurfalı (2022) and Nyberg (2022) for Swedish, to name just a few.

The Matthew effect in GEC and GED? It can be said that the current state of NLP reflects the Matthew effect – i.e., 'the rich get richer, and the poor get poorer' (Perc, 2014; Bol et al., 2018). The Matthew effect has been observed and studied in various disciplines, including economics, sociology, biology, education and even research funding, but is similarly applicable to NLP, as Søgaard (2022) convincingly argued in the article with the provocative title "Should We Ban English NLP for a Year?". The growing bias of NLP research, models and datasets towards English ('the rich') creates inequality by not only making English a 'better equipped language', but also by lowering chances of being cited for researchers working on other languages than English ('the poor'). We witness therefore a tendency in NLP research where reseachers prefer to work on English as it is both the best resourced and best cited language.

To counter-balance the current dynamics in the field towards English dominance, we have taken the initiative to form a *Computational SLA working group* whose main aim is to support and promote work on less represented languages in the area of GED, GEC and other potential tasks in SLA. The MultiGED-2023 shared task is the first one organized by this Computational SLA working group. By bringing non-English datasets, in combination with the English ones, to the attention of the international NLP community, we aim to foster an increasing interest in working on these languages.

2 Task and challenges

The main focus of the first Computational SLA shared task was **error detection**, which we argue should be given more attention as a first step towards pedagogical feedback generation. Through this task, several needs and challenges became clearer which we summarize below.

(i) *Use of authentic L2 data for training al-*

[3] with few exceptions, e.g., UNLP-2023 for Ukranian: https://github.com/asivokon/unlp-2023-shared-task

gorithms. Leacock et al. (2014) convincingly showed that tools for error correction and feedback for foreign language learners benefit from being trained on real L2 students' texts, and that these systems are better suited for use in Intelligent Computer-Assisted Language Learning (ICALL) or Automatic Writing Evaluation (AWE) contexts. Hence the importance of *authentic language learner data*.

(ii) *Focus on less represented languages in GEC/GED*. Both GEC and GED have predominantly been explored in the context of English data. There is a strong incentive to broaden the language spectrum and draw the attention of the international NLP community to other, less represented, languages. We therefore target a few of the less represented languages, namely Czech, German, Italian and Swedish, along with English for comparison with previous work.

(iii) The requirement (i) to use authentic L2 data for the task sets further challenges. First of all, it brings attention to the *scarceness of authentic learner data for a number of languages*. Most languages have modest or tiny collections of L2 data, if any, which contain error annotation and correction. As a consequence, the data is too small to be offered for a shared task by itself. As a way to overcome that problem, we suggest that several languages with smaller datasets coordinate their efforts in a *multilingual low-resource context*, creating possibilities for augmentation of data and/or use of datasets from several languages through domain adaptation, transfer learning, and other modern techniques. The *low-resource context* above refers to a limitation on dataset sizes: there is a maximum of ≈36,000 sentences for each MultiGED language to stimulate creativity in solving problems relating to data scarcity, the smallest datasets comprising ≈8,000 sentences.

(iv) However, (iii) brings further the need to *harmonize datasets* between the languages participating in a multilingual shared task. Harmonization includes both data formatting and data annotation (i.e., converting all language-specific error tags into a set of shared tags). This in itself is a tremendous challenge since languages differ in both linguistic terms and in terms of the annotation approaches and taxonomies adopted by research teams who collated the various corpora. Our initial attempts to convert existing error taxonomies for the five languages to a set of five head categories – punctuation, orthography, lexis, morphology and syntax [POLMS] (Casademont Moner and Volodina, 2022) – proved to be more challenging than expected. As a result, we simplified the task from a multi-class error detection to a binary error detection task, leaving the idea of multi-class detection for future work.

Token	Label	Token	Label
I	c	I	c
saws	i	saws	i
the	c	show	i
show	c	last	c
last	c	nigt	i
nigt	i	.	c
.	c		

Table 1: Data example with two sentences. The sentence on the right demonstrates an error that requires the addition of an extra token, which is indicated by 'i' attached to the next token (see 'i' attached to the token *show* to indicate the missing article *the* before *show*)

MultiGED task in a nutshell The above challenges defined the way the task of *multilingual grammatical error detection in low-resource contexts* was formulated:

> Given an authentic, learner-written sentence, detect tokens within the sentence that contain errors (i.e. perform binary classification on a per-token level) for each provided language separately, or as a multilingual system.

The tokens should be labeled as either correct ('c') or incorrect ('i'), as shown in Table 1.

We encouraged development of multilingual systems that would process all or several languages using a single model, but this was not a mandatory requirement. The submitted systems were evaluated using per-language precision, recall, and $F_{0.5}$ scores. $F_{0.5}$ gives a double weighting to precision over recall, and is conventionally used as the primary metric for GED and GEC on the basis that high precision is more important than high recall for educational applications (Section 4).

The shared task was organized as an open track, in the sense that teams were freely permitted to enhance the provided training and development data for all languages, provided they report the use of additional data, and share them for research

Language	Source corpus	Nr. sentences	Nr. tokens	Nr. errors	Error rate	MultiGED License
Czech	GECCC	35,453	399,742	84,041	0.210	CC BY-SA 4.0
English	FCE	33,243	531,416	50,860	0.096	custom
English	REALEC[*]	8,136	177,769	16,608	0.093	CC BY-SA 4.0
German	Falko-MERLIN	24,079	381,134	57,897	0.152	CC BY-SA 4.0
Italian	MERLIN	7,949	99,698	14,893	0.149	CC BY-SA 4.0
Swedish	SweLL-gold[†]	8,553	145,507	27,274	0.187	CC BY-SA 4.0

[*] We only provide a dev and test set for English-REALEC.

[†] The original SweLL-gold corpus is released under a CLARIN ID+BY+PRIV+NORED license.

Table 2: MultiGED data statistics.

use and replication studies. This contrasts with a closed track shared task, where teams are prohibited from using additional training and development data beyond that provided by the organizers.

The task aimed to promote research into languages which have received less attention in GED or GEC (Czech, Italian, German, and Swedish alongside English), and for which appropriately annotated datasets are available, even if modest in size (8,000 – 36,000 sentences).

Our **main contributions** are three-fold.

1. We present the first shared task on GED that includes original L2 learner data from Swedish, Italian, German and Czech.

2. We introduce a new dataset of Russian learner English, the REALEC corpus, for the first time.

3. We standardize the formats of several multilingual datasets to faciliate development of multilingual models.

3 Data

We provided training, development and test data for each of the five languages: Czech, English, German, Italian and Swedish.[4] Test sets were released during the test phase through CodaLab and are available there for future work and system comparisons.[5] It is important to note that most corpora are made available on a CC BY-SA 4.0 data license, however the English-FCE uses a custom license, and the original SweLL-gold corpus uses a CLARIN PRIV+ID+BY+NORED license.

[4]The training and development splits are available for download on the publicly available MultiGED-2023 github repository: https://github.com/spraakbanken/multiged-2023

[5]https://codalab.lisn.upsaclay.fr/competitions/9784

3.1 Source data

For each language, a MultiGED dataset was generated from a corpus of original error-annotated learner essays. Table 2 provides an overview of the source corpora, and data statistics of the resulting MultiGED datasets expressed in number of sentences, tokens, errors and error rates. Some of the source corpora mentioned in the Table have already been used in Grammatical Error Detection/Correction research, but we also release two new datasets: one based on REALEC (English) and another on SweLL-gold (Swedish). Where possible, we use the same train/dev/test splits as established in previous work (as is the case for GECCC, FCE, Falko-MERLIN), and only create new splits when necessary (REALEC, Italian MERLIN, SweLL). All datasets were derived from error-annotated L2 learner essays. Below, we provide an overview of each of the source corpora used to create these datasets.

Czech The Grammar Error Correction Corpus for Czech – GECCC (Náplava et al., 2022), consisting of 83,000 sentences, is based on native and non-native texts collected in several earlier projects.[6] The native part consists of essays written by children and teenagers attending primary and secondary schools, either (i) native in standard Czech, or (ii) in its Romani ethnolect, and (iii) informal website texts. However, only the non-native part of GECCC is included in the MultiGED datasets: (iv) essays written by learners of Czech as a foreign or second language, collected mostly for the CzeSL project (Rosen et al., 2020) at nearly all levels of proficiency, from beginners to advanced learners[7] (Rosen et al., 2020),

[6]The corpus is publicly available at http://hdl.handle.net/11234/1-4639

[7]The relatively high share of beginners is the reason why the error rate for Czech in MultiGED is higher than for other languages (Table 2).

but also for the Czech section of MERLIN (Boyd et al., 2014). Instead of relying on the manual and automatic error annotations available in CzeSL and MERLIN, errors in spelling and grammar in the entire GECCC were detected and normalized manually, then categorized automatically using the ERRor ANnotation Toolkit – ERRANT (Bryant et al., 2017), which was modified for Czech.[8] The GECCC corpus is available in its raw untokenized form and in M^2 format (Dahlmeier and Ng, 2012). Basic metadata are available about sex, age and L1 family, with links to a richer set.

English-FCE The FCE Corpus (Yannakoudakis et al., 2011) consists of essays written by candidates for the First Certificate in English (FCE) exam (now "B2 First") designed by Cambridge English to certify learners of English at CEFR level B2. It is part of the larger Cambridge Learner Corpus that has been annotated for grammatical errors (Nicholls, 2003). The FCE Corpus has been used in grammatical error detection (and correction) experiments on numerous occasions, including the BEA 2019 Shared Task (Bryant et al., 2019).

English-REALEC REALEC (Russian Error-Annotated Learner English Corpus) is a corpus of essays written by Russian L1 university students in their final English language examinations designed for students at B1–B2 CEFR levels (Vinogradova and Lyashevskaya, 2022). The requirements for the two types of essays in this examination are the same as in IELTS[9] Task 1 and Task 2. The grammar errors in these essays were annotated manually by specially trained students in the Linguistics Bachelor program. The sentences from all essays were shuffled for the MultiGED shared task to avoid any breach of anonymity, and sentences without any errors identified by the annotators were manually double-checked once more. At both stages of annotating errors and processing sentences for the MultiGED shared task, no stylistic improvements were suggested; all sentences remained authentic.

German For German L2 data, we made use of the Falko-MERLIN GEC corpus as introduced in Boyd (2018). Falko-MERLIN involved the amalgamation of the Falko Corpus – specifically the 248 texts from 'FalkoEssayL2' v2.42 and the 196 texts from 'FalkoEssayWhig' v2.02 (Reznicek et al., 2012) – and 1033 texts from the German section of MERLIN v1.1 (Boyd et al., 2014). Both corpora were annotated in a similar fashion, according to guidelines which demanded only minimal corrections for grammaticality. Falko contains essays at a more advanced proficiency level whereas MERLIN covers a broader range of proficiencies.

Italian The Italian data is drawn from the trilingual learner corpus MERLIN, which contains not only Czech and German texts but also 813 Italian written learner productions (letters and emails), collected within the framework of standardised language tests (Boyd et al., 2014). Similar to the German texts, the handwritten originals of the Italian texts in MERLIN were transcribed and normalised manually, with error annotations added on various levels of linguistic accuracy. Like in the German data, for the shared task we also used the provided minimal corrections for grammaticality, which ignore uncommon stylistic choices.

Swedish For Swedish, we used the SweLL-gold corpus (Volodina et al., 2019), that contains 502 essays written by adult learners at different proficiency levels. The essays were manually transcribed, pseudonymized, normalized and correction annotated. Due to the presence of personal information in the texts, the corpus is under GDPR protection[10] and is distributed for individual use on signing an agreement form. For this reason, texts in their entirety cannot be freely distributed, for example, for use in shared tasks. Shuffling of sentences and removal of demographic information was therefore necessary to make SweLL-gold data openly available for the MultiGED shared task.

3.2 Data pre-processing

The starting point for the corpora featuring in MultiGED varied from dataset to dataset. We took steps to reformat and reshape the corpora so that they were in a common format, as described in Section 3.3 and shown in Table 1. This meant that each corpus needed to be transformed into tabular form with one token per row in the first col-

[8]The modified version of ERRANT, potentially useful for related languages, is available at `https://github.com/ufal/errant_czech`. However, error tags produced by ERRANT are not used in the MultiGED dataset.

[9]https://www.ielts.org/

[10]`https://gdpr-info.eu/`

umn and labels in the second column, in line with one of the conventional formats for GED and NLP tasks used more widely. Pre-processing steps for each corpus are described below, starting with the three corpora which have been previously used for GED experiments: Czech GECCC, English FCE and German Falko-MERLIN.

3.2.1 Established GED corpora

For **Czech**, we retained only the learner section of the corpus, which involved first obtaining a list of identifiers for the texts written by L2 learners of Czech (recorded in the 'Domain' field of the metadata file). The GECCC text ID file is aligned with the 'input' file of one sentence per line, but not with the error annotations file (in M^2 format: because M^2 format involves multiple lines per sentence). We therefore attempted to align the original input sentences with the tokenized sentences given in the M^2 file, where tokenization meant that exact matches were often unlikely. We used optimal string alignment as implemented in the `stringdist` package for R (van der Loo, 2014), allowing for a distance up to two-thirds the character length of the original sentence, and breaking any ties manually. Text sequences[11] written by L2 learners were then converted from M^2 to CoNLL format. We used the training, development and test splits already defined in the GECCC.

For the **English-FCE** we started with the M^2 format files made available in the BEA-2019 shared task[12]. The train/dev/test splits are long-established for the FCE Corpus: we simply converted the M^2 files to CoNLL-format and left the splits as they are. To produce files for GED – i.e. with binary error labels – we labelled any token bearing a correction (or following a missing word) as 'i' and all other tokens were labelled 'c'.

Boyd (2018) described the **German** Falko-MERLIN corpus and defined the train/dev/test splits that we use. We obtained the dataset as M^2 files from Adriane Boyd's GitHub repository[13]; note that the data link there carries a security warning and so we made the files available in the German directory of the MultiGED GitHub repository. We converted the M^2 files to CoNLL format[14], and again used the error corrections to arrive at our final token labels, binary 'c' (correct) or 'i' (incorrect).

3.2.2 New GED corpora

Next, we turn to the three corpora which have not previously featured in GED experiments to the best of our knowledge: English REALEC, Italian MERLIN and Swedish SweLL.

Using manually annotated parts of **English REALEC** in .brat format from `https://realec.org/index.xhtml#/exam/`, a tabular representation was produced. Given that the manually annotated subsection of REALEC is relatively small, we only released a development set and a test set for this corpus (i.e., not a training set), randomly assigning each sentence to dev or test. The annotation style in REALEC is different from the other corpora in the shared task: errors are annotated over spans at least one token long. As a result, non-errorful tokens may be included in the span; e.g., [*present-day* rythme $\rightarrow$ the *present-day* rhythm], which means it is less straightforward to precisely map edit labels to tokens. We nevertheless attempted to automatically infer which tokens should be marked as incorrect using heuristics; e.g. by removing unchanged tokens from the peripheries of both sides of the edit span. Because this conversion process became noisier the longer the error span however, we opted not to attempt it for spans longer than eight tokens, meaning that these longer corrections (just 2.9% of the multiword corrections) are left as they are (i.e. all tokens are labelled as incorrect).

For **Italian MERLIN** we started with the Exmaralda[15] files provided with the 2018 release of the MERLIN corpus (v1.1)[16]. The .exb files contain manually corrected tokenisation and annotations on various layers, including span annotations for error annotation and correction, or token level annotation for edit operations, etc. While the corpus contains annotations for both TH1 (i.e. target hypothesis 1, which only contains form-based corrections of linguistic accuracy) and TH2 (i.e. target hypothesis 2, which also contains meaning-based corrections considering semantics) as de-

[11] Note that not all sequences in the corpora are necessarily *sentences* in a grammatical sense (well-punctuated and containing a finite verb at least), which is why we prefer to refer to them as 'sequences'.

[12] `https://www.cl.cam.ac.uk/research/nl/bea2019st/`

[13] `https://github.com/adrianeboyd/boyd-wnut2018/`

[14] The Python script for this conversion process, `m2_to_conll_conversion-script.py`, is available in the MultiGED repository: `https://github.com/spraakbanken/multiged-2023/`

[15] `https://exmaralda.org/en/`

[16] `http://hdl.handle.net/20.500.12124/6`

fined in Reznicek et al. (2013), we only used the aligned original and TH1 layers of the multilayer annotation.

We transferred the aligned layers into a vertical tab-separated table format, marking any corrections in the normal way as 'i' and uncorrected tokens as 'c'. We omitted lines with unreadable tokens in the original (marked with '-unreadable-' in the token layer), segmented the text where we found sentence-final punctuation in order to insert empty lines between sequences, and applied corrections involving token insertion to the following token in the sequence (in the multilayer annotation of Exmaralda these are indicated against empty tokens). We randomly assigned each sequence to train/dev/test with a probability of .8, .1, .1 respectively.

Finally, for **Swedish** we started with the tabular representation of the data first produced by Casademont Moner and Volodina (2022), which was derived from SweLL-gold in JSON format. As part of processing the corpus, we removed $ symbols (indicating illegible characters), replaced the "-gen" marker with a possessive 's' suffix, and randomly selected one of four options wherever we encountered an anonymisation placeholder. For instance, for any occurrence of the "*-hemland" ('homeland') placeholder, we sampled one of {'Brasil', 'Spanien', 'Irak', 'Kina'} (Brazil, Spain, Iraq, China); and for any occurrence of the "*-svensk-stad" ('Swedish town') placeholder, we sampled a made-up place-name from {'Sydden', 'Norrebock', 'Rosaborg', 'Ögglestad'}. Similar fake replacements were made for '*-geoplats' ('geolocation'), '*-plats' ('place'), '*-institution', '*-skola' ('school'), '*-land' ('country'), '*-region', '*-stad' ('town'), '*-linjen' ('transport line').

As a GDPR-related requirement of using SweLL, we randomly shuffled the order of sentences in order to protect individual privacy. We then assigned the sentences to train/dev/test splits with a probability of .8, .1, .1 respectively. As with Italian MERLIN, in SweLL the insertion correction type is marked against an empty token: therefore we carried such annotations forward to the next token, in line with other corpora in MultiGED, and omitted the empty tokens. Subsequently, the usual 'i' and 'c' labels were generated based on the presence of corrections (or not) against each token in the file.

3.3 Data format

MultiGED data is, thus, provided in a tab-separated format consisting of two columns and no headers: the first column contains the token and the second column contains the label (`c` or `i`), as shown in Table 1. Each sequence is separated by an empty line, and double quotes are escaped (\"). Error labels (`i`) are attached on the same line where the errors are, with one exception: if an insertion is necessary, the `i` label is attached to the next token; e.g., the right-hand side of Table 1. System outputs should be generated in the same format.

4 Evaluation

System evaluation was carried out in terms of token-based $F_{0.5}$ to be consistent with previous work in error detection (Bell et al., 2019; Kaneko and Komachi, 2019; Yuan et al., 2021). It has been customary to evaluate GED/GEC systems in terms of $F_{0.5}$, which weights precision twice as much as recall, since the CoNLL-2014 shared task, given that it is more important to an end user that a system makes a correct prediction than to necessarily detect all errors (Ng et al., 2014). Precision (P), Recall (R) and F-score (F_β) were hence calculated in the standard way based on the total number of true positives (TP), false positives (FP) and false negatives (FN) (Equation 1–3) with the parameter $\beta = 0.5$.

$$P = \frac{TP}{TP + FP} \quad (1) \qquad R = \frac{TP}{TP + FN} \quad (2)$$

$$F_\beta = (1 + \beta^2) \times \frac{P \times R}{(\beta^2 \times P) + R} \quad (3)$$

One notable limitation of token-based $F_{0.5}$ is that systems will receive multiple rewards for detecting each erroneous token in a multi-word edit, e.g. [*In other hand* $\rightarrow$ *On the other hand*], when it might otherwise be more realistic to treat such cases as a single error. This approximation is generally acceptible, however, given that multi-token errors are typically much rarer than single token errors, and it may in fact be beneficial to reward systems for the partial detection of multi-token errors. It is nevertheless worth keeping this property of token-based evaluation in mind.

Team	System description
EliCoDe Colla et al. (2023)	XLM-RoBERTa language model pretrained on ≈100 languages with a stacked linear classifier on top, with a dropout layer in-between fine-tuned 5 different models for 5 languages on train (or train+dev) data
DSL-MIM-HUS Ngo et al. (2023)	XLM-RoBERTa language model from the HuggingFace repo pretrained on ≈100 languages, fine-tuned jointly on all MultiGED datasets i.e. there is only one trained model for prediction of all the test datasets
Brainstorm Thinkers	mBERT, for all six datasets
VLP-char (no eng-realec) Ngo et al. (2023)	character-based LSTM model with two recurrent layers, unidirectional supervised approach, separate model for each dataset, REALEC excluded no external datasets
NTNU-TRH Bungum et al. (2023)	multilingual system based on LSTMs, GRUs and standard RNNs with multilingual Flair embeddings for a sequence-to-sequence labeling multitask learning
su-dali (only swe) Kurfalı and Östling (2023)	distantly-supervised transformer-based machine translation (MT) system trained solely on artificial dataset of 200 million sentences, only Swedish no supervision, training or fine-tuning on any labeled data

Table 3: Overview of submitted systems, lister in the order of registration

4.1 CodaLab

Evaluation was formally carried out on the Code-Lab competition platform[17], with participants being allowed to anonymously make a maximum of 2 submissions on the test data during the test phase. Each submission was expected to contain output for as many languages as the team wished to participate in, and so participants could effectively make a maximum of 2 submissions for each dataset in the shared task.

It is **extremely important** to note that we treated the best score *from either submission* as the official result for each team. This means that if a team scored 50 in Language A and 60 in Language B from Submission 1, but 45 in Language A and 70 in Language B from Submission 2, the official score for the team is 50 in Language A (Submission 1) and 70 in Language B (Submission 2). In other words, we did not penalise teams for uploading their best system output in different submissions.

5 Teams, Approaches, Results

In total, six teams participated in the task, representing five different countries: China, Italy, Norway, Sweden and Vietnam. Four teams developed systems for all five languages (and six datasets): EliCoDe (Colla et al., 2023), NTNU-TRH (Bungum et al., 2023), DDSL-MIM-HUS (Ngo et al., 2023, System 1) and Brainstorm Thinkers (no submitted system description); one team submitted results for all five languages excluding the English-REALEC dataset: VLP-char (Ngo et al., 2023, System 2); and one team submitted results for Swedish only: su-dali (Kurfalı and Östling, 2023).

The different approaches that each team took are summarized in Table 3. The most successful approaches relied on BERT-like large language models (see Table 4). The team with the best average result across all languages, EliCoDe, fine-tuned a different model for each dataset and showed considerably superior recall capabilities on most datasets (Colla et al., 2023). The second-best average result came from the DSL-MIM-HUS team, who fine-tuned one pre-trained model on all 6 datasets at once (Ngo et al., 2023). The same team also trained a character-based LSTM, VLP-char. The NTNU-TRH team used LSTMs as well, implementing their systems with FlairNLP and comparing monolingual and multilingual scenarios (Bungum et al., 2023). These latter approaches require less data for training but show weaker performance in recall and precision, either tending to detect fewer errors or produce a greater number of false positives. The su-dali team used artificial data mimicking the error distribution from the Swedish source corpus, and achieved very good results on Swedish showing that access to manually annotated training data can be avoided (Kur-

[17] https://codalab.lisn.upsaclay.fr/competitions/9784

a. Results on Czech

Team	P	R	$F_{0.5}\downarrow$
EliCoDe	82.01	51.79	**73.44**
DSL-MIM-HUS	58.31	55.69	57.76
Brainstorm Thinkers	62.35	23.44	46.81
VLP-char	34.93	63.95	38.42
NTNU-TRH	80.65	6.49	24.54
Majority	84.32	43.22	70.85

b. Results on English – FCE

Team	P	R	$F_{0.5}\downarrow$
EliCoDe	73.64	50.34	**67.40**
DSL-MIM-HUS	72.36	37.81	61.18
Brainstorm Thinkers	70.21	37.55	59.81
VLP-char	20.76	29.53	22.07
NTNU-TRH	81.37	1.84	8.45
Majority	85.35	32.48	64.39

c. Results on English – REALEC

Team	P	R	$F_{0.5}\downarrow$
DSL-MIM-HUS	62.81	28.88	**50.86**
EliCoDe	44.32	40.73	43.55
Brainstorm Thinkers	48.19	31.22	43.46
NTNU-TRH	51.34	1.13	5.19
Majority	65.46	27.23	51.11

d. Results on German

Team	P	R	$F_{0.5}\downarrow$
EliCoDe	84.78	73.75	**82.32**
DSL-MIM-HUS	77.80	51.92	70.75
Brainstorm Thinkers	77.94	47.55	69.11
NTNU-TRH	83.56	15.58	44.61
VLP-char	25.18	44.27	27.56
Majority	87.80	49.88	76.21

e. Results on Italian

Team	P	R	$F_{0.5}\downarrow$
EliCoDe	86.67	67.96	**82.15**
DSL-MIM-HUS	75.72	38.67	63.55
Brainstorm Thinkers	70.65	36.46	59.49
NTNU-TRH	93.38	19.84	53.62
VLP-char	25.79	44.24	28.14
Majority	90.25	40.95	72.74

f. Results on Swedish

Team	P	R	$F_{0.5}\downarrow$
EliCoDe	81.80	66.34	**78.16**
DSL-MIM-HUS	74.85	44.92	66.05
Brainstorm Thinkers	73.81	39.94	63.11
su-dali	82.41	27.18	58.60
VLP-char	26.40	55.00	29.46
NTNU-TRH	80.12	5.09	20.31
Majority	89.90	45.37	75.15

Table 4: Results for each language and team in terms of Precision (P), Recall (R) and F-score ($F_{0.5}$). The *Majority* score is based on the majority predicted token-based labels across all systems.

fali and Östling, 2023).

Czech Systems that relied on Transformer-based architectures (the top three in Table 4) achieved the top-3 $F_{0.5}$ scores. Despite that, the best recall comes from the LSTM-based system (VPL-char).

English-FCE The performance of the RoBERTa-based architecture, fine-tuned exclusively on the FCE dataset by EliCoDe team, outperformed other architectures in all evaluation metrics, indicating its superior efficacy for the FCE dataset.

English-REALEC The results obtained from the REALEC dataset were relatively low compared to other datasets, which may be attributed to the different annotation style in REALEC (see Section 3.2), and the fact that REALEC was both released later in the shared task and without a training split.

German The highest scores were obtained by all teams on the German Falko-MERLIN dataset. Remarkably, the teams NTNU-TRH and VLP-char, who did not use external data, exhibited substantially better performance on the German dataset.

Italian The solutions submitted for the German and Italian datasets exhibited the highest performance levels compared to the other datasets. This finding could potentially be attributed to the fact that these datasets were sourced from the MERLIN corpus and possessed a high level of consistency in their annotations.

Swedish The Swedish dataset received the highest participation rate among all the datasets. The best performance was achieved by Transformer-based architectures, which is consistent with the performance on other datasets. Nevertheless, satisfactory results were also achieved by solutions using LSTMs without pre-training or additional data.

Altogether, shared task participants submitted different systems representing a variety of approaches, including machine translation, LSTMs, mBERT and XLM-RoBERTa (Table 3). The best results were achieved by teams employing the multilingual XLM-RoBERTa (large) language model pre-trained on ≈100 languages (Conneau et al., 2020). The systems trained and fine-tuned

Language	Team	Best $F_{0.5}$ ↓
German	EliCoDe	82.32
Italian	EliCoDe	82.15
Swedish	EliCoDe	78.16
Czech	EliCoDe	73.44
Eng-FCE	EliCoDe	67.40
Eng-REALEC	DSL-MIM-HUS	50.87

Table 5: Best results for each language dataset.

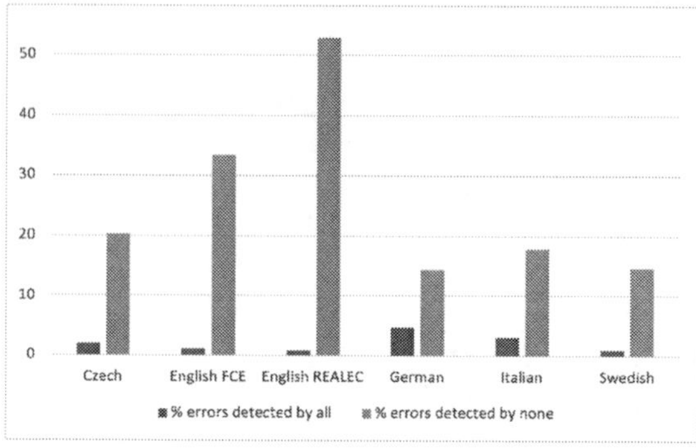

Figure 2: Percentage of errors in the test set which were either detected by all (blue bars, on the left) or none (orange bars, on the right) of the participating teams.

separately for each language dataset by the EliCoDe team performed substantially better than the ones that used one multilingual model for all languages (team DSL-MIM-HUS), with the exception of the English-REALEC dataset, where the results were reversed (see the results for the top-performing systems in Table 5). This is an important insight, because the EliCoDe team also showed that for some language datasets multilingual models, fine-tuned on all datasets, performed better than monolingually fine-tuned ones (Colla et al., 2023). On the one hand, it is intuitive that monolingual models might perform better than multilingual models because they are more specially trained for a particular target language, but on the other hand, multilingual models might be expected to perform better because they have access to richer multilingual representations from linguistically-related languages. In either case, both approaches have different advantages which are worth exploring further.

Table 4 also lists the scores from a token-based majority vote for each language in gray. This is based on the performance of a system relying on a majority vote among all system outputs. For the two languages with an even number of system outputs – English-REALEC and Swedish – a fallback was implemented in case of a tie, namely to choose the output of the best system (EliCoDe in both languages). As can be observed, this majority system led to better precision in all languages and lower recall. If this score were to be included in the ranking, it would end up on place two for all languages, except for English-REALEC where, with an $F_{0.5}$ of 51.11 it would obtain first place.

In Figure 2 we combine all system output to get more insights in the error detection (the `i` labels). The blue bars (on the left) represent the percentage of errors that were detected by all participatings systems in each language, whereas the orange bars (on the right) illustrate the percentage of errors none of which the systems were able to detect. What draws the attention are the high percentages of errors none of the approaches were able to detect for English (33% for English FCE and 53% for English REALEC, respectively). Also, when ranked by best results for all languages (Table 5) it is counter-intuitive to see that English comes at the bottom, as English has typically received the most attention in GED. REALEC is a special case – we did not provide training data for it, and obviously models trained on other languages or other datasets for the same language did not generalize well to REALEC – hypothetically because REALEC had a different type of annotation approach. However, an interesting question is why performance on the English-FCE dataset was lower than on all other languages? In this respect, the EliCoDe team (Colla et al., 2023) carried out an analysis of training/development splits versus the test split per language for linguistic similarity and identified bigger differences between English splits than any other MultiGED languages; they conclude this may be the reason why scores were lower on English.

A short look at the six system output files for Swedish shows that most of the errors that all systems missed (i.e. labeled them as `c` instead of `i`) are those that cover:

- lexical choices, for example non-idiomatic use of vocabulary, e.g. `Jag tror att religion *`**`har`**` ingen roll...`[18] ('I think that religion ***has** no role...')
- verb tense harmonization with other verb

[18]The missed token shown in bold.

tenses used in the sentence, e.g. `Hon tycker att Hans är hennes äkta kärlek men så *var det inte` ('She thinks that Hans is her real love, but it ***was** not the case')

- a few preposition and syntactic construction choices, e.g. `Hur går det *med dig?` ('How is it going ***with** you?')

- few of the errors missed by all systems would in fact require longer context than one sentence for determiniting the need of a correction

Note that these are only indicative insights and a more thorough analysis would be necessary to draw any proper conclusions.

Rather obviously, spelling errors resulting in 'non-words' (OOVs – out-of-vocabulary strings) were easier to detect than errors resulting in some existing word forms ('real-word errors'). Whereas the entire Czech test data included 6.937% of non-words, there were much fewer non-words among the 1716 incorrect word forms that all the systems failed to detect: 0.047%. The almost 15:1 ratio was lower for the English data (about 7:1 for FCE: 1.440% vs. 0.199%; 4:1 for REALEC: 1.135% vs. 0.310%), but it is still clear that real-word errors were harder to detect.

In future, it would be useful to see error distributions made by systems by types of (gold) error labels [e.g. POLMS[19]] and account for their effect on different language systems performance. Another possible interesting analysis could be to correlate system performance with learners' language proficiency, their first languages, as well as with the effect of essay tasks on system performance.

6 Comparison with previous work

To provide some context for the MultiGED results on the English FCE benchmark, we present Table 6, which summarisee results on English GED in the past five years. The state-of-the-art has been gradually pushed: Bell et al. (2019) explored the effect of using different contexual embeddings and their generalizability to different datasets, showing the potential of "leveraging information learned in an unsupervised manner from high volumes of unlabeled data" and their sensitivity to error types, with BERT embeddings (Peters et al., 2017) being especially promising ($F_{0.5}$ 57.28). Kaneko and Komachi (2019) complemented $BERT_{BASE}$ with a Multi-Head Multi-Layer Attention (MHMLA) function to achieve a new state of the art for GED, reaching $F_{0.5}$ 61.65 on FCE. Yuan et al. (2021) meanwhile showed that ELECTRA (Clark et al., 2020) has a "discriminative pre-training objective that is conceptually similar to GED", which improved GED results by a large margin on several public English datasets, reaching $F_{0.5}$ 72.93 on the FCE benchmark. Two years later, the results by Yuan et al. (2021) are still state-of-the-art. The bulk of work on English provides potential ways for improvement on other MultiGED languages – if nothing else, to see whether the same trends hold cross-linguistically.

System / English FCE	P	R	$F_{0.5}$
MultiGED-23			
EliCoDe	73.64	50.34	**67.40**
DSL-MIM-HUS	72.36	37.81	61.18
State-of-the-art			
Yuan-2021, BERT	75.73	47.98	67.88
Yuan-2021, XLNet	77.50	49.81	69.75
Yuan-2021, ELECTRA	82.05	50.49	**72.93**
Previous results			
Kaneko-Komachi-2019	68.87	43.45	61.65
Bell-2019, $BERT_{BASE}$	64.96	38.89	57.28

Table 6: Comparison to previous GED results on English FCE dataset (Yuan et al., 2021; Kaneko and Komachi, 2019; Bell et al., 2019).

We are unable to make similar comparisons for the other languages in MultiGED because this is the first time these languages have been evaluated in the context of GED. More specifically:

- For Czech, previous research explores grammatical error correction (GEC) rather than detection (e.g. Náplava and Straka, 2019; Náplava et al., 2022). There has been some previous work on the evaluation of Czech error detection in the context of a spellchecking tool, Korektor (Ramasamy et al., 2015), however, this is not fully compatible with the scope of errors in MultiGED.

- For German, although there is some work on sentence-level error detection (e.g. Boyd, 2012) and error correction (e.g. Boyd, 2018; Sun et al., 2022; Pająk and Pająk, 2022), there is no previous work on token-level GED.

[19]POLMS = P-unctuation, O-rthography, L-exical, M-orphology, S-yntax

Feedback type	Example	NLP task
1. correct/incorrect	*incorrect*	sentence-level acceptability judgment
2. highlighting	I saw show last night .	GED – grammatical error detection (per token)
3. metalinguistic	*note definiteness / morphology*	multi-class GED
4. error explanation	*note rules for noun definiteness*	instructive feedback generation
5. correct answer	I saw **the** show last night .	GEC – grammatical error correction
6. level/grade	CEFR level A2	AEG – automatic essay grading

Table 7: NLP tasks for different feedback types

- For Italian, we are unaware of any work on GED or GEC at all.
- For Swedish, rule-based error detection was developed within the Granska project, (e.g. Birn, 2000; Arppe, 2000), however, it is difficult to use these results for comparison since the evaluation metrics and test sets are different, as is the scope of errors.

We can therefore conclude that the MultiGED-2023 shared task has established a new set of benchmark datasets and state-of-the-art GED baselines for four new languages in this domain: Czech, German, Italian and Swedish.

7 Concluding remarks

We have presented datasets and results for the task of multilingual grammatical error detection for five languages and six corpora, three of which have not previously featured in the domain of GED.

We view this contribution *primarily* as a step towards empowering "smaller" languages and decreasing the Matthew effect in this field (Søgaard, 2022; Perc, 2014; Bol et al., 2018). It is our hope that the availability of these datasets and baselines will spark further GED research for these languages. *Secondly*, we view this shared task as a step towards instructional feedback generation in ICALL tutoring systems – corrections, error classification and grammar explanations being reserved as potential future shared tasks, see Table 7 for some ideas.

Besides this, we summarise a few of our insights that might be useful to keep in mind for further GED experiments:

1. Pre-trained large language models have no doubt pushed the field far forward (cf. Yuan et al., 2021; Colla et al., 2023; Ngo et al., 2023). It is left to see in the future how GPT[20] models can influence the field (e.g. Radford et al., 2018; Wu et al., 2023; Lund and Wang, 2023).
2. Monolingual fine-tuning tends to outperform multilingual approaches, however, there are some exceptions (Colla et al., 2023; Ngo et al., 2023; Bungum et al., 2023), and more attention should be given to multilingual approaches.
3. Embeddings of various types can have a significant impact on system performance (Bungum et al., 2023).
4. Artificial data containing error distributions similar to the test data facilitates reaching competitive performance with relatively low costs (Kurfalı and Östling, 2023), and is a promising way to go.
5. The quality of data annotation is critical for high performance, as has been indicated by the results on different MultiGED languages, the ones coming from MERLIN (German and Italian) showing better results compared to other annotation paradigms (see Section 5 for descriptions of Italian).

Finally, we would like to encourage those who have L2 data and are willing to use it for a shared task on L2 language *in combination with other languages*, to make contact with the *Computational SLA working group*.[21] It would be especially welcome if languages from beyond the Indo-European group could feature in future shared tasks.

Acknowledgements

The first author has been supported by the Swedish *Språkbanken Text* and by *HumInfra* through funding from the Swedish Research Council (contracts

[20]GPT stands for Generative Pretrained Transformers

[21]https://spraakbanken.gu.se/en/compsla

2017-00626 and 2021-00176). The second and third authors are supported by Cambridge University Press & Assessment.

References

Antti Arppe. 2000. Developing a grammar checker for Swedish. In *Proceedings of the 12th Nordic Conference of Computational Linguistics (NODALIDA 1999)*, pages 13–27, Trondheim, Norway. Department of Linguistics, Norwegian University of Science and Technology, Norway.

Nicolas Ballier, Stéphane Canu, Caroline Petitjean, Gilles Gasso, Carlos Balhana, Theodora Alexopoulou, and Thomas Gaillat. 2020. Machine learning for learner English: A plea for creating learner data challenges. *International Journal of Learner Corpus Research*, 6(1):72–103.

Samuel Bell, Helen Yannakoudakis, and Marek Rei. 2019. Context is key: Grammatical error detection with contextual word representations. In *Proceedings of the Fourteenth Workshop on Innovative Use of NLP for Building Educational Applications*, pages 103–115, Florence, Italy. Association for Computational Linguistics.

Juhani Birn. 2000. Detecting grammar errors with lingsoft's Swedish grammar checker. In *Proceedings of the 12th Nordic Conference of Computational Linguistics (NODALIDA 1999)*, pages 28–40, Trondheim, Norway. Department of Linguistics, Norwegian University of Science and Technology, Norway.

Thijs Bol, Mathijs de Vaan, and Arnout van de Rijt. 2018. The Matthew effect in science funding. *Proceedings of the National Academy of Sciences*, 115(19):4887–4890.

Adriane Boyd. 2012. *Detecting and diagnosing grammatical errors for beginning learners of german: From learner corpus annotation to constraint satisfaction problems*. Ph.D. thesis, The Ohio State University.

Adriane Boyd. 2018. Using Wikipedia Edits in Low Resource Grammatical Error Correction. In *Proceedings of the 2018 EMNLP Workshop W-NUT: The 4th Workshop on Noisy User-generated Text*, pages 79–84, Brussels, Belgium. Association for Computational Linguistics.

Adriane Boyd, Jirka Hana, Lionel Nicolas, Detmar Meurers, Katrin Wisniewski, Andrea Abel, Karin Schöne, Barbora Štindlová, and Chiara Vettori. 2014. The MERLIN corpus: Learner Language and the CEFR. In *Proceedings of the Ninth International Conference on Language Resources and Evaluation (LREC'14)*, pages 1281–1288, Reykjavik, Iceland. European Language Resources Association (ELRA).

Christopher Bryant, Mariano Felice, Øistein E. Andersen, and Ted Briscoe. 2019. The BEA-2019 Shared Task on Grammatical Error Correction. In *Proceedings of the Fourteenth Workshop on Innovative Use of NLP for Building Educational Applications*, pages 52–75, Florence, Italy. Association for Computational Linguistics.

Christopher Bryant, Mariano Felice, and Ted Briscoe. 2017. Automatic Annotation and Evaluation of Error Types for Grammatical Error Correction. In *Proceedings of the 55th Annual Meeting of the Association for Computational Linguistics (Volume 1: Long Papers)*, pages 793–805, Vancouver, Canada. Association for Computational Linguistics.

Christopher Bryant, Zheng Yuan, Muhammad Reza Qorib, Hannan Cao, Hwee Tou Ng, and Ted Briscoe. 2023. Grammatical Error Correction: A Survey of the State of the Art. *arXiv preprint arXiv:2211.05166*.

Lars Bungum, Björn Gambäck, and Arild Brandrud Næss. 2023. NTNU-TRH System at the MultiGED-2023 Shared Task on Multilingual Grammatical Error Detection. In *Proceedings of the 12th Workshop on NLP for Computer Assisted Language Learning (NLP4CALL)*.

Judit Casademont Moner and Elena Volodina. 2022. Swedish MuClaGED: A new dataset for Grammatical Error Detection in Swedish. In *Proceedings of the 11th Workshop on NLP for Computer Assisted Language Learning*, pages 36–45.

Kevin Clark, Minh-Thang Luong, Quoc V. Le, and Christopher D. Manning. 2020. ELECTRA: Pretraining Text Encoders as Discriminators Rather Than Generators. In *8th International Conference on Learning Representations, ICLR*. OpenReview.net.

Davide Colla, Matteo Delsanto, and Elisa Di Nuovo. 2023. ELICODE at MultiGED2023: fine-tuning XLM-RoBERTa for multilingual grammatical error detection. In *Proceedings of the 12th Workshop on NLP for Computer Assisted Language Learning (NLP4CALL)*.

Alexis Conneau, Kartikay Khandelwal, Naman Goyal, Vishrav Chaudhary, Guillaume Wenzek, Francisco Guzmán, Edouard Grave, Myle Ott, Luke Zettlemoyer, and Veselin Stoyanov. 2020. Unsupervised cross-lingual representation learning at scale. In *Proceedings of the 58th Annual Meeting of the Association for Computational Linguistics*, pages 8440–8451, Online. Association for Computational Linguistics.

Teodor-Mihai Cotet, Stefan Ruseti, and Mihai Dascalu. 2020. Neural grammatical error correction for romanian. In *2020 IEEE 32nd International Conference on Tools with Artificial Intelligence (ICTAI)*, pages 625–631.

Daniel Dahlmeier and Hwee Tou Ng. 2012. Better Evaluation for Grammatical Error Correction. In *Proceedings of the 2012 Conference of the North American Chapter of the Association for Computational Linguistics: Human Language Technologies*, pages 568–572, Montréal, Canada. Association for Computational Linguistics.

Robert Dale, Ilya Anisimoff, and George Narroway. 2012. HOO 2012: A Report on the Preposition and Determiner Error Correction Shared Task. In *Proceedings of the Seventh Workshop on Building Educational Applications Using NLP*, pages 54–62, Montréal, Canada. Association for Computational Linguistics.

Robert Dale and Adam Kilgarriff. 2011. Helping Our Own: The HOO 2011 Pilot Shared Task. In *Proceedings of the 13th European Workshop on Natural Language Generation*, pages 242–249, Nancy, France. Association for Computational Linguistics.

Vidas Daudaravicius, Rafael E. Banchs, Elena Volodina, and Courtney Napoles. 2016. A Report on the Automatic Evaluation of Scientific Writing Shared Task. In *Proceedings of the 11th Workshop on Innovative Use of NLP for Building Educational Applications*, pages 53–62, San Diego, CA. Association for Computational Linguistics.

Sam Davidson, Aaron Yamada, Paloma Fernandez Mira, Agustina Carando, Claudia H. Sanchez Gutierrez, and Kenji Sagae. 2020. Developing NLP Tools with a New Corpus of Learner Spanish. In *Proceedings of the Twelfth Language Resources and Evaluation Conference*, pages 7238–7243, Marseille, France. European Language Resources Association.

Masahiro Kaneko and Mamoru Komachi. 2019. Multi-Head Multi-Layer Attention to Deep Language Representations for Grammatical Error Detection. *Computación y Sistemas*, 23(3).

Murathan Kurfalı and Robert Östling. 2023. A distantly supervised Grammatical Error Detection/Correction system for Swedish. In *Proceedings of the 12th Workshop on NLP for Computer Assisted Language Learning (NLP4CALL)*.

Claudia Leacock, Martin Chodorow, Michael Gamon, and Joel Tetreault. 2014. *Automated Grammatical Error Detection for Language Learners*. Morgan and Claypool.

Mark P.J. van der Loo. 2014. The stringdist Package for Approximate String Matching. *The R Journal*, 6(1):111–122.

Brady D Lund and Ting Wang. 2023. Chatting about ChatGPT: how may AI and GPT impact academia and libraries? *Library Hi Tech News*.

Behrang Mohit, Alla Rozovskaya, Nizar Habash, Wajdi Zaghouani, and Ossama Obeid. 2014. The First QALB Shared Task on Automatic Text Correction for Arabic. In *Proceedings of the EMNLP 2014 Workshop on Arabic Natural Language Processing (ANLP)*, pages 39–47, Doha, Qatar. Association for Computational Linguistics.

Jakub Náplava and Milan Straka. 2019. Grammatical Error Correction in Low-Resource Scenarios. In *Proceedings of the 5th Workshop on Noisy User-generated Text (W-NUT 2019)*, pages 346–356, Hong Kong, China. Association for Computational Linguistics.

Jakub Náplava, Milan Straka, Jana Straková, and Alexandr Rosen. 2022. Czech grammar error correction with a large and diverse corpus. *Transactions of the Association for Computational Linguistics*, 10:452–467.

Hwee Tou Ng, Siew Mei Wu, Ted Briscoe, Christian Hadiwinoto, Raymond Hendy Susanto, and Christopher Bryant. 2014. The CoNLL-2014 shared task on grammatical error correction. In *Proceedings of the Eighteenth Conference on Computational Natural Language Learning: Shared Task*, pages 1–14, Baltimore, Maryland. Association for Computational Linguistics.

Hwee Tou Ng, Siew Mei Wu, Yuanbin Wu, Christian Hadiwinoto, and Joel Tetreault. 2013. The CoNLL-2013 shared task on grammatical error correction. In *Proceedings of the Seventeenth Conference on Computational Natural Language Learning: Shared Task*, pages 1–12, Sofia, Bulgaria. Association for Computational Linguistics.

The Quyen Ngo, Thi Minh Huyen Nguyen, and Phuong Le-Hong. 2023. Two Neural Models for Multilingual Grammatical Error Detection. In *Proceedings of the 12th Workshop on NLP for Computer Assisted Language Learning (NLP4CALL)*.

Diane Nicholls. 2003. The Cambridge Learner Corpus: error coding and analysis for lexicography and ELT. In *Proceedings of the Corpus Linguistics 2003 conference; UCREL technical paper number 16*. Lancaster University.

Malvina Nissim, Lasha Abzianidze, Kilian Evang, Rob van der Goot, Hessel Haagsma, Barbara Plank, and Martijn Wieling. 2017. Last words: Sharing is caring: The future of shared tasks. *Computational Linguistics*, 43(4):897–904.

Martina Nyberg. 2022. *Grammatical Error Correction for Learners of Swedish as a Second Language*. Master's thesis, Uppsala university.

Krzysztof Pająk and Dominik Pająk. 2022. Multilingual fine-tuning for grammatical error correction. *Expert Systems with Applications*, 200:116948.

Carla Parra Escartín, Wessel Reijers, Teresa Lynn, Joss Moorkens, Andy Way, and Chao-Hong Liu. 2017. Ethical Considerations in NLP Shared Tasks. In *Proceedings of the First ACL Workshop on Ethics in*

Natural Language Processing, pages 66–73, Valencia, Spain. Association for Computational Linguistics.

Matjaž Perc. 2014. The Matthew effect in empirical data. *Journal of The Royal Society Interface*, 11(98):20140378.

Matthew E. Peters, Waleed Ammar, Chandra Bhagavatula, and Russell Power. 2017. Semi-supervised sequence tagging with bidirectional language models. In *Proceedings of the 55th Annual Meeting of the Association for Computational Linguistics (Volume 1: Long Papers)*, pages 1756–1765, Vancouver, Canada. Association for Computational Linguistics.

Aigner Picou, Alex Franklin, Maggie Meg Benner, Perpetual Baffour, Phil Culliton, Ryan Holbrook, Scott Crossley, and Terry_yutian Ulrichboser. 2021. Feedback Prize - Evaluating Student Writing.

Alec Radford, Karthik Narasimhan, Tim Salimans, Ilya Sutskever, et al. 2018. Improving language understanding by generative pre-training. *OpenAI*.

Loganathan Ramasamy, Alexandr Rosen, and Pavel Straňák. 2015. Improvements to Korektor: A Case Study with Native and Non-Native Czech. In *Proceedings ITAT 2015: Information Technologies - Applications and Theory*, volume 1422 of *CEUR Workshop Proceedings*, pages 73–80. CEUR-WS.org.

Gaoqi Rao, Erhong Yang, and Baolin Zhang. 2020. Overview of NLPTEA-2020 shared task for Chinese grammatical error diagnosis. In *Proceedings of the 6th Workshop on Natural Language Processing Techniques for Educational Applications*, pages 25–35, Suzhou, China. Association for Computational Linguistics.

Marc Reznicek, Anke Lüdeling, and Hagen Hirschmann. 2013. Competing target hypotheses in the falko corpus. *Automatic treatment and analysis of learner corpus data*, 59:101–123.

Marc Reznicek, Anke Lüdeling, Cedric Krummes, and Franziska Schwantuschke. 2012. *Das FalkoHandbuch. Korpusaufbau und Annotationen Version 2.0.*

Alexandr Rosen, Jiří Hana, Barbora Hladká, Tomáš Jelínek, Svatava Škodová, and Barbora Štindlová. 2020. *Compiling and annotating a learner corpus for a morphologically rich language – CzeSL, a corpus of non-native Czech*. Karolinum, Charles University Press, Praha.

Alla Rozovskaya, Houda Bouamor, Nizar Habash, Wajdi Zaghouani, Ossama Obeid, and Behrang Mohit. 2015. The second QALB shared task on automatic text correction for Arabic. In *Proceedings of the Second Workshop on Arabic Natural Language Processing*, pages 26–35, Beijing, China. Association for Computational Linguistics.

Alla Rozovskaya and Dan Roth. 2019. Grammar error correction in morphologically rich languages: The case of Russian. *Transactions of the Association for Computational Linguistics*, 7:1–17.

Burr Settles, Chris Brust, Erin Gustafson, Masato Hagiwara, and Nitin Madnani. 2018. Second language acquisition modeling. In *Proceedings of the Thirteenth Workshop on Innovative Use of NLP for Building Educational Applications*, pages 56–65, New Orleans, Louisiana. Association for Computational Linguistics.

Anders Søgaard. 2022. Should we ban English NLP for a year? In *Proceedings of the 2022 Conference on Empirical Methods in Natural Language Processing*, pages 5254–5260, Abu Dhabi, United Arab Emirates. Association for Computational Linguistics.

Xin Sun, Tao Ge, Shuming Ma, Jingjing Li, Furu Wei, and Houfeng Wang. 2022. A Unified Strategy for Multilingual Grammatical Error Correction with Pre-trained Cross-Lingual Language Model. In *Proceedings of the Thirty-First International Joint Conference on Artificial Intelligence*, pages 4367–4374, Vienna, Austria. International Joint Conferences on Artificial Intelligence Organization.

Oleksiy Syvokon and Olena Nahorna. 2022. UA-GEC: Grammatical error correction and fluency corpus for the Ukrainian language. *arXiv preprint arXiv:2103.16997*.

Olga Vinogradova and Olga Lyashevskaya. 2022. Review Of Practices Of Collecting And Annotating Texts In The Learner Corpus REALEC. In *Text, Speech, and Dialogue: 25th International Conference, TSD 2022*, page 77–88, Berlin, Heidelberg. Springer-Verlag.

Elena Volodina, Lena Granstedt, Arild Matsson, Beáta Megyesi, Ildikó Pilán, Julia Prentice, Dan Rosén, Lisa Rudebeck, Carl-Johan Schenström, Gunlög Sundberg, et al. 2019. The SweLL language learner corpus: From design to annotation. *Northern European Journal of Language Technology (NEJLT)*, 6:67–104.

Haoran Wu, Wenxuan Wang, Yuxuan Wan, Wenxiang Jiao, and Michael Lyu. 2023. ChatGPT or Grammarly? Evaluating ChatGPT on Grammatical Error Correction Benchmark. *arXiv preprint arXiv:2303.13648*.

Helen Yannakoudakis, Ted Briscoe, and Ben Medlock. 2011. A New Dataset and Method for Automatically Grading ESOL Texts. In *Proceedings of the 49th Annual Meeting of the Association for Computational Linguistics: Human Language Technologies*, pages 180–189, Portland, Oregon, USA. Association for Computational Linguistics.

Zheng Yuan, Shiva Taslimipoor, Christopher Davis, and Christopher Bryant. 2021. Multi-Class Grammatical Error Detection for Correction: A Tale of

Two Systems. In *Proceedings of the 2021 Conference on Empirical Methods in Natural Language Processing*, pages 8722–8736, Online and Punta Cana, Dominican Republic. Association for Computational Linguistics.

Yuanyuan Zhao, Nan Jiang, Weiwei Sun, and Xiaojun Wan. 2018. Overview of the NLPCC 2018 Shared Task: Grammatical Error Correction. In *Natural Language Processing and Chinese Computing*, pages 439–445. Springer International Publishing.

Robert Östling and Murathan Kurfalı. 2022. Really good grammatical error correction, and how to evaluate it. *Proceedings of Swedish Language Technology Conference*.

The NTNU System in MultiGED-2023: Contextual Flair Embeddings for Multilingual Grammatical Error Detection

Lars Bungum and **Björn Gambäck**
Department of Computer Science
NTNU, Trondheim, Norway
{lars.bungum,gamback}@ntnu.no

Arild Brandrud Næss
NTNU Business School
NTNU, Trondheim, Norway
arild.naess@ntnu.no

Abstract

The paper presents a monolithic approach to grammatical error detection, which uses one model for all languages, in contrast to the individual approach, which creates separate models for each language. For both approaches, pre-trained embeddings are the only external knowledge sources. Two sets of embeddings (Flair and BERT) are compared as well as two approaches to the problem of multilingual rammar detection, building individual and monolithic systems for multilingual grammar error detection. The system submitted to the test phase of the MultiGED-2023 shared task ranked 5th of 6 systems. In the subsequent open phase, more experiments were conducted, improving results. These results show the individual models to perform better than the monolithic ones and BERT embeddings working better than Flair embeddings for the individual models, while the picture is more mixed for the monolithic models.

1 Introduction

The MultiGED-2023 shared task on Multilingual Grammatical Error Detection (MGED; Volodina et al., 2023) presents six datasets, in the languages Czech, German, Italian, and Swedish as well as two in English; all well-resourced languages with more than 10 million speakers. Although not strictly required, the task did encourage the submission of multilingual systems. This work compares both approaches, multilingual and individual models for each language.

The NTNU system aimed to answer two research questions with its submission:

(i) the feasibility of using Flair embeddings (Akbik et al., 2018) provided by the FlairNLP framework (Akbik et al., 2019a) vs. the more traditional BERT embeddings, and

(ii) the impact of training RNNs using language-specific and multilingual embeddings, respectively, to address the problem.

Consequently, no other external resources — or synthetic data — were used. The submission to the test phase of the shared task was a multilingual system, which ranked 5th of 6 systems.

The rest of the paper is structured as follows: first, Section 2 discusses relevant background, and Section 3 briefly describes the dataset. Section 4 outlines the proposed method and Section 5 presents the results, while Section 6 provides a discussion. Finally, Section 7 concludes and outlines ideas for future work.

2 Background

Grammatical error detection (GED) has received increased attention in the research community. Figure 1 shows the number of publications about GED registered in the Web of Science[1] over the last 31 years, most of which are categorized as computer science disciplines. The results were obtained by searching for the query "Grammatical Error Detection" and asking for a citation report, from which the chart was downloaded at the time of submission.

Bryant et al. (2023) summarized the state-of-the-art of the closely related field of grammati-

[1] http://www.webofscience.com

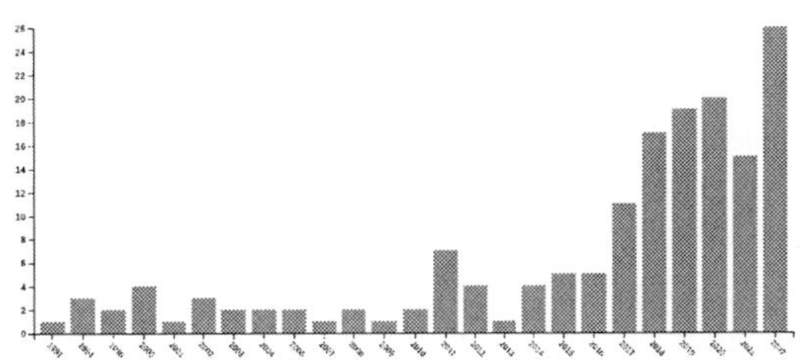

Figure 1: Number of GED publications registered in the Web of Science per year from 1991 (1) to 2022 (27).

Lars Bungum, Björn Gambäck and Arild Brandrud Næss. NTNU-TRH system at the MultiGED-2023 Shared on Multilingual Grammatical Error Detection. *Proceedings of the 12th Workshop on Natural Language Processing for Computer Assisted Language Learning (NLP4CALL 2023).* Linköping Electronic Conference Proceedings 197: 17–23.

cal error correction (GEC) as of November 2022, citing various neural network methods, including LSTMs and Transformers, but not contextualized Flair embeddings. The authors cite the following core approaches: 1) classifiers, 2) statistical machine translation, 3) neural machine translation, 4) edit-based approaches, and 5) language models for low-source and unsupervised GEC.

2.1 Flair Embeddings

Flair embeddings (Akbik et al., 2018) are *contextualized embeddings* trained without explicit notions of words and contextualized by their surrounding text. As they were launched, the embeddings were evaluated on four classic sequence labeling tasks: Named Entity Recognition (NER)-English, NER-German, Chunking, and Part-of-Speech (POS)-tagging. Akbik et al. reported improved scores on several datasets. The embeddings are trained with a forward-backward Recurrent Neural Network (RNN), and can be stacked before being applied to a particular problem.

Flair embeddings are pre-trained on large unlabeled corpora, they capture word meaning in context, and they model words as sequences of characters, which helps them with modeling rare and misspelled words. Thus, applying them to a sequence labeling problem such as GED is an interesting research option. Akbik et al. (2019b) launched *pooled* contextual embeddings to address the shortcoming of dealing with rare words in underspecified context. The pooled embeddings aggregate contextualized embeddings as they are encountered in a dataset. The Flair embeddings are released for all of the languages studied in MultiGED-2023, as well as in a multilingual version, covering more than 300 languages.[2]

In addition to the authors' experiments, Flair embeddings have previously been applied to sequence labeling in the biomedical domain (Sharma and Jr., 2019; Akhtyamova and Cardiff, 2020), achieving similar performance to alternatives like BERT (Bidirectional Encoder Representations from Transformers; Devlin et al., 2019), despite being computationally cheaper. Santos et al. (2019) and Consoli et al. (2020) achieved state-of-the-art results on doing NER on Portuguese literature in the geoscience domain. Wiedemann et al. (2019) compared Flair embeddings to BERT in a word sense disambiguation task, and argued that the latter models were better able to find the right sense of polysemic words. Syed et al. (2022) combined Flair and BERT embeddings for concept compilation in the medical domain, reporting improved results with a hybrid artificial neural network model, which concatenates the two embedding types. The FlairNLP framework also offers this functionality.

3 Data and preprocessing

Six datasets in five languages were used for the MultiGED-2023 shared task, ranging from 8k to 35k sentences.[3] The data loaded unproblematically, with the exception of line 96487 in the Swedish training corpus, a UTF-8 character that broke scripts. Specifically, embeddings were created with wrong dimensions. This character was replaced by the string 'FOO' in the experiments on this corpus to work around this problem. Additionally, line 149 in the Swedish test corpus and line 5351 in the Italian test corpus caused some problems. Because the FlairNLP framework, in contrast to, for instance, OpenNMT (Klein et al., 2017), parses the vertical format directly, no other preprocessing steps were necessary.

For the English Realec corpus, only a development and a test file were provided. More details are provided by Volodina et al. (2023).

4 Method

The FlairNLP framework was used to conduct the experiments presented below. After the data was loaded, it was passed to a processing pipeline, which is a sequence-to-sequence labeler consisting of a bi-directional LSTM (long short-term memory; Hochreiter and Schmidhuber, 1997) with an optional Conditional random field (CRF; Lafferty et al., 2001) classifier on top. Next, the model uses the training and development corpora for training, as well as F_1 scoring.

The architecture of the models can be adapted, e.g., in terms of recurrent neural network (RNN) layers, RNN type (RNN, LSTM or GRU — gated recurrent unit), the number of hidden units and training epochs, and the optional use of CRF. Additionally, the Tensorboard[4] system was used to monitor training progress.

[2] https://github.com/flairNLP/flair/blob/master/resources/docs/embeddings/FLAIR_EMBEDDINGS.md

[3] https://github.com/spraakbanken/multiged-2023/

[4] Part of TensorFlow (Abadi et al., 2015).

FlairNLP can combine several corpora into a `MultiCorpus` object, which builds a *monolithic* model of several corpora. This object can be used to train and test a single model on a collection of corpora, analogously to how a `Corpus` object can be used to do training and inference of one corpus for same. In the following, such a monolithic MGED model is considered multilingual, in contrast to several smaller, *individual* models, one for each language or dataset. While it is possible to have different models for different languages and direct input by means of language identification prior to inference, this distinction is made for clarity in separating the approaches.

Since the Realec corpus only came with development and test files, it was used differently than the other corpora: the English language was covered by the monolithic models and the individual model for the English FCE corpus, so the Realec test corpus was tested on this model and submitted to CodaLab (Pavao et al., 2022) for evaluation. The Realec dev corpus was not used in training.

4.1 Exploring Embeddings vs. Architecture

As a Bi-LSTM-CRF model is sensitive to initialization, a wide range of RNN layers (2, 6, 12, 24), hidden units (128, 256, 512) were explored as well as using GRUs and standard LSTMs. While there is a scope for tweaking the results, none of these configurations resulted in markedly better performance, with the exception of models with very few layers that were unable to converge to anything but same-labeling the entire corpus. For the results reported in Section 5, the choice for RNN type was LSTM, and the number of layers was 10.

4.2 System Submitted to the Test Phase of the Shared Task

The system submitted to the test phase was a monolithic multilingual system, which used the multilingual Flair embeddings. The architecture was a Bi-LSTM-CRF sequence labeler with only one layer and using no CRF. While the system was able to learn for all languages simultaneously, the performance was weak, especially in terms of recall and $F_{0.5}$.

5 Experimental Results

The experiments presented below were all carried out with the RNN type LSTM, using 10 layers with 256 hidden units, no use of CRF, and with a tag dictionary of only $[c, i]$. The experiments consisted of two stages: initially, five systems (including only one English model) were developed for each language using both Flair and BERT embeddings; subsequently, two monolithic models were created employing cased multilingual Flair and BERT embeddings. After presenting the scores of the simple system submitted to the shared task, these two types of experiments will be presented.

Table 1: Monolithic system submitted to the test phase of the shared task.

Dataset	Precision	Recall	$F_{0.5}$
Czech	80.65	6.49	24.54
English (FCE)	81.37	1.84	8.45
English (Realec)	51.34	1.13	5.19
German	83.56	15.58	44.61
Italian	93.38	19.84	53.62
Swedish	80.12	5.09	20.31

5.1 System Submitted to the Test Phase of the Shared Task

Table 1 shows the results of the system that was submitted to the test phase of the shared task, which was discussed above. Using only one RNN, layer, the monolithic model using Flair embeddings did get good precision on some datasets, but at the cost of recall and $F_{0.5}$ score. Only the score on the Italian dataset came close to the models using 10 layers in $F_{0.5}$ terms.

5.2 Individual Models for each Language

Figure 2 shows how the English FCE model (as an example) developed toward convergence and Table 2 exhibits the results in tabular form. The FCE models were chosen randomly as two samples of the ten models that were built in total. The results are better for BERT embeddings across all languages, and the differences are the largest for the smaller datasets, Swedish and Italian, than the larger English, German, and Czech, which is highlighted in the extra column of Table 2b.

BERT models are available for these languages in the Huggingface[5] interface: Czech (Sido et al., 2021), English (Devlin et al., 2019), German[6], Italian[7], and Swedish (Malmsten et al., 2020).

[5]https://huggingface.co/

[6]https://www.deepset.ai/german-bert

[7]https://huggingface.co/dbmdz/bert-base-italian-cased

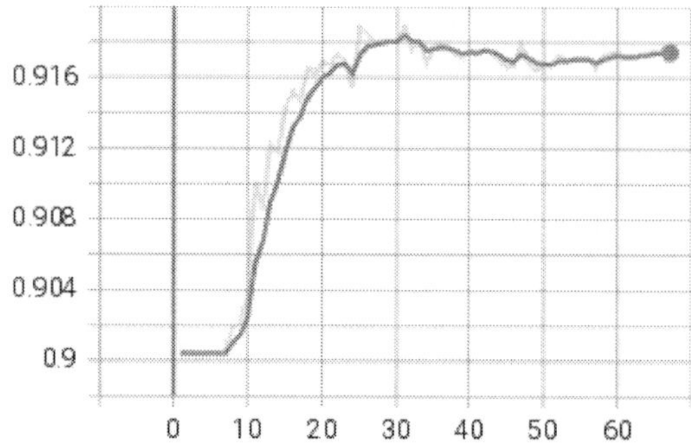

(a) With Flair embeddings.

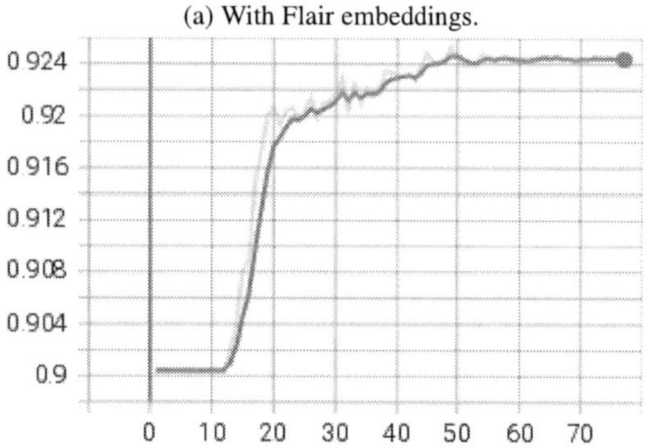

(b) With BERT embeddings.

Figure 2: Development corpus score per epoch until convergence for the English FCE model.

Table 2: Comparison of individual models. The 'Diff' column shows the difference between the two models (Flair vs. BERT). The biggest difference in **bold**, the smallest in *italics*.

(a) Individual models built with Flair embeddings.

Dataset	Prec.	Rec.	$F_{0.5}$
Czech	75.3	39.46	63.73
En (FCE)	65.49	33.01	54.72
En (Realec)	41.52	28.12	37.91
German	78.06	56.37	72.48
Italian	70.29	27.28	53.44
Swedish	57.44	26.85	46.78

(b) Individual models built with BERT embeddings.

Dataset	Prec.	Rec.	$F_{0.5}$	Diff
Czech	80.2	47.22	70.37	6.64
En (FCE)	71.13	41.5	62.25	7.53
En (Realec)	44.9	35.2	42.56	*4.65*
German	81.99	65.48	78.05	5.57
Italian	83.45	63.54	78.53	25.09
Swedish	80.64	60.1	75.48	**27.7**

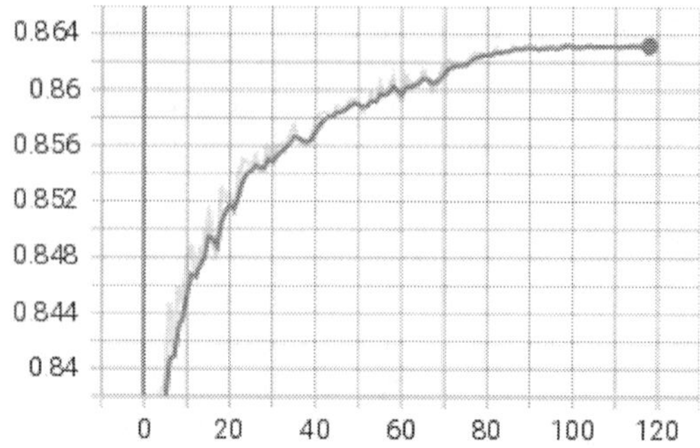

(a) With Flair embeddings.

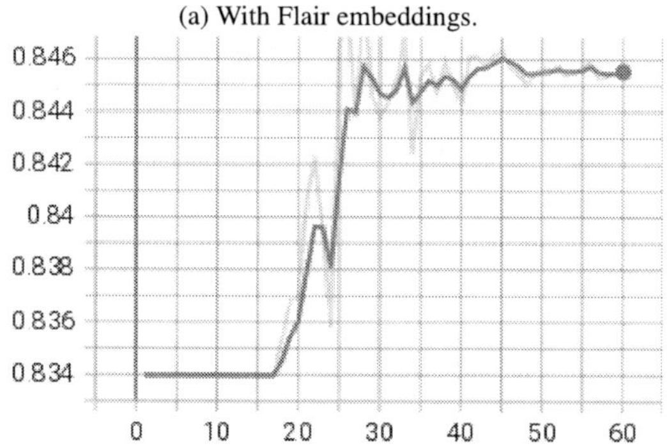

(b) With BERT embeddings.

Figure 3: Development corpus score per epoch until convergence for the monolithic models.

Table 3: Comparison of monolithic models. The 'Diff' column shows the difference between the two models (Flair vs. BERT). The biggest difference in **bold**, the smallest in *italics*.

(a) Monolithic model built with Flair embeddings.

Dataset	Prec.	Rec.	$F_{0.5}$
Czech	70.21	21.05	47.85
En (FCE)	66.76	10.13	31.52
En (Realec)	41.91	9.23	24.54
German	72.35	33.2	58.54
Italian	84.02	28.89	60.81
Swedish	67.57	19.45	45.2

(b) Monolithic model built with BERT embeddings.

Dataset	Prec.	Rec.	$F_{0.5}$	Diff
Czech	54.07	20.43	40.68	-7.17
En (FCE)	68.51	41.04	60.42	**28.9**
En (Realec)	42.07	35.1	40.46	15.92
German	59.6	26.55	47.72	-10.82
Italian	47.55	20.78	37.8	*-23.0*
Swedish	50.04	24.36	41.32	-3.88

5.3 Monolithic Models for all Languages

Figure 3 shows how the monolithic model developed towards convergence for both embedding types, and Table 3 exhibits the results in tabular form. The multilingual and cased BERT model and the corresponding Flair model were used for the embeddings. The results are markedly better for the English datasets but worse for the others, in particular Italian.

6 Discussion

As expected, the Flair embeddings performed worse than the more expensive BERT models individually. The results show that the Flair embeddings were performing closer to the BERT models for the larger corpora, with a larger difference for the smaller Italian and Swedish corpora. The masked language model training of BERT could introduce more imbalances when the corpora have different sizes. Possibly, the Flair embeddings need more training data to perform well.

It was a more mixed picture for the monolithic MGED models, where the BERT embeddings scored better for the English but worse for the other languages. Unlike for the individual models, performance was actually worse than with Flair embeddings, the reasons for which should be further explored.

In some experiments, the training process would get stuck in local minima, which converged to models that categorized all words as *c*. Anecdotally, fewer experiments were necessary to make the experiments using Flair embeddings to converge to a result other than a one-category (thus, meaningless) result. In contrast, the monolithic models using BERT embeddings were harder to get to converge to a result with both correct and incorrect predictions. Thus, several experiments were necessary to get a meaningful result out, although those models were performing better.

Furthermore, some experiments on model architecture were conducted by changing the RNN type, number of layers, or the dimensionality of the hidden state vector. While no notable differences in results were discovered in this exploratory phase, a potential for tweaking the models to increase performance on the test set likely remains.

As a consequence of an implementation error, the results submitted to the test phase of MultiGED-2023 were revised and turned out to be better. The errors were due to the FlairNLP system outputting a labeling of the test set, which was different from using the best model from training on the dataset, which caused minor differences in scoring. However, the substantial performance gain in the results presented above compared to the results submitted to the test phase stems from the architectural change to the system, whereby more RNN layers were added. The submitted system was simple, as the exploratory phase of getting the setup to produce results reliably had just been completed. As the scoring in CodaLab was (and is) available in the open phase, more work could be done, both in development and comparison terms.

For monolithic models, the multilingual BERT models are resource-demanding. Since the experiments were carried out on a multiuser HPC (high-performance computing) grid with many outside factors influencing performance, training times cannot be compared directly. Approximately and informally, however, the monolithic jobs with BERT embeddings could take 36 hours to converge, while the corresponding jobs with Flair embeddings converged in 6–8 hours.

7 Conclusion and Future Work

The research questions posed concerned (i) the feasibility of using Flair embeddings on an MGED task and (ii) monolithic vs. individual models.

The Flair embeddings were definitely feasible. For the larger datasets, performance neared BERT models, and did better on non-English languages for the monolithic approach. The monolithic approach did, however, perform worse than the individual models for both Flair and BERT embeddings. Thus, more research is needed to improve the monolithic approaches, with the gap in performance in the presented results too big to ignore.

For future work, hybrid solutions could be explored, where Flair and BERT embeddings are stacked. There is also room for further exploring the parameter space of the sequence-to-sequence labeling architecture, as well as leveraging newer and larger language models for embeddings. In addition, it would be interesting to apply $F_{0.5}$ scoring in training, as opposed to the default F_1 scoring in the FlairNLP framework that was used in the experiments reported here.

Acknowledgments

The computations were performed on resources provided by Sigma2 — the National Infrastructure for High Performance Computing and Data Storage in Norway.[8]

References

Martín Abadi, Ashish Agarwal, Paul Barham, Eugene Brevdo, Zhifeng Chen, Craig Citro, Greg S. Corrado, Andy Davis, Jeffrey Dean, Matthieu Devin andand Sanjay Ghemawat, Ian Goodfellow, Andrew Harp, Geoffrey Irving, Michael Isard, Yangqing Jia, Rafal Jozefowicz, Lukasz Kaiser, Manjunath Kudlur, Josh Levenberg, Dandelion Mané, Rajat Monga, Sherry Moore, Derek Murray, Chris Olah, Mike Schuster, Jonathon Shlens, Benoit Steiner, Ilya Sutskever, Kunal Talwar, Paul Tucker, Vincent Vanhoucke, Vijay Vasudevan, Fernanda Viégas, Oriol Vinyals, Pete Warden, Martin Wattenberg, Martin Wicke, Yuan Yu, and Xiaoqiang Zheng. 2015. TensorFlow: Large-scale machine learning on heterogeneous systems. Software available from tensorflow.org.

Alan Akbik, Tanja Bergmann, Duncan Blythe, Kashif Rasul, Stefan Schweter, and Roland Vollgraf. 2019a. FLAIR: An easy-to-use framework for state-of-the-art NLP. In *Proceedings of the 2019 Conference of the North American Chapter of the Association for Computational Linguistics (Demonstrations)*, pages 54–59, Minneapolis, Minnesota, USA. Association for Computational Linguistics.

Alan Akbik, Tanja Bergmann, and Roland Vollgraf. 2019b. Pooled contextualized embeddings for named entity recognition. In *Proceedings of the 2019 Conference of the North American Chapter of the Association for Computational Linguistics: Human Language Technologies, Volume 1 (Long and Short Papers)*, pages 724–728, Minneapolis, Minnesota, USA. Association for Computational Linguistics.

Alan Akbik, Duncan Blythe, and Roland Vollgraf. 2018. Contextual string embeddings for sequence labeling. In *Proceedings of the 27th International Conference on Computational Linguistics*, pages 1638–1649, Santa Fe, New Mexico, USA. Association for Computational Linguistics.

Liliya Akhtyamova and John Cardiff. 2020. LM-based word embeddings improve biomedical named entity recognition: A detailed analysis. In *Bioinformatics and Biomedical Engineering*, pages 624–635, Cham. Springer International Publishing.

Christopher Bryant, Zheng Yuan, Muhammad Reza Qorib, Hannan Cao, Hwee Tou Ng, and Ted Briscoe. 2023. Grammatical error correction: A survey of the state of the art. *CoRR*, abs/2211.05166.

[8]http://www.sigma2.no

Bernardo Consoli, Joaquim Santos, Diogo Gomes, Fabio Cordeiro, Renata Vieira, and Viviane Moreira. 2020. Embeddings for named entity recognition in geoscience Portuguese literature. In *Proceedings of the Twelfth Language Resources and Evaluation Conference*, pages 4625–4630, Marseille, France. European Language Resources Association.

Jacob Devlin, Ming-Wei Chang, Kenton Lee, and Kristina Toutanova. 2019. BERT: Pre-training of deep bidirectional transformers for language understanding. *CoRR*, abs/1810.04805.

Sepp Hochreiter and Jürgen Schmidhuber. 1997. Long short-term memory. *Neural Computation*, 9(8):1735–1780.

Guillaume Klein, Yoon Kim, Yuntian Deng, Jean Senellart, and Alexander Rush. 2017. OpenNMT: Open-source toolkit for neural machine translation. In *Proceedings of ACL 2017, System Demonstrations*, pages 67–72, Vancouver, Canada. Association for Computational Linguistics.

John D. Lafferty, Andrew McCallum, and Fernando C. N. Pereira. 2001. Conditional Random Fields: Probabilistic models for segmenting and labeling sequence data. In *Proceedings of the Eighteenth International Conference on Machine Learning*, pages 282–289, San Francisco, CA, USA. Morgan Kaufmann Publishers Inc.

Martin Malmsten, Love Börjeson, and Chris Haffenden. 2020. Playing with words at the national library of Sweden — making a Swedish BERT. *CoRR*, abs/2007.01658.

Adrien Pavao, Isabelle Guyon, Anne-Catherine Letournel, Xavier Baró, Hugo Escalante, Sergio Escalera, Tyler Thomas, and Zhen Xu. 2022. CodaLab competitions: An open source platform to organize scientific challenges. Technical report, Université Paris-Saclay, Paris, France.

Joaquim Santos, Bernardo Consoli, Cicero dos Santos, Juliano Terra, Sandra Collonini, and Renata Vieira. 2019. Assessing the impact of contextual embeddings for Portuguese named entity recognition. In *2019 8th Brazilian Conference on Intelligent Systems (BRACIS)*, pages 437–442, Salvador, Brazil. IEEE.

Shreyas Sharma and Ron Daniel Jr. 2019. BioFLAIR: Pretrained pooled contextualized embeddings for biomedical sequence labeling tasks. *CoRR*, abs/1908.05760.

Jakub Sido, Ondřej Pražák, Pavel Přibáň, Jan Pašek, Michal Seják, and Miloslav Konopík. 2021. Czert — Czech BERT-like model for language representation. *CoRR*, abs/2103.13031.

Shorabuddin Syed, Adam Jackson Angel, Hafsa Bareen Syeda, Carole France Jennings, Joseph VanScoy, Mahanazuddin Syed, Melody Greer, Sudeepa Bhattacharyya, Meredith Zozus, Benjamin

Tharian, and Fred Prior. 2022. The h-ANN model: Comprehensive colonoscopy concept compilation using combined contextual embeddings. In *Proceedings of the 15th International Joint Conference on Biomedical Engineering Systems and Technologies — HEALTHINF*, pages 189–200, Virtual. INSTICC, SciTePress.

Elena Volodina, Christopher Bryant, Andrew Caines, Orphée De Clercq, Jennifer-Carmen Frey, Elizaveta Ershova, Alexandr Rosen, and Olga Vinogradova. 2023. MultiGED-2023 shared task at NLP4CALL: Multilingual grammatical error detection. In *Proceedings of the 12th workshop on Natural Language Processing for Computer Assisted Language Learning (NLP4CALL)*, Tórshavn, Faroe Islands.

Gregor Wiedemann, Steffen Remus, Avi Chawla, and Chris Biemann. 2019. Does BERT make any sense? interpretable word sense disambiguation with contextualized embeddings. In *Proceedings of the 15th Conference on Natural Language Processing, KONVENS*, Erlangen, Germany.

ELICODE at MultiGED2023: fine-tuning XLM-RoBERTa for multilingual grammatical error detection

Davide Colla and **Matteo Delsanto** and **Elisa Di Nuovo**
University of Turin - Italy
Computer Science Department
davide.colla@unito.it, matteo.delsanto@unito.it, elisa.dinuovo@unito.it

Abstract

In this paper we describe the participation of our team, ELICODE, to the first shared task on Multilingual Grammatical Error Detection, MultiGED, organised within the workshop series on Natural Language Processing for Computer-Assisted Language Learning (NLP4CALL). The multilingual shared task includes five languages: Czech, English, German, Italian and Swedish. The shared task is tackled as a binary classification task at token level aiming at identifying correct or incorrect tokens in the provided sentences. The submitted system is a token classifier based on XLM-RoBERTa language model. We fine-tuned five different models—one per each language in the shared task. We devised two different experimental settings: first, we trained the models only on the provided training set, using the development set to select the model achieving the best performance across the training epochs; second, we trained each model jointly on training and development sets for 10 epochs, retaining the 10-epoch fine-tuned model. Our submitted systems, evaluated using F0.5 score, achieved the best performance in all evaluated test sets, except for the English REALEC data set (second classified). Code and models are publicly available at `https://github.com/davidecolla/EliCoDe`.

1 Introduction

Grammatical Error Detection (GED) is the task of automatically identifying errors in learner language. Despite its name, the errors to be identified are not only grammatical errors, but different error types are considered, e.g. spelling, punctuation, lexical. In Second Language Acquisition and Learner Corpus Research, indeed, an error is defined as "a linguistic form or combination of forms which, in the same context and under similar conditions of production, would, in all likelihood, not be produced by the speakers' native speaker counterparts" (Lennon, 1991). As can be noticed, this definition includes different causes, i.e. grammaticality and correctness, or acceptability, strangeness and infelicity (James, 1998). This difference results in different resources annotating different errors, with some annotating as grammatical errors also appropriateness errors—i.e. pragmatics, register and stylistic choices (Lüdeling and Hirschmann, 2015, p. 140)—others excluding appropriateness, but including orthographical and semantic well-formedness together with acceptability (Di Nuovo, 2022).

In both GED task and the related Grammatical Error Correction (GEC) task, research has focused mainly on learner English (as second or foreign language) (Bell et al., 2019; Ng et al., 2014; Bryant et al., 2019). Recently, also non-English error-annotated data sets have been released (Boyd, 2018; Náplava et al., 2022). Thanks to these recent trends, the authors of MultiGED (Volodina et al., 2023) organised this year the first multilingual GED shared task, hosted at the workshop series on Natural Language Processing for Computer-Assisted Language Learning (NLP4CALL).

Both GED and GEC can be seen as low or mid-resource tasks, because of three main characteristics: requiring time-expensive and highly-specialised human annotation, annotated data sets are usually small in size; the incorrect tokens in a text are significantly scarce if compared to the correct ones; since errors pertain to different error categories, each error type in the data sets is represented unevenly.

The data sets included in MultiGED shared task are in Czech, English, German, Italian and Swedish. Some of these data sets have been al-

Davide Colla, Matteo Delsanto and Elisa Di Nuovo. EliCoDe at MultiGED2023: fine-tuning XLM-RoBERTa for multilingual grammatical error detection. *Proceedings of the 12th Workshop on Natural Language Processing for Computer Assisted Language Learning (NLP4CALL 2023)*. Linköping Electronic Conference Proceedings 197: 24–34.

ready used for GED or GEC tasks—i.e. *Falko* and *Merlin* corpora (Boyd, 2018), *Grammar Error Correction Corpus for Czech* (GECCC) (Náplava et al., 2022), *First Certificate in English* (FCE) corpus (Yannakoudakis et al., 2011)—others have been released *ad hoc* for this shared task—i.e. *Russian Error-Annotated Learner English Corpus* (REALEC) (Kuzmenko and Kutuzov, 2014), released only as development and test data sets, and learner Swedish *SweLL-gold* (Volodina et al., 2019), comprising training, development and test data sets.

The aim of MultiGED is to detect tokens to be corrected labelling them as correct or incorrect, performing a binary classification task at token level. Training and development data sets were segmented into sentences and tokens (no information at text level was released).

Following previous GED shared tasks, the used evaluation metric is F0.5, which weights precision twice as much as recall, carried out on the Codalab competition platform.[1]

The authors of the shared task encouraged submissions using a multilingual approach and additional resources, provided that these resources are publicly available for research purposes. However, since different resources can annotate different errors, the use of other additional data might be a double-edged sword. In fact, the additional data would increase the tool's ability to identify a greater variety of errors, but at the same time, as the tool is evaluated in-domain, it moves away from the characteristics of the test set.

In this paper, we present the systems submitted by our team, ELICODE, to MultiGED 2023 shared task. Our systems are both based on XLM-RoBERTa language model (Conneau et al., 2019), and do not use additional resources. We fine-tuned five models—one per each language in the shared task—for ten epochs. We devised two different experimental settings both using early stopping: in the first experimental setting, we trained the models only on the training data set and used the early stopping according to the F0.5 score obtained on the development data set (ELICODE); in the second experimental setting, we trained each model on both training and development data sets (ELICODE_{ALL}). Since in both experimental settings the early stopping was based on the development data set, in the second one, being it part of training, the training continued for all the ten epochs. We comment the results of the above-mentioned systems comparing them with a baseline—a Naive Bayes model—and an XLM-RoBERTa-based model trained jointly on the five-language training data sets (ELICODE_{MLT}) and on both training and development data sets ($\text{ELICODE}_{MLT_{ALL}}$), tackling the shared task with a multilingual approach.

The remainder of this paper is organised as follows: in Section 2 we present related work; in Section 3 we quantitatively describe the multilingual data set; in Section 4 we describe in detail our submitted models; in Section 5 we report and discuss the obtained results; in Section 6 we conclude the paper highlighting possible future work.

2 Related work

The detection of errors in interlanguage texts (Selinker, 1972) is a challenging task that has received significant attention in the natural language processing community, since GED systems can be used to provide feedback and guidance to language learners. In this section, we review some of the most relevant and recent studies in this area and in the related task of GEC.

Initially tackled using rule-based approaches, GED systems have evolved from being able to identify only certain types of errors to being more and more able to handle the complexity and variability of natural language, thanks to modern machine learning techniques which make use of large annotated text corpora, usually released in the occasion of shared tasks. This switch is evident in the evolution of the shared task from CoNLL-2013 (Ng et al., 2013) to CoNLL-2014 (Ng et al., 2014), when it changed from annotating only five error types to *all* error types.[2]

In CoNLL-2014 shared task, the majority of the systems made use of hybrid approaches able to deal with all error types together, as compared to previous year's submissions, where a specific classifier per each error type was trained. The most popular approaches made use of one or more of

[1] https://codalab.lisn.upsaclay.fr/competitions/9784

[2] Twenty-eight error types are annotated in the CoNLL-2014 benchmark data set. However, it should be noticed that this is still far from annotating all error types. For example, in the English Corpus of Learner English (ICLE) (Granger et al., 2020) there are 54 error tags, in the error-annotated learner Italian corpus, VALICO-UD (Di Nuovo, 2022, p. 94), 120 error tags.

the following: the Language Model (LM) based approach (using n-gram language models), which has been used for both GED and GEC; the phrase-based Statistical Machine Translation (SMT) approach, used mainly for GEC; and rule-based approaches to tackle regular error types.

In 2019, the Building Educational Applications (BEA) shared task on GEC (Bryant et al., 2019) introduces a new data set, joining the Cambridge English Write & Improve (W&I) (Yannakoudakis et al., 2018) and LOCNESS corpus (Granger, 1998), making the test data set bigger than the one on which CoNLL-2014 systems were tested (from 50 essays on two different topics, to 350 essays on about 50 topics). Another major change concerns the use of neural machine translation (Bryant et al., 2022)—being it based on recurrent neural networks (Bahdanau et al., 2014), convolutional neural networks (Gehring et al., 2016), or transformers (Vaswani et al., 2017)—instead of SMT and n-gram-based LMs. BEA reported results highlighted that the same system had different performances in texts at different CEFR levels (Little, 2006), lexical errors were the most difficult to detect and correct, and multi-token errors were better handled than in the previous shared task.

Bell et al. (2019) integrate contextual embeddings—BERT, ELMo and Flair embeddings (Peters et al., 2017; Devlin et al., 2018; Akbik et al., 2018)—in Rei (2017) architecture for GED (a bi-LSTM sequence labeler at token and sentence level, making use also of character-level bi-LSTM, to benefit from morphological information). Their best model used BERT embeddings and proved to better generalise in out-of-domain texts. Their analyses show that missing tokens are the most difficult errors to indentify.

Kaneko and Komachi (2019) proposed an extension of BERT base (Devlin et al., 2018) with multi-head multi-layer attention, since research has shown that different layers are best-suited for different tasks, e.g. lower layers capture local syntactic relationships, higher layers longer-range relationships (Peters et al., 2018).

Recently, Yuan et al. (2021) fine-tuned BERT, XLNet (Yang et al., 2019) and ELECTRA (Clark et al., 2020) models to perform GED in English. The three models obtained the new state of the art in binary GED training on FCE data set and testing on BEA-dev, FCE-test and CoNLL-2014, with ELECTRA performing the best overall. Thus, they used ELECTRA to carry out some multi-class GED experiments to boost performance on GEC data sets using it as auxiliary input or for re-ranking.

Our system treats GED as a binary sequence labelling task, like all the above-described systems, and since the best results have been obtained by fine-tuning transformer-based models, we followed this approach by fine-tuning XLM-RoBERTa model (Conneau et al., 2019). We decided to use multilingual RoBERTa because its training focuses on the discrimination of the masked token, and thus, it is conceptually similar to GED. In the following section we quantitatively analyse MultiGED data set, before describing in detail our submitted systems in Section 4.

3 Data set quantitative analysis

MultiGED data set contains labelled training and development sets in Czech (GECCC), English (FCE), Italian (Merlin), German (Falko and Merlin) and Swedish (SweLL-gold). In particular, for English language an additional data set (REALEC) has been released only as development set. In addition, for each data set an unlabelled test set has been released.

Following the work of Siino et al. (2022), we quantitatively analyse the 5-language data sets using established corpus linguistics methods implemented in Sketch Engine (Kilgarriff et al., 2014).[3] We report general data set figures in Table 1, as computed using Sketch Engine.

We used Compare Corpora, the built-in function of Sketch Engine that applies chi-square (χ^2) test (Kilgarriff, 2001), to compare training, development and test sets per each language. The result of this comparison is a confusion matrix per each language, reported in Figure 1, showing values greater or equal to 1, with 1 indicating identity. The higher the value, the larger the difference between the compared data sets.[4] For English we created a comprehensive confusion matrix comparing the two different corpora (FCE and REALEC).

[3]Available here: https://www.sketchengine.eu (last accessed on 28 March 2023).

[4]Please consider that correct or incorrect labels are not taken into account in this comparison. This comparison, instead, gives as an idea of how different the data sets are according to the different words used. Compare Corpora tool is affected by set size: this is why development and test sets, being the smallest, have a higher similarity score than when compared individually to the bigger training sets.

Source corpus	Language	Split	# Tokens	# Unique words
GECCC	Czech	train	333,995	37,228
		dev	32,071	8,145
		test	35,075	8,764
FCE	English	train	465,038	13,972
		dev	35,463	3,569
		test	42,545	3,800
REALEC	English	train	–	–
		dev	88,698	6,208
		test	90,391	6,300
Falko-MERLIN	German	train	306,847	20,561
		dev	39,627	5,606
		test	36,763	5,478
MERLIN	Italian	train	82,040	6,957
		dev	9,326	2,041
		test	10,300	2,176
SweLL-gold	Swedish	train	115,547	10,791
		dev	15,713	3,225
		test	14,666	3,141

Table 1: MultiGED data set in figures. # stands for *number of.*

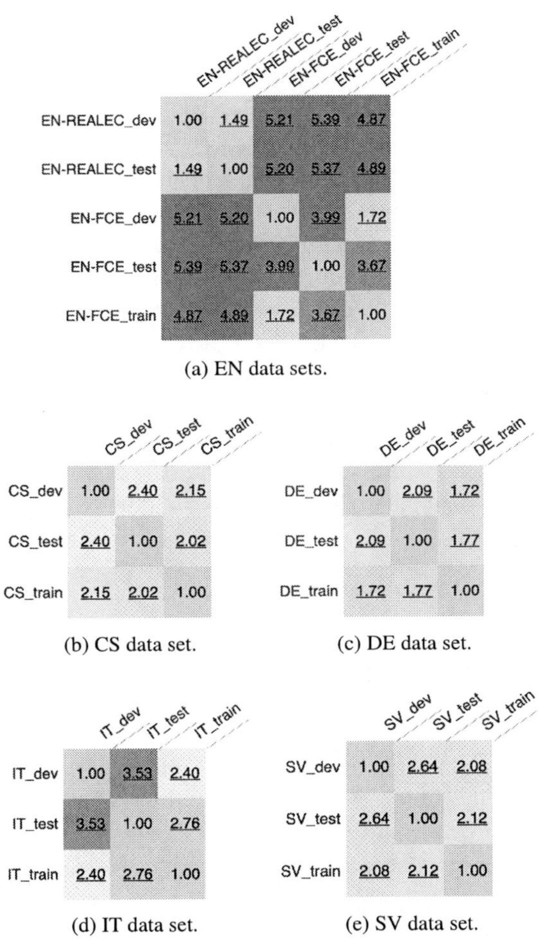

Figure 1: Confusion matrices obtained with word-based chi-square test. The value 1.00 indicates identity between the compared data sets. The greater the value, the more different the data sets.

Looking at the matrices, we could suppose that systems should have less trouble in handling the task in German, Czech, Swedish (in order) than in Italian and English.

English (EN) data set – Since the big difference between FCE and REALEC, the lowest results should be obtained using models trained on FCE and tested on REALEC. Better results could be instead obtained fine-tuning in-domain using REALEC development set and testing it on the test set (because of the smaller similarity score between REALEC development and training sets). It is interesting to notice that REALEC development and test data sets have a similarity score (i.e. 1.49) significantly lower than FCE development and test data sets (i.e. 3.99). FCE training and development data sets have a similarity score of 1.72. FCE training and test data sets of 3.67. These results might suggest that the English data set is challenging for the models.

Czech (CS) data set – The lower similarity scores between the data sets suggest that systems should perform better on Czech than in English test set. Also if compared to the similarity scores obtained in Italian data sets, the lower similarity scores might indicate that the systems should perform better on Czech than in the Italian test set.

German (DE) data set – Since the low similarity score, indicating a bigger similarity between the sets, should mean that German should be the easiest to tackle for the models.

Italian (IT) data set – Here again, since similarity scores between the sets are lower than in

English one, models should perform better on the Italian data set than in the English. In addition, the higher similarity score between development and test data sets suggests that choosing the best performance model according to the results on the development set should be avoided. Instead training on both training and development data sets should ensure the best performance in this data set.

Swedish (SV) data set – According to the reported similarity scores, Swedish training set is in an order of similarity with development and test sets as the Czech sets. This might suggest that similar performances might be expected.

4 System description

In this section, we describe in detail the specifications of our submission.

Given the nature of the MultiGED shared task, we framed the problem as a token classification task, where systems are required to provide a label for each token within the input sequence. More precisely, we employed a sequence labelling strategy using the BIO labelling schema (Ramshaw and Marcus, 1999). The standard schema is formed by B-I-O tags, where each token in a sentence is labelled with one of the three tags: B indicates the beginning of the error span, i.e. the first token of an incorrect use; I is used to label tokens inside the error unit; O marks tokens that are out of the error span, hence correct. However, since in our task we did not have information about the number of errors nor the error span, we decided to use always B to mark an incorrect token, even when preceded by another incorrect token, and O to mark the correct tokens.

The adopted model allows framing the problem as token classification task that, given a sentence $W = w_1 w_2 \dots w_n$, amounts to labelling each word w_i with B or O tags because of the abovementioned reason. Figure 2 reports an example of the system output of a sentence from the English FCE training data. Considering the example, we can see that the token *disappointing* is correctly tagged with B, indicating an incorrect usage, and then it is followed by another incorrect token *a*—marked again with the label B because of the information loss from the conversion from error-tagged corpora to binary token labelling. In the same example, the token *week* is labelled as correct while the token *holiday* is labelled as incorrect token.

The model we employed is based on XLM-RoBERTa large: we stacked a linear classifier—with input size of 1024 units and the output size is set to the number of labels—on top of the pretrained XLM-RoBERTa model, inserting in between the two a dropout layer—with a dropout probability set to 0.1—to avoid overfitting. Finally, in order to compute the distance between the actual data and the predictions we adopted the Cross Entropy loss function. The model architecture is depicted in Figure 3.

To run the experiments, we devised two different experimental settings. In the first one, we trained the models only on the provided training set for 10 epochs, using the development set to select the model achieving the best performance across the training epochs (ELICODE). In the second setting, we trained each model jointly on the training and development sets for 10 epochs, and retained the 10-epoch trained model (ELICODE_{ALL}).[5]

To build our models, we started from the ClinicalTransformerNER framework (Yang et al., 2020) and we adapted the code so as to deal with XLM-RoBERTa language model.[6]

Our experiments were performed on machinery provided by the Competence Centre for Scientific Computing (Aldinucci et al., 2017). In particular, we exploited nodes with 2x Intel Xeon Processor E5-2680 v3 and 128GB memory. The training time is about 15 hours per epoch for the provided languages with a large training data—i.e. Czech, English and German—and drops to 8 hours per epoch for Italian and Swedish. The time taken in the prediction phase is about 25 minutes per language.

5 Results and discussion

We report in Table 2 the results obtained by all teams participating to MultiGED shared task (upper part of the table),[7] and additional experimental results—i.e. a baseline and our submitted models but trained in a multilingual fashion (bottom part of the table). As far as the baseline is concerned, we extracted the token counts from the training data and adopted the multinomial Naive Bayes

[5]In both experimental settings we adopted a batch size of 4 and an early stop of 5 epochs.

[6]The code and the models will be publicly available on GitHub after the review phase of this paper to ensure blind review.

[7]We took the results from the official MultiGED repository: `https://github.com/spraakbanken/multiged-2023`.

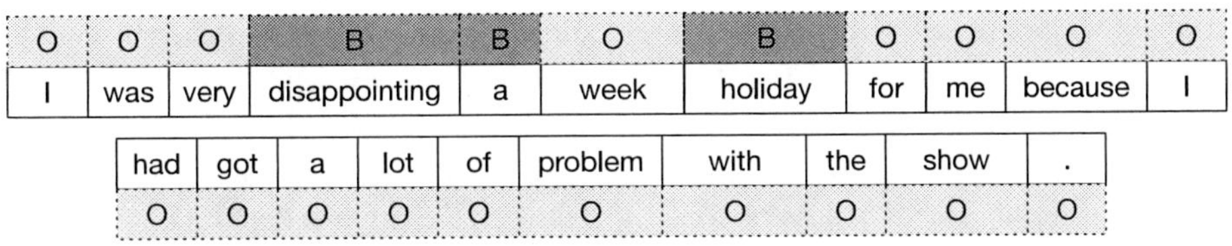

Figure 2: The output of the model for the sentence *I was very disappointing a week holiday for me because I had got a lot of problem with the show.* Here the token *disappointing* is marked as the beginning of an error unit. By the same token, *a* is marked as beginning of a new error due to the information loss caused by the conversion from error-tagged corpora to binary token labelling. The token *holiday* is also marked as an incorrect use. The other tokens are marked as correct uses.

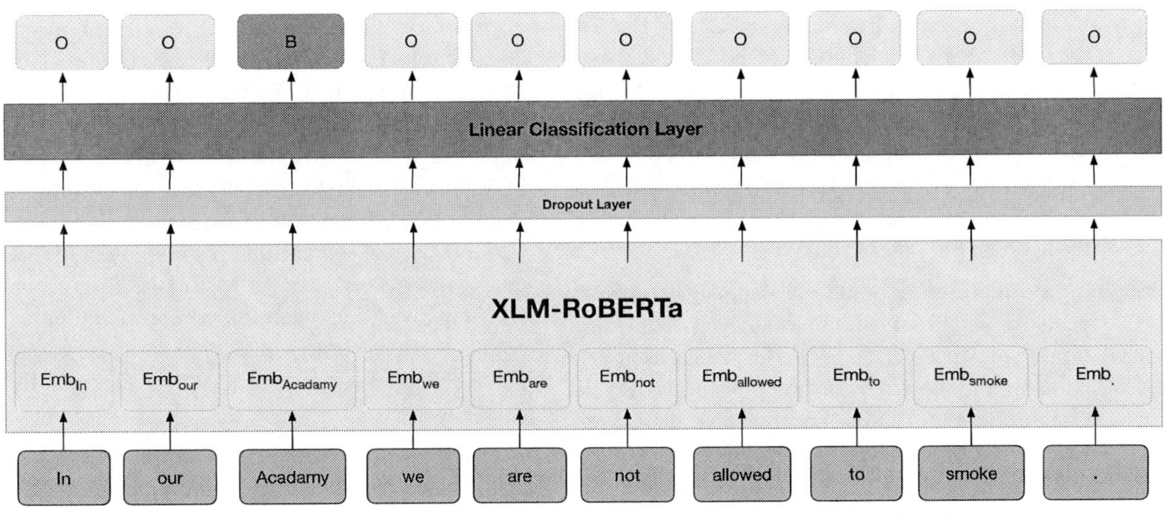

Figure 3: Graphic representation of the model. The grey boxes represent the tokens in the example. These tokens are vectorised and converted into embeddings by XLM-RoBERTa. Tokenisation in XLM-RoBERTa is simplified in this figure for readability reasons. XML-RoBERTa output is inputted to the linear classifier, after passing a dropout layer. The classifier predicts the label B or O for each token.

classifier for sequence labelling (Baseline). As far as the multilingual models are concerned, we followed the same experimental settings of the submitted monolingual models, training two multilingual models: a first model trained only on the concatenation of training data sets (ELICODE$_{MLT}$), the second concatenating also the development data sets (ELICODE$_{MLT_{ALL}}$).

The overall results obtained by both ELICODE and ELICODE$_{ALL}$ are higher than those obtained by the other competing systems, except for the English REALEC test set.

Concerning Precision (P), the baseline and both our ELICODE and ELICODE$_{ALL}$ submissions perform well overall. However, on the FCE partition of the English data set the scores consistently decrease by about 10% and, as expected, the REALEC partition is the most challenging data set: Precision scores drop from about 80% on average to about 40%. As far as Recall (R) is concerned, the token count-based baseline performs poorly: the average Recall of the baseline across languages is about 12% while the average score of ELICODE and ELICODE$_{ALL}$ is about 58%. Following the same trend as Precision, Recall scores for both our submitted systems drop from about 62% of average to 40% on the REALEC English data set. Given the definition of F0.5 metric—i.e. it puts more importance on Precision with respect to Recall—, the overall scores reflect the trend of Precision: the average F0.5 score is about 76% for both ELICODE and ELICODE$_{ALL}$ on all languages but the English REALEC data set, where the average F0.5 drops to 43%.

Considering the different languages, as expected from the quantitative analysis from Section 3, the ELICODE$_{ALL}$ performance improves compared to the scores obtained by ELICODE on Czech, German, Italian and Swedish languages: training on both training and development set allows accounting for the similarities between development set and test set too. Consistently with the above-mentioned analysis, the performances achieved on the Swedish and Czech data sets are comparable and lower than the scores obtained on the German data set, that recorded the highest F0.5 score of 82.32%. Concerning the differences in the English data, as expected, ELICODE performs better than ELICODE$_{ALL}$ on both FCE and REALEC partitions, this is likely due to the high dissimilarity between the English FCE development and test data sets, thus training the model on the development set as well amounts to introducing noise during the learning phase. Additionally, given the great difference between FCE and REALEC partitions, the results of models trained on the FCE data set are consistently lower on REALEC data compared to the results on the FCE data.

In order to explore the impact of the difference between the English data sets, we trained a model only on the REALEC development set. The model has been trained for 10 epochs and by maintaining fixed all the other parameters so as to make the results of such model comparable to the others. The model trained only on REALEC data achieved 58.44 of Precision, 33.19 of Recall and the F0.5 is 50.72, thus improving the F0.5 of about 7% compared to the ELICODE result; in particular, the model becomes more precise in predicting errors, but given the reduced amount of training data is less incline to label tokens as incorrect.

Concerning the baseline, its poor performance is likely due to the employed representation: count-based features consider terms in isolation rather than in context, in so doing, the model is able to detect errors based on words frequency only, thus detecting errors related only to vocabulary—i.e. non-existing words or unseen tokens at training time. In this respect, the results achieved by the baseline on the REALEC partition of the English data set are lower than those for the FCE data set—especially on Precision—, thus reflecting the difference between such two data sets. Conversely, the representations employed by language models such as XLM-RoBERTa are context sensitive—i.e. each token representation accounts for the whole sequence information—and this is reflected in a consistent improvement in Recall scores.

In order to assess the multilingual competence of the language model, we trained a model on the concatenation of the training sets of all the different languages: typologically similar languages may mutually improve the model representations, while languages with different structures may negatively impact the error detection in both languages. The trained multilingual models, as said, follow the same experimental setting than the submitted monolingual models. Differently than the monolingual models which were trained for 10 epochs, the multilingual models have been trained

System	Czech			English - FCE			English - REALEC		
	P	R	F0.5	P	R	F0.5	P	R	F0.5
DSL-MIM-HUS	58.31	55.69	57.76	72.36	37.81	61.18	62.81	28.88	**50.86**
Brainstorm Thinkers	62.35	23.44	46.81	70.21	37.55	59.81	48.19	31.22	43.46
VLP-char	34.93	63.95	38.42	20.76	29.53	22.07	-	-	-
NTNU-TRH	80.65	6.49	24.54	81.37	1.84	8.45	51.34	1.13	5.19
su-dali	-	-	-	-	-	-	-	-	-
ELICODE	82.29	50.61	73.14	73.64	50.34	67.40	44.32	40.73	43.55
ELICODE$_{ALL}$	82.01	51.79	73.44	71.67	50.74	66.21	43.69	40.74	43.07
Baseline	85.69	21.19	53.26	72.81	7.55	26.69	36.40	5.67	17.46
ELICODE$_{MLT}$	83.06	50.72	**73.66**	73.85	50.08	67.45	44.36	42.29	43.93
ELICODE$_{MLT_{ALL}}$	82.79	49.56	73.01	75.01	48.94	**67.79**	45.34	40.29	44.23

System	German			Italian			Swedish		
	P	R	F0.5	P	R	F0.5	P	R	F0.5
DSL-MIM-HUS	77.80	51.92	70.75	75.72	38.67	63.55	74.85	44.92	66.05
Brainstorm Thinkers	77.94	47.55	69.11	70.65	36.46	59.49	73.81	39.94	63.11
VLP-char	25.18	44.27	27.56	25.79	44.24	28.14	26.40	55.00	29.46
NTNU-TRH	83.56	15.58	44.61	93.38	19.84	53.62	80.12	5.09	20.31
su-dali	-	-	-	-	-	-	82.41	27.18	58.60
ELICODE	83.87	71.89	81.16	85.63	66.69	81.03	80.56	67.50	77.56
ELICODE$_{ALL}$	84.78	73.75	**82.32**	86.67	67.96	**82.15**	81.80	66.34	78.16
Baseline	80.99	10.25	34.02	85.11	10.72	35.65	78.09	13.65	40.16
ELICODE$_{MLT}$	83.47	72.52	81.02	85.30	69.64	81.63	82.24	65.94	78.36
ELICODE$_{MLT_{ALL}}$	84.80	71.09	81.65	85.71	65.95	80.87	83.34	64.37	**78.70**

Table 2: Results of experiments in the token classification task. To increase readability, we partitioned the results on two tables grouped by language. We reported the results for all the systems submitted to the MultiGED competition—in the upper part of each sub-table—together with the results of our submission (ELICODE and ELICODE$_{ALL}$). The bottom part of each sub-table report the Naive Bayes-based baseline and the multilingual models (ELICODE$_{MLT}$ and ELICODE$_{MLT_{ALL}}$) results. For each system we report the scores obtained on all the languages included in the competition; for each language, the corresponding columns report the Precision (P), Recall (R) and F0.5 scores. The highest F0.5 scores are in bold.

for 7 epochs: in this setting the training took on average 55 hours per epoch for ELICODE$_{MLT}$ and 62 hours for ELICODE$_{MLT_{ALL}}$.[8]

The multilingual models perform similarly on the shared task test sets compared to monolingual models. If we consider the two languages with a smaller training and development sets, i.e. Italian and Swedish, we might notice that the performance on the Italian test set does not improve using the multilingual approach. This might be due to the fact that the other languages included in the shared task are not typologically similar to Italian. On the contrary, the performance on the Swedish language, which is slightly higher than the monolingual model performance, might benefit from the German training and development data sets, being both Germanic languages.

6 Conclusion and future work

In this paper, we presented the ELICODE system submitted to the first shared task on Multilingual Grammatical Error Detection (MultiGED). We studied the effect of fine-tuning the pre-trained XLM-RoBERTa language model on the multilingual grammatical error detection framed as sequence labelling task. The submitted system achieved the highest scores on five out of six different data sets in a multilingual setting: the provided data are in five languages, namely Czech, English, German, Italian and Swedish.

We compared our system with a simple Naive Bayes classifier based on token counting. The comparison shows that a system based on local representations is able to detect a small subset of errors (good Precision and low Recall) such as typos or out-of-vocabulary words; conversely, a system exploiting contextual representations detects a larger number of error types (increased Recall). Additionally, we compared our monolingual system with a multilingual model trained jointly on the five-language training data sets. We found that the results achieved by the multilingual model are comparable to those obtained by the monolingual models, thus indicating that the token representations built by the language model are suited to generalise over different languages.

As part of future work, we plan to qualitatively analyse the error types recognised by the presented models, to find possible ways to improve grammatical error detection, e.g. by creating hybrid or ensemble models, but also to verify that models based on local representations are able to recognise mainly error categories based on the *signifier*, which do not need to take context into account. Another interesting solution could be that described in Omelianchuk et al. (2020), in which the authors address the GEC task iteratively.

Concerning error types and interlanguage, it would be interesting to train Second Language Acquisition theory-aware models taking interlanguage stages into account by grouping data according to CEFR level information. Indeed, learners at the same learning stage share the same error types, irrespective to their mother tongue (Giacalone Ramat, 2003). These models might perform better in applicative cases in which we know learners' language level (Bryant et al., 2019).

In addition, it would be interesting to analyse the embeddings generated by models fine-tuned on this task, using visualisation techniques as principal component analysis, to verify if embeddings representing the same word are localised in different space areas according to their correct or incorrect usage.

Furthermore, we plan to explore the performance of other language models already tested in GEC and GED tasks to compare RoBERTa and other transformer-based models trained using a different technique (e.g. ELECTRA trained to discriminate the wrongly generated token in a sequence).

[8]The multilingual model trained only on the training data sets (ELICODE$_{MLT}$) for 7 epochs achieved the same results of the 8-epoch model. Thus, we assume that ELICODE$_{MLT}$ reached the learning upper bound at the 7th epoch.

References

Alan Akbik, Duncan Blythe, and Roland Vollgraf. 2018. Contextual string embeddings for sequence labeling. In *Proceedings of the 27th international conference on computational linguistics*, pages 1638–1649.

M Aldinucci, S Bagnasco, S Lusso, P Pasteris, S Rabellino, and S Vallero. 2017. OCCAM: a flexible, multi-purpose and extendable HPC cluster. *Journal of Physics: Conference Series*, 898(8):082039.

Dzmitry Bahdanau, Kyunghyun Cho, and Yoshua Bengio. 2014. Neural machine translation by jointly learning to align and translate. *arXiv preprint arXiv:1409.0473*.

Samuel Bell, Helen Yannakoudakis, and Marek Rei. 2019. Context is key: Grammatical error detection with contextual word representations. In *Proceedings of the Fourteenth Workshop on Innova-*

tive Use of NLP for Building Educational Applications, pages 103–115, Florence, Italy. Association for Computational Linguistics.

Adriane Boyd. 2018. Using wikipedia edits in low resource grammatical error correction. In *Proceedings of the 2018 EMNLP Workshop W-NUT: The 4th Workshop on Noisy User-generated Text*, pages 79–84.

Christopher Bryant, Mariano Felice, Øistein E. Andersen, and Ted Briscoe. 2019. The BEA-2019 shared task on grammatical error correction. In *Proceedings of the Fourteenth Workshop on Innovative Use of NLP for Building Educational Applications*, pages 52–75, Florence, Italy. Association for Computational Linguistics.

Christopher Bryant, Zheng Yuan, Muhammad Reza Qorib, Hannan Cao, Hwee Tou Ng, and Ted Briscoe. 2022. Grammatical Error Correction: A Survey of the State of the Art. *arXiv preprint arXiv:2211.05166*.

Kevin Clark, Minh-Thang Luong, Quoc V Le, and Christopher D Manning. 2020. ELECTRA: Pre-training text encoders as discriminators rather than generators. *arXiv preprint arXiv:2003.10555*.

Alexis Conneau, Kartikay Khandelwal, Naman Goyal, Vishrav Chaudhary, Guillaume Wenzek, Francisco Guzmán, Edouard Grave, Myle Ott, Luke Zettlemoyer, and Veselin Stoyanov. 2019. Unsupervised cross-lingual representation learning at scale. *arXiv preprint arXiv:1911.02116*.

Jacob Devlin, Ming-Wei Chang, Kenton Lee, and Kristina Toutanova. 2018. BERT: Pre-training of deep bidirectional transformers for language understanding. *arXiv preprint arXiv:1810.04805*.

Elisa Di Nuovo. 2022. *VALICO-UD: annotating an Italian learner corpus*. Doctoral Thesis. University of Genoa and University of Turin.

Jonas Gehring, Michael Auli, David Grangier, and Yann N Dauphin. 2016. A convolutional encoder model for neural machine translation. *arXiv preprint arXiv:1611.02344*.

Anna Giacalone Ramat. 2003. *Verso l'italiano. Percorsi e strategie di acquisizione*. Roma, Carocci.

Sylviane Granger. 1998. The computer learner corpus: a versatile new source of data for SLA research. In *Learner English on computer*, pages 3–18. Routledge.

Sylviane Granger, Maïté Dupont, Fanny Meunier, and Magali Paquot. 2020. International Corpus of Learner English. Version 3 (Handbook and web interface). *Louvain-la-Neuve: Presses Universitaires de Louvain*, page 134.

Carl James. 1998. *Errors in language learning and use*. Pearson Educational Limited.

Masahiro Kaneko and Mamoru Komachi. 2019. Multi-head multi-layer attention to deep language representations for grammatical error detection. *Computación y Sistemas*, 23(3):883–891.

Adam Kilgarriff. 2001. Comparing corpora. *International journal of corpus linguistics*, 6(1):97–133.

Adam Kilgarriff, Vít Baisa, Jan Bušta, Miloš Jakubíček, Vojtěch Kovář, Jan Michelfeit, Pavel Rychlý, and Vít Suchomel. 2014. The sketch engine: ten years on. *Lexicography*, 1(1):7–36.

Elizaveta Kuzmenko and Andrey Kutuzov. 2014. Russian error-annotated learner English corpus: a tool for computer-assisted language learning. In *Proceedings of the third workshop on NLP for computer-assisted language learning*, pages 87–97, Uppsala, Sweden. LiU Electronic Press.

Paul Lennon. 1991. Error: Some problems of definition, identification, and distinction. *Applied linguistics*, 12(2):180–196.

David Little. 2006. The Common European Framework of Reference for Languages: Content, purpose, origin, reception and impact. *Language Teaching*, 39(3):167–190.

Anke Lüdeling and Hagen Hirschmann. 2015. Error annotation systems. In Sylviane Granger, Gaëtanelle Gilquin, and Fanny Meunier, editors, *The Cambridge handbook of learner corpus research*, pages 135–157. Cambridge University Press, Cambridge.

Jakub Náplava, Milan Straka, Jana Straková, and Alexandr Rosen. 2022. Czech grammar error correction with a large and diverse corpus. *Transactions of the Association for Computational Linguistics*, 10:452–467.

Hwee Tou Ng, Siew Mei Wu, Ted Briscoe, Christian Hadiwinoto, Raymond Hendy Susanto, and Christopher Bryant. 2014. The conll-2014 shared task on grammatical error correction. In *Proceedings of the Eighteenth Conference on Computational Natural Language Learning: Shared Task*, pages 1–14.

Hwee Tou Ng, Siew Mei Wu, Yuanbin Wu, Christian Hadiwinoto, and Joel Tetreault. 2013. The CoNLL-2013 shared task on grammatical error correction. In *Proceedings of the Seventeenth Conference on Computational Natural Language Learning: Shared Task*, pages 1–12, Sofia, Bulgaria. Association for Computational Linguistics.

Kostiantyn Omelianchuk, Vitaliy Atrasevych, Artem Chernodub, and Oleksandr Skurzhanskyi. 2020. GECToR – grammatical error correction: Tag, not rewrite. In *Proceedings of the Fifteenth Workshop on Innovative Use of NLP for Building Educational Applications*, pages 163–170, Seattle, WA, USA → Online. Association for Computational Linguistics.

Matthew E. Peters, Waleed Ammar, Chandra Bhagavatula, and Russell Power. 2017. Semi-supervised sequence tagging with bidirectional language models. In *Proceedings of the 55th Annual Meeting of the Association for Computational Linguistics (Volume 1: Long Papers)*, pages 1756–1765, Vancouver, Canada. Association for Computational Linguistics.

Matthew E Peters, Mark Neumann, Luke Zettlemoyer, and Wen-tau Yih. 2018. Dissecting contextual word embeddings: Architecture and representation. In *EMNLP, Association for Computational Linguistics*, pages 1499–1509.

Lance A Ramshaw and Mitchell P Marcus. 1999. Text chunking using transformation-based learning. In *Natural language processing using very large corpora*, pages 157–176. Springer.

Marek Rei. 2017. Semi-supervised multitask learning for sequence labeling. In *Proceedings of the 55th Annual Meeting of the Association for Computational Linguistics*, pages 2121–2130.

Larry Selinker. 1972. Interlanguage. *International Review of Applied Linguistics*, 10(3):209–231.

Marco Siino, Elisa Di Nuovo, Ilenia Tinnirello, and Marco La Cascia. 2022. Fake news spreaders detection: Sometimes attention is not all you need. *Information*, 13(9):426.

Ashish Vaswani, Noam Shazeer, Niki Parmar, Jakob Uszkoreit, Llion Jones, Aidan N Gomez, Łukasz Kaiser, and Illia Polosukhin. 2017. Attention is all you need. *Advances in neural information processing systems*, 30.

Elena Volodina, Christopher Bryant, Andrew Caines, Orphée De Clercq, Jennifer-Carmen Frey, Elizaveta Ershova, Alexandr Rosen, and Olga Vinogradova. 2023. MultiGED-2023 shared task at NLP4CALL: Multilingual Grammatical Error Detection. In *Proceedings of the 12th workshop on Natural Language Processing for Computer Assisted Language Learning (NLP4CALL)*, pages 1–15, Tórshavn, Faroe Islands.

Elena Volodina, Lena Granstedt, Arild Matsson, Beáta Megyesi, Ildikó Pilán, Julia Prentice, Dan Rosén, Lisa Rudebeck, Carl-Johan Schenström, Gunlög Sundberg, et al. 2019. The swell language learner corpus: From design to annotation. *Northern European Journal of Language Technology (NEJLT)*, 6:67–104.

Xi Yang, Jiang Bian, William R Hogan, and Yonghui Wu. 2020. Clinical concept extraction using transformers. *Journal of the American Medical Informatics Association*. Ocaa189.

Zhilin Yang, Zihang Dai, Yiming Yang, Jaime Carbonell, Russ R Salakhutdinov, and Quoc V Le. 2019. XLNet: Generalized autoregressive pretraining for language understanding. *Advances in neural information processing systems*, 32.

Helen Yannakoudakis, Ted Briscoe, and Ben Medlock. 2011. A new dataset and method for automatically grading ESOL texts. In *Proceedings of the 49th Annual Meeting of the Association for Computational Linguistics: Human Language Technologies*, pages 180–189, Portland, Oregon, USA. Association for Computational Linguistics.

Helen Yannakoudakis, Øistein E Andersen, Ardeshir Geranpayeh, Ted Briscoe, and Diane Nicholls. 2018. Developing an automated writing placement system for ESL learners. *Applied Measurement in Education*, 31(3):251–267.

Zheng Yuan, Shiva Taslimipoor, Christopher Davis, and Christopher Bryant. 2021. Multi-class grammatical error detection for correction: A tale of two systems. In *Proceedings of the 2021 Conference on Empirical Methods in Natural Language Processing*, pages 8722–8736, Online and Punta Cana, Dominican Republic. Association for Computational Linguistics.

A distantly supervised Grammatical Error Detection/Correction system for Swedish

Murathan Kurfalı*
Department of Psychology†
Stockholm University
murathan.kurfali@su.se

Robert Östling*
Department of Linguistics
Stockholm University
robert@ling.su.se

Abstract

This paper presents our submission to the first Shared Task on Multilingual Grammatical Error Detection (MultiGED-2023). Our method utilizes a transformer-based sequence-to-sequence model, which was trained on a synthetic dataset consisting of 3.2 billion words. We adopt a distantly supervised approach, with the training process relying exclusively on the distribution of language learners' errors extracted from the annotated corpus used to construct the training data. In the Swedish track, our model ranks fourth out of seven submissions in terms of the target $F_{0.5}$ metric, while achieving the highest precision. These results suggest that our model is conservative yet remarkably precise in its predictions.

1 Introduction

In today's interconnected world, learning a language is not optional for the majority of people. With digital platforms now the primary medium for individuals to express their thoughts and ideas, written communication has taken precedence over verbal communication, many people often find themselves producing text in a language that is not their first language. Consequently, natural language processing (NLP) systems that can assist non-native speakers in producing grammatically correct text are now more essential than ever. Grammatical error detection (GED) and grammatical error correction (GEC) are two well-established tasks that are designed to improve the writing skills of language users by identifying their errors as well as offering possible suggestions to correct them (Ng et al., 2014; Bryant et al., 2019; Ranalli and Yamashita, 2022).

*The authors contributed equally to this work

†Work carried out while at the Department of Linguistics.

This paper presents a system description of our submission to the first Shared task on Multilingual Grammatical Error Detection, MultiGED-2023 (Volodina et al., 2023). Our approach relies on training a transformer-based sequence-to-sequence model on a synthetic dataset, building upon previous work (e.g. Grundkiewicz et al., 2019; Nyberg, 2022). The distantly supervised training process requires manually error-annotated corpus exclusively to extract the distribution of language learners' errors which is mimicked in the synthetic data creation process. Hence, the employed pipeline aims to capture the characteristics of errors made by language learners while sidestepping the problem of sparsity by eliminating the need for direct supervision or large labeled datasets.

Our submission is confined to Swedish as the developed model is intended as a baseline for our ongoing work on Swedish grammatical error correction using large language models (Östling and Kurfalı, 2022). According to the official results, our model[1] is very accurate with a high precision score, indicating that it has a low false positive rate; yet, it cannot recognize various error types, as suggested by the low recall scores. The rest of the paper discusses previous work on Swedish (Section 2), presents the system in detail (Section 3), analyzes the results and implications (Section 4), and concludes with suggestions for future research directions (Section 5).

2 Related Work

Following our focus on Swedish, we restrict this section to research on Swedish grammatical error correction. Granska (Domeij et al., 2000) is one of the earliest Swedish grammar-checking systems, using part-of-speech tagging, morphological features, and error rules to identify grammat-

[1] https://github.com/MurathanKurfali/swedish-gec

Murathan Kurfalı and Robert Östling. A distantly supervised Grammatical Error Detection/Correction system for Swedish. *Proceedings of the 12th Workshop on Natural Language Processing for Computer Assisted Language Learning (NLP4CALL 2023)*. Linköping Electronic Conference Proceedings 197: 35–39.

Method	Original Sentence	Corrupted Sentence
1. Rearrange words	Jag älskar att läsa läroböcker.	Jag **läroböcker** att **älskar** läsa.
2. Insert spurious words or phrases	Jag älskar att läsa läroböcker.	Jag älskar att **plötsligt** läsa läroböcker.
3. Replace words or phrases	Jag älskar att läsa läroböcker.	Jag älskar att **skriva** läroböcker.
4. Change inflections, split compounds	Jag älskar att läsa läroböcker.	Jag **älskade** att läsa **läro bok**.
5. Letter substitutions	Jag älskar att läsa läroböcker.	Jag **älskat** att **läda** läroböcker.
6. Change capitalization	Jag älskar att läsa läroböcker.	**jag** älskar **ATT** läsa **LÄROBÖCKER**.

Table 1: Illustration of corruption methods applied to a simple sentence, "I love reading textbooks." Note that the table is not exhaustive and showcases only one of the several possible ways a sentence can be corrupted by a specific strategy, and not necessarily the most probable way. For simplicity, the illustration does not show errors added on top of each other, as done in the real data.

ical issues. More recent studies have explored methods to correct errors in learner texts, such as using word embeddings to obtain correction candidates (Pilán and Volodina, 2018) and a tool developed by (Getman, 2021) that detects erroneous words and sequences, suggesting corrections based on sub-word language models and morphological features.

Nyberg (2022) is the most notable, if not the only, example of integrating neural approaches into Swedish GEC, which also serves as the basis for our approach. Nyberg (2022) conducts GEC using two different but related methods: one employing a Transformer model for a neural machine translation approach, and the other utilizing a Swedish version of the pre-trained language model BERT to estimate the likelihood of potential corrections. These methods have demonstrated promising results in correcting different error types, with the first approach excelling at handling syntactical and punctuation errors, while the latter outperforms in addressing lexical and morphological errors.

3 System Overview

In the following section, we provide a detailed description of our submission. Our system is primarily a grammatical error correction model which is trained on a synthetic dataset consisting of original sentences and their artificially corrupted versions. The rest of the section details our training data generation procedure, model architecture, and the post-processing step to arrive at the locations of the identified errors.

3.1 Training data

We generally follow the approach of (Nyberg, 2022) in generating artificial data by corrupting text, but use more extensive corruption heuristics.

Data is collected from the collection of Språkbanken[2], and consists of a number of mixed-domain corpora of modern Swedish. This includes blog texts, news, and fiction. Since all data is processed sentence by sentence, we use sentence-scrambled data which we deduplicate after merging all the subcorpora. The final amount of data is 3.2 billion words. Empirical distributions for error types is derived from the DaLAJ (Volodina et al., 2021) dataset of linguistic acceptability in Swedish.

Corruption of sentences is performed as a pipeline, where each of the following procedures is applied in order:

1. *Rearrange words.* With probability 0.1, the word at position i is moved to a position sampled from $\mathcal{N}(i, 1.5)$ and rounded to the nearest integer. Words are not moved across punctuation marks.

2. Insert spurious words or phrases. For each sentence position i, with probability 0.025 an n-gram (possibly a unigram) is inserted at this position. The n-gram to be inserted is sampled from the DaLAJ distribution.

3. *Replace words or phrases.* For each sen-

[2]https://spraakbanken.gu.se/ – specifically we used the following corpora, which constitutes Språkbanken's collection of modern Swedish corpora at the time of download: *sweachum, sweacsam, romi, romii, rom99, storsuc, bloggmix1998, bloggmix1999, bloggmix2000, bloggmix2001, bloggmix2002, bloggmix2003, bloggmix2004, bloggmix2005, bloggmix2006, bloggmix2007, bloggmix2008, bloggmix2009, bloggmix2010, bloggmix2011, bloggmix2012, bloggmix2013, bloggmix2014, bloggmix2015, bloggmix2016, bloggmix2017, bloggmixodat, gp1994, gp2001, gp2002, gp2003, gp2004, gp2005, gp2006, gp2007, gp2008, gp2009, gp2010, gp2011, gp2012, gp2013, gp2d, press65, press76, press95, press96, press97, press98, webbnyheter2001, webbnyheter2002, webbnyheter2003, webbnyheter2004, webbnyheter2005, webbnyheter2006, webbnyheter2007, webbnyheter2008, webbnyheter2009, webbnyheter2010, webbnyheter2011, webbnyheter2012, webbnyheter2013, attasidor, dn1987, ordat, fof, snp7879, suc3, wikipedia-sv, talbanken*

tence position i, sample a replacement n-gram from the empirical replacement distribution in DaLAJ. Word deletion may also be performed at this stage, by replacing by a shorter n-gram. In most cases, this leads to no change.

4. *Change inflections and split compounds.* With probability 0.1, pick a random new inflection of the word (assuming it can be inflected – otherwise do nothing). With probability 0.25, split compounds by inserting spaces. The compound analysis is performed using the morphological lexicon of SALDO (Borin et al., 2013).

5. *Letter substitutions.* For each letter in the sentence, sample it using the empirical letter replacement distribution from DaLAJ. In most cases this results in no change. A temperature parameter of $t = 1.5$ is used when sampling.

6. *Change capitalization.* With probability 0.2, turn the whole sentence into lowercase. With probability 0.01, turn the whole sentence into upper-case. With probability 0.025, perform the following: for each individual *word* in the sentence, turn it to uppercase with probability 0.1.

We note that the DaLAJ dataset is derived from the SweLL corpus (Volodina et al., 2019), and the statistics used to estimate the sampling distributions for text corruption may overlap to some extent with the source of the shared task test set. It is unfortunately difficult to quantify exactly how large the overlap is, since both datasets (DaLAJ and the SweLL-derived MultiGED test set) have been created independently from the SweLL corpus using different types of processing that makes it challenging to map sentences between the two resources. We hope that future work will be able to remedy this problem by ensuring that fully disjoint sets of data are used to estimate the corruption model parameters and evaluate the final grammatical error detection system.

3.2 Model Architecture

We model grammatical error correction as a translation problem where the input sentence with errors is treated as the source language and the corrected sentence as the target language. Our model

Team Name	P	R	F0.5
EliCoDe	81.80	**66.34**	**78.16**
DSL-MIM-HUS	74.85	44.92	66.05
Brainstorm Thinkers	73.81	39.94	63.11
Our system	**82.41**	27.18	58.60
VLP-char	26.40	55.00	29.46
NTNU-TRH	80.12	5.09	20.31

Table 2: Official results for the Swedish language.

is based on the transformer architecture (Vaswani et al., 2017), which has become the default choice for many natural language processing tasks due to its self-attention mechanism which is highly effective in capturing long-range dependencies in sequences.

We implement our model with the OpenNMT-py library (Klein et al., 2017), following the suggested base configuration. The model is trained for 100,000 training steps, with a validation step interval of 10,000 and an initial warm-up phase of 8,000 steps. Both the encoder and decoder are of the transformer type, with 6 layers, a hidden size of 512, and 8 attention heads. We learn a sentence-piece vocabulary (Kudo and Richardson, 2018) of 32,000 sub-word units to tokenize the sentences.

Training configuration We trained our model using mini-batches containing 400 sentence pairs, distributed across four GPUs, and accumulated gradients for 4 iterations. This resulted in an effective mini-batch size of 6,400 sentence pairs. The training was carried out on A100 GPUs, taking approximately 16 hours in total to complete.

3.3 Post-processing: Correction to Detection

As mentioned earlier, despite the shared task's focus on grammatical error detection, our model is originally trained as a grammatical error correction model which we developed as a baseline in our ongoing work (Östling and Kurfalı, 2022). Therefore, the output of our model is in the form of corrected sentences rather than detected errors. To convert the corrected sentences into detected errors, we perform post-processing on the model's output.

We use the difflib library[3] to compare the original sentences with the corrected sentences and identify the differences between them. Given the goal of the shared task is to identify incorrect

[3]https://docs.python.org/3/library/difflib.html

	P	R	F0.5
Training set	78.72	26.63	56.59
Development set	81.52	26.73	57.82
Test set	82.41	27.18	58.60

Table 3: Additional results on the training and development set. The last line refers to the official results on the test set.

words, we disregard all additions made by our model and focus on the changes performed on the original sentences. Specifically, any words that are not copied unchanged from the original sentence to the corrected sentence are marked as errors that needed correction.

4 Results and Discussion

In this section, we present the results of the shared task on grammatical error detection for the Swedish language. The performance of our system is compared to other participating teams in terms of precision (P), recall (R), and F0.5 score, which is the harmonic mean between precision and recall, with a higher emphasis on precision. Table 2 provides an overview of the performance metrics for each team.

As shown in Table 2, our system achieved the highest precision of 82.41% among all participants. This indicates that our model's predictions for grammatical errors were highly accurate. However, our recall score of 27.18% demonstrates that our model failed to identify a significant proportion of the actual errors in the dataset. This trade-off between precision and recall resulted in an F0.5 score of 58.60%, which places our system in the fourth position among the six participating teams.

In addition to the official results on the test, we present additional results on the shared task's training and development sets in Table 3 as none of these sets are utilized during the model training. We observe that the results are stable across the sets and our model exhibits the same conservative behavior.

Lastly, it is worth noting that the task of grammatical error correction is significantly more challenging than the task of grammatical error detection. While error detection is essentially a binary classification problem at the token level, error correction requires identifying the specific type and location of the error as well as suggesting a suitable correction. Consequently, our pipeline is counter-intuitive in the sense that we are using a more sparse task (error correction) to tackle a simpler one (error detection). Therefore, we would like to emphasize that the results are unlikely to reflect the full potential of such a transformers-based model for grammatical error detection. It's highly probable that the model could perform much better if trained specifically to predict whether an individual token requires correction or not.

5 Conclusion

In this paper, we described our submission to the first Shared task on Multilingual Grammatical Error Detection (MultiGED-2023) for the Swedish language. Our approach relied on a transformer-based sequence-to-sequence model trained on a synthetic dataset, using a distantly supervised training process. Our system achieved the highest precision score among the participating teams, indicating that our model's predictions for grammatical errors are highly accurate. However, our low recall score indicated that our model was not able to detect all errors in the dataset, possibly a limitation of the training process.

6 Future work

While our current proposal focuses exclusively on Swedish, the proposed pipeline can be readily adapted to other languages with an error-annotated corpus and a large monolingual corpus. Additionally, an interesting direction for further research would be to explore the effectiveness of following the error distribution derived from the error-annotated corpus through an ablation study.

Acknowledgments

The computations were enabled by resources provided by the Swedish National Infrastructure for Computing (SNIC) at C3SE partially funded by the Swedish Research Council through grant agreement no. 2018-05973.

This work was funded in part by the Swedish Research council through grant agreement no. 2019-04129.

References

Lars Borin, Markus Forsberg, and Lennart Lönngren. 2013. Saldo: a touch of yin to wordnet's yang. *Language resources and evaluation*, 47:1191–1211.

Christopher Bryant, Mariano Felice, Øistein E Andersen, and Ted Briscoe. 2019. The bea-2019 shared task on grammatical error correction. In *Proceedings of the Fourteenth Workshop on Innovative Use of NLP for Building Educational Applications*, pages 52–75.

Rickard Domeij, Ola Knutsson, Johan Carlberger, and Viggo Kann. 2000. Granska–an efficient hybrid system for swedish grammar checking. In *Proceedings of the 12th Nordic Conference of Computational Linguistics (NODALIDA 1999)*, pages 49–56.

Yaroslav Getman. 2021. Automated writing support for swedish learners. In *Swedish Language Technology Conference and NLP4CALL*, pages 21–26.

Roman Grundkiewicz, Marcin Junczys-Dowmunt, and Kenneth Heafield. 2019. Neural grammatical error correction systems with unsupervised pre-training on synthetic data. In *Proceedings of the Fourteenth Workshop on Innovative Use of NLP for Building Educational Applications*, pages 252–263.

Guillaume Klein, Yoon Kim, Yuntian Deng, Jean Senellart, and Alexander M Rush. 2017. Opennmt: Open-source toolkit for neural machine translation. In *Proceedings of ACL 2017, System Demonstrations*, pages 67–72.

Taku Kudo and John Richardson. 2018. Sentencepiece: A simple and language independent subword tokenizer and detokenizer for neural text processing. In *Proceedings of the 2018 Conference on Empirical Methods in Natural Language Processing: System Demonstrations*, pages 66–71.

Hwee Tou Ng, Siew Mei Wu, Ted Briscoe, Christian Hadiwinoto, Raymond Hendy Susanto, and Christopher Bryant. 2014. The conll-2014 shared task on grammatical error correction. In *Proceedings of the Eighteenth Conference on Computational Natural Language Learning: Shared Task*, pages 1–14.

Martina Nyberg. 2022. Grammatical error correction for learners of swedish as a second language. Master's thesis, Uppsala University, Department of Linguistics and Philology.

Ildikó Pilán and Elena Volodina. 2018. Exploring word embeddings and phonological similarity for the unsupervised correction of language learner errors. In *Proceedings of the Second Joint SIGHUM Workshop on Computational Linguistics for Cultural Heritage, Social Sciences, Humanities and Literature*, pages 119–128.

Jim Ranalli and Taichi Yamashita. 2022. Automated written corrective feedback: Error-correction performance and timing of delivery. *Language Learning & Technology*, 26(1):n1.

Ashish Vaswani, Noam Shazeer, Niki Parmar, Jakob Uszkoreit, Llion Jones, Aidan N Gomez, Łukasz Kaiser, and Illia Polosukhin. 2017. Attention is all you need. *Advances in neural information processing systems*, 30.

Elena Volodina, Christopher Bryant, Andrew Caines, Orphée De Clercq, Jennifer-Carmen Frey, Elizaveta Ershova, Alexandr Rosen, and Olga Vinogradova. 2023. MultiGED-2023 shared task at NLP4CALL: Multilingual Grammatical Error Detection. In *Proceedings of the 12th workshop on Natural Language Processing for Computer-Assisted Language Learning (NLP4CALL)*, Tórshavn, Faroe Islands.

Elena Volodina, Lena Granstedt, Arild Matsson, Beáta Megyesi, Ildikó Pilán, Julia Prentice, Dan Rosén, Lisa Rudebeck, Carl-Johan Schenström, Gunlög Sundberg, et al. 2019. The swell language learner corpus: From design to annotation. *Northern European Journal of Language Technology (NEJLT)*, 6:67–104.

Elena Volodina, Yousuf Ali Mohammed, and Julia Klezl. 2021. DaLAJ – a dataset for linguistic acceptability judgments for Swedish. In *Proceedings of the 10th Workshop on NLP for Computer Assisted Language Learning*, pages 28–37, Online. LiU Electronic Press.

Robert Östling and Murathan Kurfalı. 2022. Really good grammatical error correction, and how to evaluate it. In *the ninth Swedish Language Technology Conference (SLTC2022)*.

Two Neural Models for Multilingual Grammatical Error Detection

The Quyen Ngo and **Thi Minh Huyen Nguyen** and **Phuong Le-Hong**[*]✉
VNU University of Science, Vietnam National University, Hanoi
FPT Technology Research Institute, FPT University, Hanoi[*]
(ngoquyenbg|huyenntm|phuonglh)@vnu.edu.vn

Abstract

This paper presents two neural models for multilingual grammatical error detection and their results in the MultiGED-2023 shared task. The first model uses a simple, purely supervised character-based approach. The second model uses a large language model which is pretrained on 100 different languages and fine-tuned on the provided datasets of the shared task. Despite simple approaches, the two systems achieved promising results. One system has the second best F-score; the other is in the top four of participating systems.

1 Introduction

Grammatical Error Detection (GED) is the task of detecting different kinds of errors in text such as spelling, punctuation, grammatical, and word choice errors. It is one of the key components in the grammatical error correction (GEC) community. This paper concerns with the development of different methods for subtoken representation and their evaluation on standard benchmarks for multiple languages. Our work is inspired by the recent shared task MultiGED-2023. The aim of this task is to detect tokens in need of correction across five different languages, labeling them as either correct ("*c*") or incorrect ("*i*"), i.e. performing binary classification at the token level.

Recent GED methods make use of neural sequence labeling models, either recurrent neural networks or transformers. The first experiments using convolutional neural network and long short-term memory networks (LSTM) models for GED was proposed in 2016 (Rei and Yannakoudakis, 2016). Later, a bidirectional, attentional LSTM was used to jointly learn token-level and sentence-level representations and combine them so as to detect grammatically incorrect sentences and to identify the location of the error tokens at the same time (Rei and Søgaard, 2019). The bidirectional LSTM model was also used together with grammaticality-specific word embeddings to improve GED performance (Kaneko et al., 2017). A bidirectional LSTM model was trained on synthetic data generated by an attentional sequence-to-sequence model to push GED score (Kasewa et al., 2018). Best-performing GED systems employ transformer block-based model for token-level labeling. A pretrained BERT model has been fine-tuned for GED and shown its superior performance in (Kaneko and Komachi, 2019). The BERT model has also been shown significant improvement over LSTM models in both GED and GEC (Liu et al., 2021). The state-of-the-art GED method uses a multi-class detection method (Yuan et al., 2021).

In this work, we also employ state-of-the-art sequence labeling methods, which are based on LSTM or BERT. In contrast to previous work, we focus on different representations of tokens at subtoken levels. Our best-performing system can process multiple languages using a single model.

2 Methods

We use two different token representations, one at the character level, and one at the subtoken level.

2.1 Character-based Representation

In this representation, the j-th input token of a sentence is represented by the concatenation of three vectors (b_j, m_j, e_j) corresponding to its characters. More precisely, the token is represented by vector $x_j = (b_j, m_j, e_j)$ where the first vector b_j and the third vectors e_j represent the first and last character of the token respectively. The second vector m_j represents *a bag of characters* of the middle subtoken without the initial and final positions.

Phuong Le-Hong, The Quyen Ngo and Thi Minh Huyen Nguyen. Two Neural Models for Multilingual Grammatical Error Detection. *Proceedings of the 12th Workshop on Natural Language Processing for Computer Assisted Language Learning (NLP4CALL 2023)*. Linköping Electronic Conference Proceedings 197: 40–44.

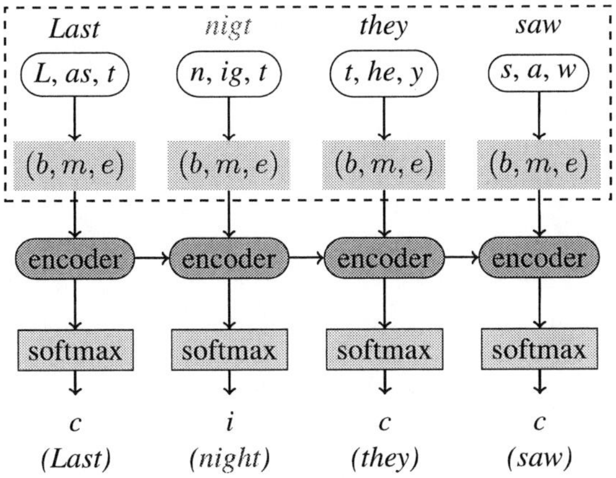

Figure 1: Our character-based model

The dotted frame in Figure 1 depicts this representation. For example, the token "*Last*" is represented as a concatenation of the following vectors: (1) an one-hot vector for character *L*; (2) an one-hot vector for character *t*, and (3) a bag-of-character multihot vector for the internal characters *a, s*. Thus, each token is represented by a vector of size $3V$ where V is the size of the alphabet. The label y_j is predicted by a softmax layer:

$$y_j = \frac{\exp(W_j \cdot h_j)}{\sum_k \exp(W_k \cdot h_j)}.$$

This representation is inspired by a semi-character word recognition method which was proposed by Sakaguchi et al. (2017). It was demonstrated that this method is significantly more robust in word spelling correction compared to character-based convolutional networks.

2.2 Subtoken-based Representation

Recent language processing systems have used unsupervised text tokenizer and detokenizer so as to make a purely end-to-end system that does not depend on language-specific pre- and post-processing. SentencePiece is a method which implements subword units, e.g., byte-pair-encoding – BPE (Sennrich et al., 2016) and unigram language model (Kudo, 2018) with the extension of direct training from raw sentences. Using this method, the vocabulary size is predetermined prior to the neural encoder training. Our system also uses subtoken representation.

2.3 LSTM and BERT Encoders

The LSTM network is a common type of recurrent neural networks which is capable of processing sequential data efficiently. This was a common method prior to 2017, before Transformers (Vaswani et al., 2017), which dispense entirely with recurrence and rely solely on the attention mechanism. Despite being outdated, we developed a purely supervised LSTM encoder to test the effectiveness of the character-based method.

We employ the XLM-RoBERTa model as another encoder in our system. RoBERTa (Liu et al., 2019) is based on Google's BERT model released in 2018 (Devlin et al., 2019). It modifies key hyperparameters, removing the next-sentence pretraining objective and training with much larger mini-batches and learning rates. RoBERTa has the same architecture as BERT, but uses a byte-level BPE as a tokenizer. The XLM-RoBERTa model was proposed in 2020 (Conneau et al., 2020), which is based on RoBERTa. It is a large multilingual language model, trained on 100 languages, 2.5TB of filtered CommonCrawl data. It has been shown that pretraining multilingual models at scale leads to significant performance gains for a wide range of cross-lingual transfer tasks. Unlike some XLM multilingual models, this model does not require language tensors to understand which language is used, and should be able to determine the correct language from the input ids.

3 Experiments

This section presents the datasets in use, experimental settings and obtained results of our system.

3.1 Datasets

The datasets are provided by the MultiGED-2023 shared task.[1] The shared task provides training, development and test data for each of the five languages: Czech, English, German, Italian and Swedish. The training and development datasets are available in the MultiGED-2023 GitHub repository, and test sets are released during the test phase for participating teams. Table 1 shows the statistics of the datasets.

3.2 Evaluation Metric

Evaluation is carried out in terms of token-based precision, recall and $F_{0.5}$, consistent with previous work on error detection. $F_{0.5}$ is used instead of F_1 because humans judge false positives more harshly than false negatives and so precision is more important than recall.

[1] *https://github.com/spraakbanken/multiged-2023*

Lang.	Sents.	Tokens	Errors	Rate
Czech	35,453	399,742	84,041	0.210
English	33,243	531,416	50,860	0.096
German	24,079	381,134	57,897	0.152
Italian	7,949	99,698	14,893	0.149
Swedish	8,553	145,507	27,274	0.187

Table 1: Statistics of datasets in five languages

3.3 Experimental Settings

Our first system, namely VLP-char, uses the character-based token representation and the LSTM encoder. Its parameters are initialized with random vectors in each run. This allows us to establish results in a pure supervised learning setting rather than a semi-supervised or transfer learning setting. The same model is trained separately for each language, resulting five models. All five language-specific models are trained with the Adam optimizer (Kingma and Ba, 2015), and with learning rate 5×10^{-4}. We use the cross-entropy loss function for multinomial classification as usual. All models are trained in 80 epochs. The maximum sequence length is set to 60 tokens – this is enough to cover most sentences in the provided datasets. Since the data is highly imbalanced – the error rates are from only 10% (for English) to 24% (for Czech), we set the incorrect label weight to 90% and the correct label weight to 10% when computing the objective function.

This system does not use any external resources; only datasets provided by the organizers are used to train and validate the models. We use the BigDL library[2] as the deep learning framework. Our code is publicly available on GitHub.[3]

Our second system, namely DSL-MIM-HUS, uses the subtoken-based representation and the pretrained XLM-RoBERTa embeddings.[4] This system uses the library NERDA[5] to fine-tune the pretrained embeddings on all datasets. That is, we combine all the provided datasets (training and development splits) into one large dataset and perform the experiment on this combined one. There is thus only one model for all the five languages. The combined dataset is divided into training, development and test split with the ratios 0.8, 0.1 and 0.1, respectively. There are 82,976 training samples, 10,371 development samples and 10,371 test samples respectively. We did not keep the proportion of different language data the same when sampling. It had been more beneficial if the proportion would have been kept since the sizes of languages are very different – there are three times more German sentences than Italian sentences. The hyper-parameters are tuned on the development set and selected as follows: the learning rate of 10^{-5}, the number of training epochs of 20.

Language	Precision	Recall	$F_{0.5}$
Czech	34.93	**63.95**	38.42
English (FCE)	20.76	29.53	22.07
English (REA)	–	–	–
German	25.18	44.27	27.56
Italian	25.79	44.24	28.14
Swedish	26.40	55.00	29.46

Table 2: Performance of the VLP-char system on the private test set. The number in bold font is the best recall of all participating systems on the Czech dataset.

3.4 Results

3.4.1 Supervised System

Without using any external datasets or pre-trained embeddings, the VLP-char system obtained mediocre results. It ranks the fourth place among participating systems. This sytem consistently gives higher recall than precision on all the languages, while other systems have better precision than recall. It achieves 63.95% of recall on the Czech test set, which is the highest recall among participating systems for this language, as shown in Table 2.

Despite mediocre results, this system represents what we can build with very limited data.

3.4.2 Pretrained System

On our test split, the system DSL-MIM-HUS achieves a precision of 80.88%, a recall of 64.07% and $F_{0.5}$ of 71.50% for incorrect token prediction. The corresponding scores on the training set is 98.54%, 96.75%, and 97.64%, respectively. Since this combined dataset contains all the provided samples of all languages, it does not make sense to evaluate on each language separately.

On the private test set of the shared task MultiGED-2023 (Volodina et al., 2023), the system DSL-MIM-HUS is the second highest ranking. It achieves the best score among participating

[2] *https://github.com/intel-analytics/BigDL*
[3] *https://github.com/phuonglh/vlp/con/*
[4] *https://huggingface.co/xlm-roberta-large*
[5] *https://github.com/ebanalyse/NERDA*

Language	Precision	Recall	$F_{0.5}$
Czech	58.31	55.69	57.76
English (FCE)	72.36	37.81	61.18
English (REA)	62.81	28.88	**50.86**
German	77.80	51.92	70.75
Italian	75.72	38.67	63.55
Swedish	74.85	44.92	66.05

Table 3: Performance of the DSL-MIM-HUS system on the private test set. The number in bold font is the best score of all participating systems on the English REALEC dataset.

systems on the English REALEC dataset. Table 3 shows the performance of this system on the private test set, as announced by the organizers.

Although the XLM-RoBERTa system clearly outperformed the LSTM system, the LSTM system was trained on a fraction of the data available to the XLM-RoBERTa system.

4 Conclusion

We have presented two neural models for multilingual grammatical error detection and their results in the MultiGED-2023 shared task. One model uses a purely supervised LSTM network on a character-based token representation. The other model uses a pretrained BERT network on a subtoken representation. The two systems have achieved promising results in the shared task.

We are going to seek a better way to exploit syntactic and semantic information which comes from a dependency parser. We believe that explicit syntactic and semantic dependency between tokens of a sentence will be fruitful in detecting grammatical errors. In a recent study, we have demonstrated the usefulness of syntactic structures in improving lexical embeddings (Dang and Le-Hong, 2021). The idea of incorporating constituent-based syntax has also been shown effective for GED as well (Zhang and Li, 2022).

References

Alexis Conneau, Kartikay Khandelwal, Naman Goyal, Vishrav Chaudhary, Guillaume Wenzek, Francisco Guzmán, Edouard Grave, Myle Ott, Luke Zettlemoyer, and Veselin Stoyanov. 2020. Unsupervised cross-lingual representation learning at scale. In *Proceedings of the 58th ACL*, pages 8440–8451, Online. ACL.

Hoang-Vu Dang and Phuong Le-Hong. 2021. A combined syntactic-semantic embedding model based on lexicalized tree-adjoining grammar. *Computer Speech and Language*, 68(2021):101202.

Jacob Devlin, Ming-Wei Chang, Kenton Lee, and Kristina Toutanova. 2019. BERT: Pre–training of deep bidirectional transformers for language understanding. In *Proceedings of NAACL*, pages 1–16, Minnesota, USA.

Masahiro Kaneko and Mamoru Komachi. 2019. Multi-head multi-layer attention to deep language representations for grammatical error detection. *Computación y Sistemas*, 23(3):883–891.

Masahiro Kaneko, Yuya Sakaizawa, and Mamoru Komachi. 2017. Grammatical error detection using error- and grammaticality-specific word embeddings. In *Proceedings of the Eighth IJCNLP*, pages 40–48, Taipei, Taiwan. AFNLP.

Sudhanshu Kasewa, Pontus Stenetorp, and Sebastian Riedel. 2018. Wronging a right: Generating better errors to improve grammatical error detection. In *Proceedings of the 2018 EMNLP*, pages 4977–4983, Brussels, Belgium. ACL.

Diederik P. Kingma and Jimmy Ba. 2015. Adam: A method for stochastic optimization. In *Proceedings of the 3rd International Conference on Learning Representations, ICLR 2015*, pages 1–15, San Diego, CA, USA.

Taku Kudo. 2018. Subword regularization: Improving neural network translation models with multiple subword candidates. In *Proceedings of the 56th ACL*, pages 66–75, Melbourne, Australia. ACL.

Yinhan Liu, Myle Ott, Naman Goyal, Jingfei Du, Mandar Joshi, Danqi Chen, Omer Levy, Mike Lewis, Luke Zettlemoyer, and Veselin Stoyanov. 2019. RoBERTa: A robustly optimized BERT pretraining approach.

Zhenghao Liu, Xiaoyuan Yi, Maosong Sun, Liner Yang, and Tat-Seng Chua. 2021. Neural quality estimation with multiple hypotheses for grammatical error correction. In *Proceedings of the 2021 NAACL*, pages 5441–5452, Online. ACL.

Marek Rei and Anders Søgaard. 2019. Jointly learning to label sentences and tokens. In *Proceeding of AAAI*, pages 6916–6923, Honolulu, Hawaii, USA.

Marek Rei and Helen Yannakoudakis. 2016. Compositional sequence labeling models for error detection in learner writing. In *Proceedings of the 54th ACL*, pages 1181–1191, Berlin, Germany. ACL.

Keisuke Sakaguchi, Kevin Duh, Matt Post, and Benjamin Van Durme. 2017. Robsut wrod reocginiton via semi-character recurrent neural network. In *Proceedings of the 31st AAAI*, AAAI'17, pages 3281–3287. AAAI Press.

Rico Sennrich, Barry Haddow, and Alexandra Birch. 2016. Neural machine translation of rare words with subword units. In *Proceedings of the 54th ACL*, pages 1715–1725, Berlin, Germany.

Ashish Vaswani, Noam Shazeer, Niki Parmar, Jakob Uszkoreit, Llion Jones, Aidan N Gomez, Lukasz Kaiser, and Illia Polosukhin. 2017. Attention is all you need. In *Advances in Neural Information Processing Systems*, volume 30. Curran Associates, Inc.

Elena Volodina, Christopher Bryant, Andrew Caines, Orphée De Clercq, Jennifer-Carmen Frey, Elizaveta Ershova, Alexandr Rosen, and Olga Vinogradova. 2023. MultiGED-2023 shared task at NLP4CALL: Multilingual Grammatical Error Detection. In *Proceedings of the 12th workshop on Natural Language Processing for Computer Assisted Language Learning (NLP4CALL)*, Tórshavn, Faroe Islands.

Zheng Yuan, Shiva Taslimipoor, Christopher Davis, and Christopher Bryant. 2021. Multi-class grammatical error detection for correction: A tale of two systems. In *Proceedings of the 2021 Conference on EMNLP*, pages 8722–8736, Online and Punta Cana, Dominican Republic. Association for Computational Linguistics.

Yue Zhang and Zhenghua Li. 2022. CSynGEC: Incorporating constituent-based syntax for grammatical error correction with a tailored GEC-oriented parser.

Experiments on Automatic Error Detection and Correction for Uruguayan Learners of English

Romina Brown **Santiago Paez** **Gonzalo Herrera** **Luis Chiruzzo** **Aiala Rosá**
Instituto de Computación, Facultad de Ingeniería
Universidad de la República
Montevideo, Uruguay
{romina.brown,santiago.paez,gonzalo.herrera,luischir,aialar}@fing.edu.uy

Abstract

This paper presents an initial experiment on Grammatical Error Correction and Automatic Grading for short texts written by Uruguayan students that are learning English. We present a set of error detection and correction heuristics, and some experiments on using these heuristics for predicting the grade. Although our experiments are limited due to the nature of the dataset, they are a good proof of concept with promising results that might be extended in the future.

1 Introduction

The kinds of errors committed by students of English as a second language could be very different depending on their background, in particular depending on their L1, but also on the different geographical varieties of their language. For example, the cognates between L1 and L2 (De Groot and Keijzer, 2000), and the homophones between languages and varieties (Kochmar and Briscoe, 2014), influence the way students learn. This could have impact on Grammatical Error Correction (GEC) and Automatic Grading systems, which are often trained in standard corpora that are not adapted to model these geographical diversities.

In Uruguay, the universalization of English teaching throughout all primary schools is one of the objectives of the National Public Education Administration (ANEP). Together with the strategic goals of ANEP, the adoption of One Laptop per Child (OLPC) program, developed as the Ceibal project in Uruguay, improved the accessibility to English classes and resources throughout the country. Uruguay is a Spanish speaking country, its Spanish variety is called Rioplatense Spanish and is shared with some regions of Argentina. This variety presents some particularities that might influence the way students learn English.

In this work, part of a research line on developing tools for Uruguayan learners of English as a second language (Chiruzzo et al., 2022), we present the results of some preliminary experiments on creating automatic GEC and grading systems adapted to the particularities of Uruguayan learners. We use a dataset of short English texts produced by students as answers to an exercise. We analyze the types of errors committed, and design heuristics for detecting and correcting them automatically. Then we carry on experiments on automatic grading using this information.

This work has an important limitation, which is that the only information available in the dataset is the answer to one specific exercise. This implies that the results obtained for this exercise might not generalize to other contexts. In order to alleviate this problem, we try to focus on creating exercise independent features for grading, but we consider this should be taken as only a proof of concept and an initial exploration on the topic, and better datasets will be needed in the future. This is, as far as we know, the first work on GEC and Automatic Grading experiments that considers text produced by Uruguayan students.

2 Related Work

Grammatical Error Correction (GEC) is an active area of research in NLP, with shared tasks and competitions organized regularly. A series of GEC related shared tasks have been proposed together with CoNLL between 2011 and 2014, for example the CoNLL-2014 shared task (Ng et al., 2014) proposed detecting and correcting errors in English essays written by students. They use the NUCLE corpus (Dahlmeier et al., 2013), that contains 1,400 essays in English written by students of the

Romina Brown, Santiago Paez, Gonzalo Herrera, Luis Chiruzzo and Aiala Rosá. Experiments on Automatic Error Detection and Correction for Uruguayan Learners of English. *Proceedings of the 12th Workshop on Natural Language Processing for Computer Assisted Language Learning (NLP4CALL 2023)*. Linköping Electronic Conference Proceedings 197: 45–52.

National University of Singapore.

BEA 2018 Duolingo (Settles et al., 2018) shared task proposed to build systems that predict (not correct) the mistakes a learner will make in the future, given a transcript of exercises written by the same learner annotated with word level mistakes. It is interesting in that it includes the country the learner is from, which could be used to capture the L1 variabilty and geographic diversity.

The BEA-2019 Shared Task on Grammatical Error Correction (Bryant et al., 2019) included two tracks with two datasets: one with 3,600 manually annotated submissions from Cambridge Write & Improve platform, and another LOCNESS dataset with texts produced by native English speakers. Other important datasets include: the Cambridge Learner Corpus (Nicholls, 2003), that contains answers to English exams from Cambridge by students from all over the world, and its FCE subset (Yannakoudakis et al., 2011) with 1,244 annotated answers to the First Certificate in English exam; and the Lang-8 corpus (Mizumoto et al., 2012), with around a million English sentences annotated in a crowd-sourced way from the Lang-8 website[1]. These resources are generally written in a register that is much more complex than the texts we are dealing with in this work, which are texts written by schoolchildren, and most of them are just beginning to learn English.

The main approaches to performing GEC (Ailani et al., 2019) include using rule-based heuristics, classification methods, and machine translation based methods, with the last two approaches requiring a relatively larger set of annotated examples. The related task of Automatic Grading of essays is usually approached with machine learning methods, using a variety of features such as length of the text, POS or n-grams features (Yannakoudakis et al., 2011), different types of errors such as misuse of tenses or spelling (Ballier et al., 2019), or even the use of larger structures such as multi-word expressions (Wilkens et al., 2022).

3 Dataset and Error Analysis

The dataset we worked with is a corpus of answers written by Uruguayan schoolchildren to a writing exercise. In the exercise, students had to describe a person in a picture, together with her likes and dislikes shown as icons below the picture (see Fig. 1).

Figure 1: Picture associated to the exercise. The students had to describe the person in the picture, and her likes and dislikes.

This was part of an exam that was taken in 2017 by many schoolchildren from ages 9 to 11 that were learning English throughout the country. All short texts were graded by teachers following a rubric, with grades between 0 and 6, which roughly correspond to categories between A0 and B1 in CEFR.

There are 65,528 texts in total, but after filtering

Grade	Count	Example
0	13746	le gusta leer comer pipza y escribir lo que no le gusta es cantar comer fruta y pescar
1	11428	i like reading,pizza and rite. i don't like apple,to sing and fish his she andrea 14 years old
2	17699	she wears a pink shirt and jeans shorts he likes to ride a bicycle
3	10281	She has got a dog. She has got a glass in her face. She has got a bike. She drive in a bike. She like read and draw. She like eat pizza. She hate sing. She doesn't like eat apples.
4	1350	Andrea is 14 years old, she is a blondy and athletic girl. She is wearing a pink t-shirt, a white short and sunglasses. She is reading a bike whit her pet, a little dog. She likes eat pizza but doesn't like apples. She has a lot of books because she likes to read. Andrea studies from monday to friday. She doesn't like to fish because it's boring, she doesn't know how to sing
5	135	She is Andrea. She is 14 years old. She tall and thin. She has blonde, long hair. She is wearing white trainers, beige shorts, a pink blouse and sunglasses. She is riding a bike. She likes reading books, eating pizza and geometry. She doesn't like singing, eating apples and fishing. She has a pet. It's a dog. She loves it. She hasn't got a car. She can ride a bike but she can't fly. She gets up early, has breakfast and ride a bike. After that she has a bath and watch tv. Then she has lunch and goes to high school. After high school she goes to hockey classes. After she has a bath again, does her homework and goes to bed. She lives in a big house with his mother, father and sister. She loves her family and she is very happy.
6	13	She is Andrea, she is fourteen years old. She's wearing a pink t-shirt, and a short of jean She is riding her bike with her dog, she likes reading books, she likes eating pizza, and she likes maths. She doesn't like singing, eating apples and fishing She's got a dog but she doesn't have a cat. She doesn't look like a professional bike riding, and she isn't fat but she isn't thin. Her bike is brown and black and her dog is gray and brown, her dog is super cute, I want to be the owner of that dog, but her dog isn't like mine (...) mine is cuter than hers. She's got yellow hair and a black glasses, she is riding her bike in a quiet place, like in a countryside, behind her is a big lake.

Table 1: Example and number of texts for each grade in the corpus, after filtering empty texts.

[1]https://lang-8.com/

empty and a few ungraded texts, we were left with around 54k texts. Table 1 shows a sample of each grade, and the total number of texts per grade in the corpus. The corpus is highly unbalanced, with an overwhelming majority of texts for the lower grades (almost half of them are graded with a score of 0 or 1) and only a few texts with the highest grades (less than 150 examples with grades 5 or 6). As can be seen in the table, lower graded texts tend to be shorter and have much more interference of Spanish words, while higher graded texts are significantly longer and contain more varied English vocabulary and structures.

3.1 Particularities of the sample

One interesting thing about this learners corpus is that it contains particularities of Uruguayan Spanish speakers trying to learn English. It has errors that Spanish speakers would make, but also errors that only speakers of Rioplatense Spanish would commit. Here is one example of an error in the dataset that any Spanish speaker could make:

*those ****hare*** *the things she does not like to do*

Because the letter "h" is silent in Spanish, misspelling *are* as **hare* could be expected, as they would sound homophonous from a Spanish perspective. However, consider the following example from the dataset:

*****llor*** *green*

In this case, the writer intended to write about *green shorts*. Here we can see two errors: writing the adjective after the noun (as is the norm in Spanish grammar), and another mistake that is very particular to Rioplatense Spanish: The misspelling of *shorts* as **llor* responds to the fact that the "ll" digraph is pronounced /ʃ/, which is equivalent to the English "sh" sound.

Also note that these are two different types of spelling errors: in the latter case *llor* is a word that does not exist in English, so it could be captured by a dictionary search, but in the former case *hare* is a perfectly valid word in English which is invalid in that context.

3.2 Types of errors

We took two small subsets of the dataset containing samples of texts for the different categories, called the *development sample* and the *evaluation sample*. The development sample contains 53 texts, and was used to manually inspect the texts and mark all the different types of English spelling and grammar errors that could be found. Two researchers participated in this annotation: They split the development sample set and each researcher evaluated one subset, then they cross-checked their corrections, and finally they discussed the cases were there was disagreement to reach a final conclusion.

After this initial manual labeling of the texts, we compiled a list of common errors and their descriptions. This list was used by two other researchers to mark down the evaluation sample, comprised of 42 texts. Table 2 shows the different types of errors considered, and how many instances of them were found in the development sample and in the evaluation sample. We focused on the most prevalent errors found in the samples

Error	Example	Dev	Eval
Spelling	✗ **reding** ✓ reading	84	69
Subject-Verb agreement	✗ She **have** a dog ✓ She has a dog	42	15
Beginning of sentence caps	✗ **she** is Andrea ✓ She is Andrea	39	68
Use of pronoun	✗ She likes riding in your bike with **your** little dog ✓ She likes riding in her bike with her little dog	26	4
Verb form	✗ She likes **sing** ✓ She likes singing	24	41
Missing subject	✗ She has blond hair, is wearing a pink sweater... ✓ She has blond hair, she is wearing a pink sweater...	15	19
Proper noun caps	✗ She is **andrea** ✓ She is Andrea	15	5
Noun number	✗ She likes **apple** ✓ She likes apples	11	6
Use of determiner	✗ and **a** white trousers ✓ and white trousers	7	14
"I" caps	✗ **i** think she is... ✓ I think she is...	6	0
Adjective order	✗ She has a t-shirt **pink** ✓ She has a pink t-shirt	4	0
Contraction	✗ **doesnt** ✓ doesn't	3	0
Missing verb	✗ She 14 years old ✓ She is 14 years old	2	3
Wrong verb	✗ She **has** 14 years old ✓ She is 14 years old	2	10
Other errors	✗ Finally she goes to bed at 0:00 a.m. **clock** ✓ Finally she goes to bed at 0:00 a.m.	24	23

Table 2: Types of errors found in the development sample and the evaluation sample.

and tried to build heuristics for detecting and correcting them, as we will see in the following section.

4 Detection and Correction Heuristics

The proposed solution for error detection and correction comprises a series of modules that try to capture each type of error, but also need to interact with each other in order to improve the effectiveness of the process. For example, some of the NLP tools we use might not work too well with noisy text such as the one found in this dataset, so it is necessary to perform spelling correction first, before running the other modules. Each heuristic focuses on detecting one type of error, and also providing an appropriate suggestion for correction.

4.1 Spelling

We experimented with three widely used spellcheckers: Hunspell[2], the spellchecker used in open source systems like LibreOffice and the Mozilla suite which combines morphological analysis and pronunciation; Norvig's Spellchecker[3], based on Levenshtein distance search with dictionary filtering; and SymSpell[4], an improvement on Norvig's focused on speed and accuracy.

To capture particular errors like the ones mentioned in section 3.1, we made an adapted dictionary including common mistakes found in the texts. We tried using the different spellcheckers and combinations of them with a voting mechanism. Furthermore, we experimented with the use of BERT (Devlin et al., 2018) for predicting the correct word: We calculated the probability of each word suggested by the spellcheckers in the context of the text, using the `bert-base-uncased` model from Hugging Face.

Method	Acc
All spellcheckers with voting resolution	0.84
All spellcheckers with adapted dictionary	0.71
All spellcheckers with BERT resolution	0.74
Only SymSpell for detection and resolution	0.89

Table 3: Performance of the different methods used for spelling errors detection and resolution over the development sample set.

[2]http://hunspell.github.io/

[3]https://norvig.com/spell-correct.html

[4]https://github.com/wolfgarbe/SymSpell

As shown in Table 3, out of the different combinations of models and tools we tested, the most accurate was using only SymSpell. It was also the fastest method, so we decided to use this tool for the rest of the experiments.

4.2 Capitalization

Note from Table 2 that there are three common errors related to capitalization, which involve not using an upper case in three cases: the beginning of a sentence, the pronoun "I", and proper nouns. The first two cases can be easily detected after sentence segmentation or finding the lowercase token "i", which is never used to refer to something different than the pronoun. However, the third case is more difficult, as the students could become creative and invent names and situations for this exercise. For example, one of the texts included the name "Paco" for the dog in the picture.

We used the Named Entity Recognition module by spaCy[5] to detect proper names. It does a good job when detecting common names used in English, like Andrea, but it failed to capture names or nicknames that are common in Spanish speaking countries, like Paco. In order to overcome this problem, we complemented the use of the NER module with a search in a list of names compiled from the Spanish National Institute of Statistics[6].

4.3 Subject-Verb agreement

In English, as well as in Spanish, the subject of a sentence and its verb must agree in number, and agreement errors are a very prevalent mistake in English learners. These errors could be easily spotted once we identify what the subject and the main verb are, which could be done using a syntactic parser, for example a dependency parser. However, consider the following text from the corpus, where the expected analysis would be the root verb *like* with the subject *she*:

*She ***like** pizza*

Parsers work best when the analyzed text is clean and well written, and this is of course not the case with these texts. The spaCy dependency parser for this example considers *like* as a SCONJ, so it fails to detect it as the root of the sentence. Similar errors occur frequently with noisy texts, so a solution based on a pre-trained parser seems not feasible, although other attempts at solutions

[5]https://spacy.io/

[6]https://www.ine.es/

based on parsing exist, like capturing wrong parses using *mal-rules* as in (Da Costa et al., 2016).

In our case, given the simplicity of the texts, we opted for a different strategy. We use rules for detecting the likely subject and main verb of the sentence: pronouns and proper nouns at the beginning of the sentence are likely subject candidates, followed by verbs that belong to a list of 1000 common verbs for English learners[7] (Turnbull et al., 2010).

We split verb forms in categories according to their inflection, then we experimented with two strategies for agreement error detection: in the first one, inspired by (Gehman et al., 2020), we use BERT to calculate the probability of the verb form used and the alternative ones; the second one, inspired by (Wang and Zhao, 2015), uses a lexicon, POS-tagging and morphology for checking agreement considering pronouns, nouns, verbs, and auxiliary constructions like negations.

Table 4 shows a comparison of both approaches on the development sample. The rules and lexicon approach, although simpler, beats the BERT method on the three considered metrics.

Method	Prec	Rec	F1
BERT	0.77	0.73	0.75
Rules and lexicon	0.82	0.76	0.79

Table 4: Performance of the different methods used for subject-verb agreement errors detection over the development sample set.

4.4 Verb form

Errors in the use of verbal forms are very common when learning English, when students must learn how to use different tenses, particularities of irregular verbs, agreement and the use of infinitives and gerunds in other constructions. The two most frequent errors found in the development sample were subject-verb agreement issues (seen in the previous section) and confusion between infinitive and gerund forms.

We considered our set of 1000 common verbs and their corresponding forms, and wrote a series of manual rules based on (Swan and Walter, 2011) that cover different situations such as: the use of verbs after adjectives, prepositions, accusative pronouns, and verbs that require a specific form. Special care had to be taken when dealing with the issue of parallelism of a construction when used in conjunctions. For example, consider the following sentence:

*She likes *__eat__ pizza, walk at night and *__singing__.*

In this case, our heuristic indicates that the verb form after "likes" should be "to eat", then the use of the verb "walk" is correct, but the verb "singing" should also be changed to "sing".

4.5 Use of determiners

There are two types of errors involving the use of determiners: they are either omitted, or included unnecessarily (wrong use). The heuristic in this case involves using the POS-tagger and morphological analyzer from spaCy to check cases of nouns with or without determiners, and using a series of rules for deciding if the use of determiner is correct. For example, plural nouns should have a plural determiner, or none in some constructions, while singular nouns could use a singular determiner depending if they are countable or not. When a missing determiner is found, the heuristic always suggests including the indefinite article ("a" or "an"), so a pronunciation dictionary[8] is used to tell apart nouns which start with vowel sounds (e.g. "an umbrella" vs. "a unicorn").

4.6 Results in sample sets

Table 5 shows the results of our heuristics over the development and evaluation samples. Note that during the development of the detection and correction heuristics, we used the information obtained by manually annotating the development sample, but the evaluation sample was not seen until later. Nonetheless, the results obtained for the evaluation sample are very similar, which gives us some confidence on how good the heuristics are for capturing the errors in the whole dataset.

	Development			Evaluation		
Error	Prec	Rec	F1	Pre	Rec	F1
Spelling	0.89	0.88	0.88	0.81	0.85	0.83
Caps - "I"	1.0	1.0	1.0	-	-	-
Caps - BoS	0.99	1.0	0.99	0.92	0.79	0.85
Caps - Proper noun	0.73	1.0	0.84	0.75	1.0	0.86
Subject-Verb agreement	0.82	0.76	0.79	0.83	0.77	0.80
Verb form	0.73	0.91	0.81	0.66	0.81	0.72
Determiner - Missing	0.71	0.87	0.78	0.50	0.81	0.62
Determiner - Wrong	0.67	0.67	0.67	0.38	0.75	0.5

Table 5: Results of the error detection heuristics over the development and the evaluation sample sets.

[7] Oxford University Press. Oxford 5000 wordlist, aug 2020. https://www.oxfordlearnersdictionaries.com/us/wordlists/

[8] http://www.speech.cs.cmu.edu/cgi-bin/cmudict

5 Automatic Grading Experiments

After creating the set of heuristics to capture many of the errors committed by the students, we wanted to assess how useful this information would be for predicting grades given by teachers. These grades were assigned following a rubric that takes into account many aspects, including the use of English or Spanish, the production of single words or phrases, the types of errors committed, the general readabilty and soundness of the text, etc. It was interesting to see if our simpler heuristics would provide sufficient information to at least roughly predict the grade. We first split the whole dataset into 70% for training, 15% for development and 15% for test (note that these are different splits than the samples described in section 3.2).

Due to the high imbalance in the dataset, we decided to cluster some grades into ranges. Grades 0 and 1 correspond to the *low* range, 2 and 3 to the *medium* range, and 4 through 6 to the *high* range. Although this does not completely fix the balance problem, by manually inspecting the texts we found these ranges left more homogeneous texts in each category. We will present results both for grade ranges and separate grades.

We ran a baseline experiment where we used bag of words and bag of bigram features. A model trained with these features would of course be highly tailored for grading this particular exercise, and would probably not generalize well to other prompts. For example, some of the most relevant BoW features found in this experiment included "Andrea", "pizza", and "14". However, we have two main motivations for these experiments: we wanted to know how likely it is to create a classifier that would emulate the grades given by teachers, and at the same time we wanted to find out if it is possible to create a classifier that works similarly but is not overfit to the specific words of this exercise.

5.1 Features and models

We trained different classifiers using different combinations of features. As mentioned before, we used BoW features, which in our case were the 750 most frequent unigrams and bigrams.

We also included one feature for each of the heuristics described in section 4, called the "correction features". The feature value is the number of errors the heuristic found for a particular text. So we have eight features counting the number of:

- spelling errors
- beginning of sentence capitalization errors
- pronoun "I" capitalization errors
- proper noun capitalization errors
- verb form errors
- subject-verb agreement errors
- missing determiner errors
- wrong determiner errors

The rationale behind the use of these features is that, if we could capture all the errors in a text, this information could help a classifier predict a grade, even when not knowing the actual words of the text. This would decouple the classifier from the prompt of the exercise and be more generalizable.

We also used a feature indicating length of the texts in tokens. This is because, as mentioned in section 3, the length of the text seems to be correlated with the grading. This could pose a problem for an automatic grading system, because it could learn that just producing a longer text would yield a better grade. However, we must also consider that when students produce longer texts they might also be introducing more errors, which could be captured by the heuristics. Of course further experiments would be needed to validate this, and it is out of the scope of this work.

All the classifiers we trained are from the `scikit-learn` suite of machine learning tools (Pedregosa et al., 2011). We experimented with Naïve Bayes (NB), Random Forest (RF), Maximum Entropy (ME), Support Vector Machine (SVM), and Multi-Layered Perceptron (MLP) classifiers.

5.2 Results

The three rounds of experiments include: using the BoW features, using only the correction features plus the length feature, and using all the combined features. Table 6 shows the results of these experiments over the test partition. The best performing classifiers are the RF model and the ME model when using all the combined features. This is expected, as using all the features provides a lot of information. However, note that the MLP and ME models with only correction and length features, although not perfect, have a performance

	BoW		Correction features + length					Combined features				
	RF	ME	NB	RF	ME	SVM	MLP	NB	RF	ME	SVM	MLP
All grades Acc.	0.67	0.62	0.48	0.56	0.59	0.59	*0.60*	0.44	**0.68**	0.63	0.33	0.32
All grades M-F1	0.48	0.40	0.32	0.37	0.35	0.36	*0.37*	0.29	**0.49**	0.41	0.12	0.08
Ranges Acc.	0.83	0.83	0.73	0.79	0.82	0.82	*0.82*	0.70	**0.86**	0.84	0.51	0.51
Ranges M-F1	0.74	0.70	0.61	0.64	0.64	0.63	*0.68*	0.61	**0.76**	0.71	0.22	0.23

Table 6: Results of the classifiers over the test set.

that is at least comparable to the top ones. This is important, because these classifiers do not use any information on the specific words of the exercise, which gives us hope that this strategy could be used to grade similar writing exercises but with other prompts. Of course, more experiments are needed to validate this with other datasets.

6 Conclusions

We presented an initial experiment on building heuristics for detecting and correcting grammatical errors in texts by Uruguayan learners of English, and then training a classifier to predict a grade to assign to those texts. The heuristics have good performance in capturing common grammar errors like spelling, capitalization, and subject-verb agreement. Our best classifier has 82% accuracy and 76% macro-F1 for separating the texts in three ranges according to grade. We found that using only features that are independent from the exercise text the performance of the classifier gets to 82% accuracy and 68% macro-F1. This is a significant drop, but we must consider that this classifier could be adaptable to other exercises as well.

This is only a proof of concept, as we are aware that it is very difficult to build a generalizable system with examples of only one exercise. There are many ideas for future work about how to improve these heuristics and make them useful in a broader context. We would like to try using a language model to produce a representation of the text that could be comparable to a set of reference texts, and measure the distance between them. Also, we could try to use positive and negative lists of words that the text should have, and create features that would be adaptable to other exercises (in this case the list would include "Andrea", "girl", "read", "bike", etc.). Another interesting research direction is trying to assess the number of texts it would take to manually grade in a corpus, so we can finetune a system that has at least a good estimate of the grades for the rest of the corpus.

We are now in the process of building a better dataset for working on these and related problems. We want to create a more varied corpus with several exercise prompts and several example answers written by Uruguayan students of English, manually corrected and graded by teachers. This dataset would help us test and compare our current heuristics and other correction methods more thoroughly.

Acknowledgements

The dataset we used in this work was created by Ceibal en Inglés, part of the Ceibal project[9]. We want to thank them for letting us use it for research purposes.

References

Sagar Ailani, Ashwini Dalvi, and Irfan Siddavatam. 2019. Grammatical error correction (gec): research approaches till now. *International Journal of Computer Application*, 178(40):1–3.

Nicolas Ballier, Thomas Gaillat, Andrew Simpkin, Bernardo Stearns, Manon Bouyé, and Manel Zarrouk. 2019. A supervised learning model for the automatic assessment of language levels based on learner errors. In *Transforming Learning with Meaningful Technologies: 14th European Conference on Technology Enhanced Learning, EC-TEL 2019, Delft, The Netherlands, September 16–19, 2019, Proceedings 14*, pages 308–320. Springer.

Christopher Bryant, Mariano Felice, Øistein E. Andersen, and Ted Briscoe. 2019. The BEA-2019 shared task on grammatical error correction. In *Proceedings of the Fourteenth Workshop on Innovative Use of NLP for Building Educational Applications*, pages 52–75, Florence, Italy. Association for Computational Linguistics.

Luis Chiruzzo, Laura Musto, Santiago Góngora, Brian Carpenter, Juan Filevich, and Aiala Rosá. 2022. Using nlp to support english teaching in rural schools. In *Proceedings of the Second Workshop on NLP for Positive Impact (NLP4PI)*, pages 113–121.

[9]https://ceibal.edu.uy/

Luis Morgado Da Costa, Francis Bond, and Xiaoling He. 2016. Syntactic well-formedness diagnosis and error-based coaching in computer assisted language learning using machine translation. In *Proceedings of the 3rd Workshop on Natural Language Processing Techniques for Educational Applications (NLPTEA2016)*, pages 107–116.

Daniel Dahlmeier, Hwee Tou Ng, and Siew Mei Wu. 2013. Building a large annotated corpus of learner english: The nus corpus of learner english. In *Proceedings of the eighth workshop on innovative use of NLP for building educational applications*, pages 22–31.

Annette MB De Groot and Rineke Keijzer. 2000. What is hard to learn is easy to forget: The roles of word concreteness, cognate status, and word frequency in foreign-language vocabulary learning and forgetting. *Language learning*, 50(1):1–56.

Jacob Devlin, Ming-Wei Chang, Kenton Lee, and Kristina Toutanova. 2018. Bert: Pre-training of deep bidirectional transformers for language understanding. *arXiv preprint arXiv:1810.04805*.

Samuel Gehman, Suchin Gururangan, Maarten Sap, Yejin Choi, and Noah A Smith. 2020. Realtoxicityprompts: Evaluating neural toxic degeneration in language models. *arXiv preprint arXiv:2009.11462*.

Ekaterina Kochmar and Ted Briscoe. 2014. Detecting learner errors in the choice of content words using compositional distributional semantics. Association for Computational Linguistics.

Tomoya Mizumoto, Yuta Hayashibe, Mamoru Komachi, Masaaki Nagata, and Yuji Matsumoto. 2012. The effect of learner corpus size in grammatical error correction of esl writings. In *Proceedings of COLING 2012: Posters*, pages 863–872.

Hwee Tou Ng, Siew Mei Wu, Ted Briscoe, Christian Hadiwinoto, Raymond Hendy Susanto, and Christopher Bryant. 2014. The CoNLL-2014 shared task on grammatical error correction. In *Proceedings of the Eighteenth Conference on Computational Natural Language Learning: Shared Task*, pages 1–14, Baltimore, Maryland. Association for Computational Linguistics.

Diane Nicholls. 2003. The cambridge learner corpus: Error coding and analysis for lexicography and elt. In *Proceedings of the Corpus Linguistics 2003 conference*, volume 16, pages 572–581. Cambridge University Press Cambridge.

Fabian Pedregosa, Gaël Varoquaux, Alexandre Gramfort, Vincent Michel, Bertrand Thirion, Olivier Grisel, Mathieu Blondel, Peter Prettenhofer, Ron Weiss, Vincent Dubourg, et al. 2011. Scikit-learn: Machine learning in python. *Journal of machine learning research*, 12(Oct):2825–2830.

Burr Settles, Chris Brust, Erin Gustafson, Masato Hagiwara, and Nitin Madnani. 2018. Second language acquisition modeling. In *Proceedings of the thirteenth workshop on innovative use of NLP for building educational applications*, pages 56–65.

Michael Swan and Catherine Walter. 2011. *Oxford English grammar course*. Oxford University Press Oxford.

Joanna Turnbull, D Lea, D Parkinson, P Phillips, B Francis, S Webb, V Bull, and M Ashby. 2010. Oxford advanced learner's dictionary. *International Student's Edition*.

Yuzhu Wang and Hai Zhao. 2015. A light rule-based approach to english subject-verb agreement errors on the third person singular forms. In *Proceedings of the 29th Pacific Asia Conference on Language, Information and Computation: Posters*, pages 345–353.

Rodrigo Wilkens, Daiane Seibert, Xiaoou Wang, and Thomas François. 2022. Mwe for essay scoring english as a foreign language. In *Proceedings of the 2nd Workshop on Tools and Resources to Empower People with REAding DIfficulties (READI) within the 13th Language Resources and Evaluation Conference*, pages 62–69.

Helen Yannakoudakis, Ted Briscoe, and Ben Medlock. 2011. A new dataset and method for automatically grading esol texts. In *Proceedings of the 49th annual meeting of the association for computational linguistics: human language technologies*, pages 180–189.

Sequence Tagging in EFL Email Texts as Feedback for Language Learners

Yuning Ding[1], Ruth Trüb[2], Stefan Keller[4], Johanna Fleckenstein[3,5] and Andrea Horbach[1,5]
[1]CATALPA, FernUniversität in Hagen, Germany,
[2]Pädagogische Hochschule der Fachhochschule Nordwestschweiz FHNW, Switzerland,
[3]Leibniz-Institut für die Pädagogik der Naturwissenschaften und Mathematik, Kiel, Germany,
[4]Pädagogische Hochschule Zürich, Switzerland, [5]Universität Hildesheim, Germany

Abstract

When predicting scores for different aspects of a learner text, automated scoring algorithms usually cannot provide information about which part of text a score is referring to. We therefore propose a method to automatically segment learner texts as a way towards providing visual feedback. We train a neural sequence tagging model and use it to segment EFL email texts into functional segments. Our algorithm reaches a token-based accuracy of 90% when trained per prompt and between 83 and 87% in a cross-prompt scenario.

1 Introduction

Writing formal emails in English is part of many English as a Foreign Language (EFL) curricula due to its high practical relevance in academic and professional life. However, manual scoring of such writing tasks and the provision of feedback to students are time-consuming tasks for teachers, especially when feedback does not solely consist of a single holistic score per text, but instead consists of more fine-grained feedback such as highlighting certain elements in a learner text and providing feedback for each element.

In this paper, we investigate the task of segmenting EFL learner emails into functional elements relating to their main communicative function (Hyland, 2019). Examples would be the salutation, closing or matter of concern (see Figure 1 for an annotated sample email). We perform the automated segmentation task on the basis of the eRubrix corpus (Keller et al., 2023) consisting of 1,102 semi-formal emails written by Swiss EFL learners at lower secondary level (8th and 9th year of schooling). In these emails, seven different core elements of an email were annotated by trained human raters. We use a neural sequence tagging architecture to automatize the segmentation task and compare it against a simple sentence-based baseline.

Overall, the paper makes the following contributions:

- We present segment annotations on the eRubrix dataset. On the basis of aspects of text quality developed by Keller et al. (2023), we show how the human annotations presented in their study can be transferred to automated span annotations.
- We apply a sequence-tagging architecture that is able to assign the right segment category for 90% of all tokens.
- We show that the automatic segmentation can be applied to new writing prompts almost without performance loss.
- We provide learning curve experiments showing that as little as 50 to 100 emails are enough to train a model that is close to the final performance on the whole dataset.
- We analyze the impact of positional information in the training data, showing that positional information is - unsurprisingly - important in this automatic segmentation task, especially on certain labels like subject line, salutation and closing.
- We discuss how the algorithm can be used as a basis for feedback to language learners and for developing language learning activities in EFL classrooms.

2 Related Work

The interdisciplinary research presented in this paper combines second language writing studies with educational science and natural language processing. In the following section, we therefore discuss related work from these three disciplines.

Yuning Ding, Ruth Trüb, Johanna Fleckenstein, Stefan Keller and Andrea Horbach. Sequence Tagging in EFL Email Texts as Feedback for Language Learners. *Proceedings of the 12th Workshop on Natural Language Processing for Computer Assisted Language Learning (NLP4CALL 2023)*. Linköping Electronic Conference Proceedings 197: 53–62.

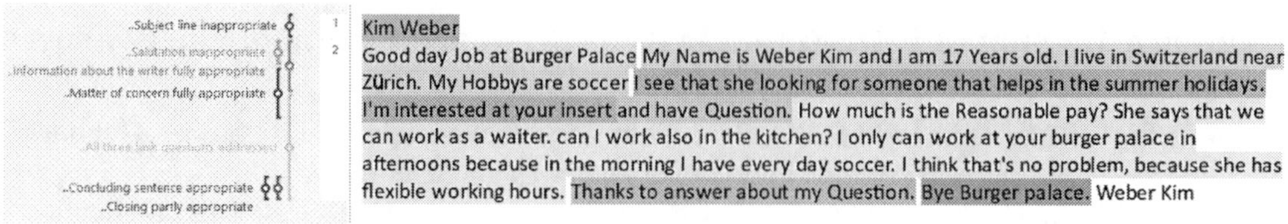

Figure 1: Sample annotation in MAXQDA (Version 22.0.1) for a learner email from the *Burger Palace* task.

2.1 Second Language Writing Studies

A number of theories have been proposed to support students' acquisition of second language writing competences (Matsuda, 2003). Among the most widely used and researched approaches are the genre-based approach and the approach based on text functions (Hyland, 2019, pp. 6-20).

A genre-based approach assumes that all writing is done in a specific social context and that a range of social constraints and choices exist that operate on writers (Hyland, 2019, p. 18). Teaching in this paradigm typically begins with the purposes of communicating before moving on to learning the "stages" of a text which can express these purposes. This often involves the analysis of model texts and typical language structures contained in them.

The approach focusing on text functions is similar in that it relates language structures to meanings. This is achieved by showing students how to compose effective paragraphs for the text functions they want to express, e.g. describing, narrating, or reporting (Hyland, 2019, p. 6). Both the genre-based and the text function-based approach would concur in the view that providing feedback on these core elements of an email can help students to understand the communicative function of an email and to apply them independently in their own writing.

The automated annotation function described in this article can be seen as a technique for enhancing genre-based writing instruction with automated span annotations: it identifies the salient structural elements required in an email to fulfil the communicative function of the text (polite greeting, expression of the writer's purpose, expected response, adequate closing, etc.), highlighting them for learners and laying the basis for feedback relating to specific text functions.

2.2 Multimedia Learning and Feedback Processing

The cognitive theory of multimedia learning (CTML) proposes that people learn more effectively from multimedia sources than from text alone (Mayer, 2001). This assumption is based on the idea that people have limited cognitive processing capacity, and that using a combination of verbal and visual information can help reduce the cognitive load on each channel (Mayer and Moreno, 2003). Research has shown that adhering to certain design principles reduces cognitive load and positively affects learning in multimedia environments (Noetel et al., 2021). The design principles derived from CTML should also pertain to automated writing feedback, but they have seldom been transferred to this context (for an exception see Burkhart et al., 2021). The visualization of different segments of a learner text - as we propose in our study - makes use of the advantages of multimedia learning and should thus support the revision process. The multimedia design principles that are particularly relevant in the context of this study are contiguity, signaling, and segmenting.

Contiguity refers to the relationship between two events or stimuli that are presented close in time or space. In multimedia learning materials, contiguity can be used to help the learner understand the relationship between different pieces of information by presenting them in close proximity to each other. For example, a graphic and a related caption might be presented together to show the relationship between the two. By using spatial contiguity, multimedia learning materials help the learner better understand the relationship between different pieces of information and reduce cognitive load by eliminating the need to search for relevant information (Schroeder and Cenkci, 2018; Burkhart et al., 2021). When transferred to the context of writing and revising, the principle of contiguity can be accomplished by providing in-text feedback rather than providing feedback in reference to an external rubric or message.

Signaling refers to the use of visual or auditory cues to help the learner understand the material and make connections between different parts of the content. Signaling can be achieved through a variety of means, including visual elements such as arrows, colours, and highlighted text. When used effectively, signaling helps the learner to more easily understand and retain the material presented in the multimedia learning resource (Richter et al., 2016). This principle applies to this study in that a central goal of sequence tagging is to highlight certain parts of the text and to assign different colors to different text elements.

Segmenting means breaking down a large learning sequence into smaller segments. This is often done with audiovisual content, for example, in allowing learners to pause an instructional video between meaningful sequences. According to Clark and Mayer (2011) the rationale for using segmentation is that it allows the learner to take essential processing steps without overloading their cognitive system. Learning has been shown to be more effective when information is presented in segments rather than in one long continuous stream (Rey et al., 2019). Sequence tagging allows us to segment a complex text into smaller parts that are easier to process and therefore more likely to be addressed by the learner.

2.3 Natural Language Processing Perspective

In a study which preceded the one presented here, Horbach et al. (2022) developed an automated scoring model for the emails in the eRubrix dataset. The purpose of that study was to prove that the human scoring of emails presented in Keller et al. (2023) could be generated automatically, and to evaluate the effectiveness of automated feedback based on that algorithm when students revised English emails. In their seminal study, Keller et al. (2023) had shown how a feedback rubric could be developed for English emails based on genre-based principles of writing instruction. They also showed that all aspects of writing quality covered in their rubric could be reliably used by human raters under the time-constraints of a live feedback study, and that the scores provided under such circumstances corresponded to differences in the linguistic quality of the texts, indicating high content validity. Horbach et al. (2022) then demonstrated that the human ratings provided by Keller et al. (2023) could be automatized as a set of binary quality criteria where each score was computed based on the whole text as input. Their study, however, did not automatize the segmentation (Horbach et al., 2022, p. 81). For that reason, it was not possible to draw the learners' attention visually to the specific segments where revisions were necessary. This current study therefore seeks to fill this research gap and provide an automated segmentation model which can be used to provide feedback on learner texts that follows central CTML design principles.

Methodologically, the approach in our study is an instance of a segmenting task where elements in a text are identified based on their function. Such tasks have been used, for example, to identify different parts (like *objective, method, results* and *conclusion*) in scientific abstracts (Hirohata et al., 2008). Mizuta and Collier (2004) identified so-called *rhetorical zones* in biology articles. In the educational domain, our task is related to other NLP tasks with the goal of identifying certain parts within a text either as feedback for learners or teachers, such as argument mining (Wachsmuth et al., 2016; Nguyen and Litman, 2018), where argumentative units are to be marked in essays. We therefore use an architecture that has been previously applied in argument mining tasks (Ding et al., 2022).

3 Data

3.1 eRubrix Dataset

The eRubrix dataset (Keller et al., 2023) contains 1,102 semi-formal emails written by Swiss lower secondary school students in grades 8 and 9. Most of them were in their 6th and 7th year of learning English as a foreign language and between 13 and 16 years old. The learners wrote three emails in randomized order and received feedback and suggestions for improvement in-between from trained human raters (Keller et al., 2023).

3.2 Writing Tasks

The writing tasks in the data-set consisted of three semi-formal emails in which students were asked to make inquiries concerning authentic, real life situations (Keller et al., 2023). In one task, they gathered information about a language school in the UK, in a second task, they inquired about a summer job at a burger restaurant, and in a third task, they collected information for a holiday at a camping site (Keller et al., 2023). Figure 2 shows the *Burger Palace* task as an example. About 370 emails were written for each task (see Table 1). To avoid the need for anonymization, students were asked to sign their emails using the (gender-neutral) name *Kim Weber*.

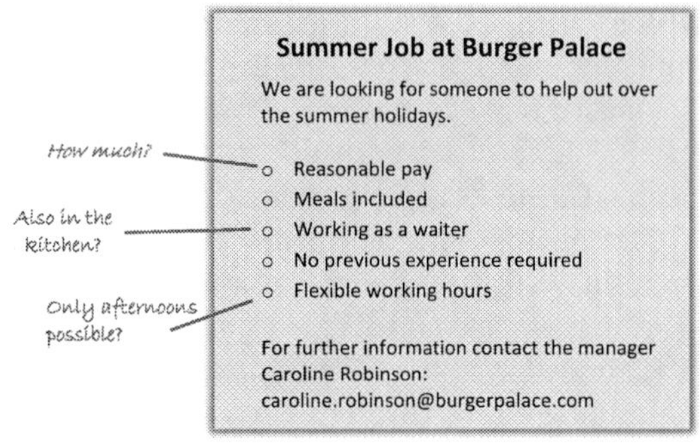

Figure 2: *Burger Palace* task from the eRubrix dataset (Keller et al., 2023, p. 25). The accompanying German instruction translates as follows: *"You want to make some money during your school holidays and are looking for a job. Read the advertisement you found on the internet and look at the notes you took (in red). Write an email to the store manager in which you introduce yourself and say what you are looking for. Inquire about the information in detail by using your notes in red"* (Keller et al., 2023, p. 24).

Prompt	# emails	∅ # tokens (SD)
Language school	367	97.9 (± 33.0)
Burger restaurant	368	104.1 (± 34.0)
Camping	367	105.0 (± 34.1)

Table 1: Basic dataset statistics.

3.3 Annotation

In Keller et al. (2023), the eRubrix text corpus was first rated on the basis of a rubric specifically developed for providing feedback to the learners. In a second step, the texts were additionally annotated in MAXQDA software by four trained human raters for a more detailed linguistic analysis (Keller et al., 2023). The different text segments were marked according to specific marking guidelines (see Table 2) and coded in terms of text quality for further linguistic analysis. These MAXQDA annotations provided the necessary data to train the automated text segmentation model presented in this paper. 40 texts had been annotated by all four raters (Keller et al., 2023) and were used in this study to calculate the raters' pairwise inter-annotater agreement (IAA) when marking the different segments.

A number of evaluation metrics have been used to calculate the IAA between two annotators in similar span annotation tasks. Ziai and Meurers (2014), for example, evaluated spans in focus annotations by computing agreement on the token level, while Reiter (2015) used boundary edit distance (see Fournier, 2013) on the segmentation of narrative texts. In our evaluation, we used a different span evaluation metric which we also applied in a similar fashion to evaluate human-machine agreement. Spans identified by one annotator were matched against spans found by the second annotator. They were considered true positive if at least 50% of the tokens found by annotator 1 were also identified by annotator 2, and vice versa. Unmatched spans by annotator 1 counted as false negatives, spans by annotator 2 without a counterpart by annotator 1 as false positives. These were combined to compute an overall Kappa score following Brennan and Prediger (1981). With this measure, we reached a pairwise IAA between 0.75 and 1.0. When increasing the required overlap from 50% to 90 %, the IAA was between 0.46 and 1.0 (see Table 3 for the averaged IAA values of all annotator pairs). The average percentage agreement of the four raters, as calculated by the average of their pairwise percentage agreements, ranged between 0.81 and 1.00 for the different criteria. Agreement for *closing* was low mainly because it was unclear to annotators whether the name after the closing should also be marked or not.

Together with the segmentation, annotators also assigned a quality label to each segment, indicating whether the content and form of the segment was appropriate (not used in this study). The annotator for the final gold standard was selected based on a many-facet Rasch analysis (Eckes, 2011) of these quality assessments, i.e. the rater whose ratings were the most balanced in terms of severity and leniency was selected.

Table 3 also shows basic statistics for the dataset. Elements are listed in order of their typical appearance in the text. We see that elements occurring later (*concluding sentence, closing*) have higher chances of being missing as learners often did not finish the email in time. We

Label	Annotation guidelines
Subject line	Code the whole subject line. If missing, code first letter of the email.
Salutation	Code the salutation including name and punctuation.
Information about writer	Code the introductory information about the writer including punctuation. Could be multiple sentences. Code entire extract, even if it contains a different type of information in between (e.g. matter of concern)
Matter of concern	Code the introductory information about the matter of concern including punctuation. Could be multiple sentences. Code entire extract, even if it contains a different type of information in between (e.g. information about the writer)
Task questions addressed	Code entirety of questions, including punctuation. If missing, code punctuation mark of previous sentence (or last letter if no punctuation present), where the questions would usually appear. Could be multiple sentences. Code entire extract even if there is additional information in between.
Concluding sentence	Code entirety of the concluding sentences, including puntuation. Could be multiple sentences, but it should be distinct from the questions.
Closing	Code entire closing, including punctuation, but do not include "Kim Weber". If closing is missing, insert code over last letter/character in the email or if only "Kim Weber" is present code the entire name.

Table 2: Guidelines for marking the segments in the eRubrix dataset

			50% overlap		90% overlap	
Label	**# segments**	**avg. length**	**∅ % agreem.**	κ	**∅ % agreem.**	κ
Subject line	1020	4.1	0.99	0.98	0.99	0.98
Salutation	1090	2.9	1.00	1.00	0.99	0.99
Information about writer	916	9.3	0.84	0.79	0.79	0.72
Matter of concern	1023	22.4	0.91	0.87	0.76	0.68
Questions	1015	45.2	0.96	0.95	0.73	0.64
Concluding sentence	747	10.2	0.93	0.91	0.76	0.69
Closing	697	2.1	0.81	0.75	0.60	0.46

Table 3: Number of segments per label as identified within the entire dataset, average length in tokens, and inter-annotater agreement. Average percentage agreement of all rater pairs, and kappa calculated according to Brennan and Prediger (1981). The segments were counted as agreement if either 50 or 90 percent of a segment matched with that of the second rater.

also see that individual elements have a very different average length with the *question* part by far the largest element on average.

In the original annotation setup, it was possible to annotate overlapping segments. It happened 93 times in the whole dataset, the majority of these cases (81) being overlaps between *matter of concern* and *information about the writer*. As our algorithm cannot work with overlapping segments, we ended a segment as soon as a new overlapping segment started, i.e. in cases of an overlap, the segment starting earlier was cut short.

4 Experimental Study

4.1 Experimental Setup

We use a sequence tagging architecture which has been successfully applied for structure-related tasks such as argument mining (Ding et al., 2022), as shown in Figure 3. In this architecture, tokens with a Inside-Outside-Beginning (IOB) tag representation of the gold-standard annotations are used as the input to a pretrained language model for token classification. We considered different pretained models and decided for RoBERTa (Liu et al., 2019) based on the Huggingface implementation [1] as it provided the best performance. We train the model for 10 epochs with a batch size of 16, CrossEntropyLoss as loss function, a learning rate at 1e-5 and an Adam optimizer.

We compare this model against several baselines: In the **random sentence baseline**, we split the data into individual sentences using the NLTK tokenizer[2] and assign each sentence a random label. In the **sentence order baseline**, we tag the first four sentences as *subject line*, *salutation*, *information about the writer* and *matter of concern* respectively, the last two sentences as *concluding sentence* and *closing*, and anything in-between as *questions*.

To examine the influence of the writing prompt, we train and test our model under several conditions: In the **all condition**, we employ 10-fold cross-validation on the complete dataset across all 3 prompts. In a **per-prompt condition**, we cross-validate on the *Language School*, *Burger Restaurant* and *Camping* prompt individually. Differences in the performance between **all** and the three **per-prompt conditions** (or rather a lack thereof) might be due to more training data available in the **all condition**. Therefore, we also introduce an **all-reduced condition** where we use only one third of the **all condition** to make the dataset size comparable to the per-prompt training sets. In a **cross-prompt condition**, we train on one prompt and test on one of the other two prompts. For each fold, we use the run with the best performance on the validation dataset.

Evaluation We follow a span evaluation F1 metric used also in similar tasks[3]. For this score, identified spans are matched against gold spans and considered a true positive if at least 50 percent of the gold span tokens are covered by the identified spans, and vice versa as described in Section 3. Unmatched gold spans count as false negatives, spans in the results without a gold counterpart as false positives. These are combined to compute an overall F-score. This score gives a good overall impression but does not account for exact matches at the segment boundaries. Therefore, we also evaluate accuracy on the token level.

4.2 Experiment 1: Prompt-Specific vs Generic Annotation

Table 4 shows the segmentation results for the two baselines, followed by the **all**, **all-reduced** and **prompt-wise** conditions.

Unsurprisingly, the **random sentence baseline** does not perform well. That also the **sentence order baselines** shows mediocre results can be taken as an indicator that the segmentation task is non-trivial.

The machine learning results show a high performance overall with token-wise accuracy between .88 and .91 and F1 scores between .84 and .89. The difference between the **all condition** and the other conditions is minimal, both for prompt-specific models and the **all-reduced** condition, indicating that the smaller models have already been provided with enough data to perform well.

4.3 Experiment 2: Cross-Prompt Segmentation

Experiment 2 investigates the model transfer potential from one email writing task to another. The lower half of Table 4 presents the results when a model trained on one prompt is applied to the other two prompts individually. Performance is slightly

[1] `https://huggingface.co/roberta-base`

[2] `https://www.nltk.org/api/nltk.tokenize.html`

[3] `https://www.kaggle.com/competitions/feedback-prize-2021/overview/evaluation`

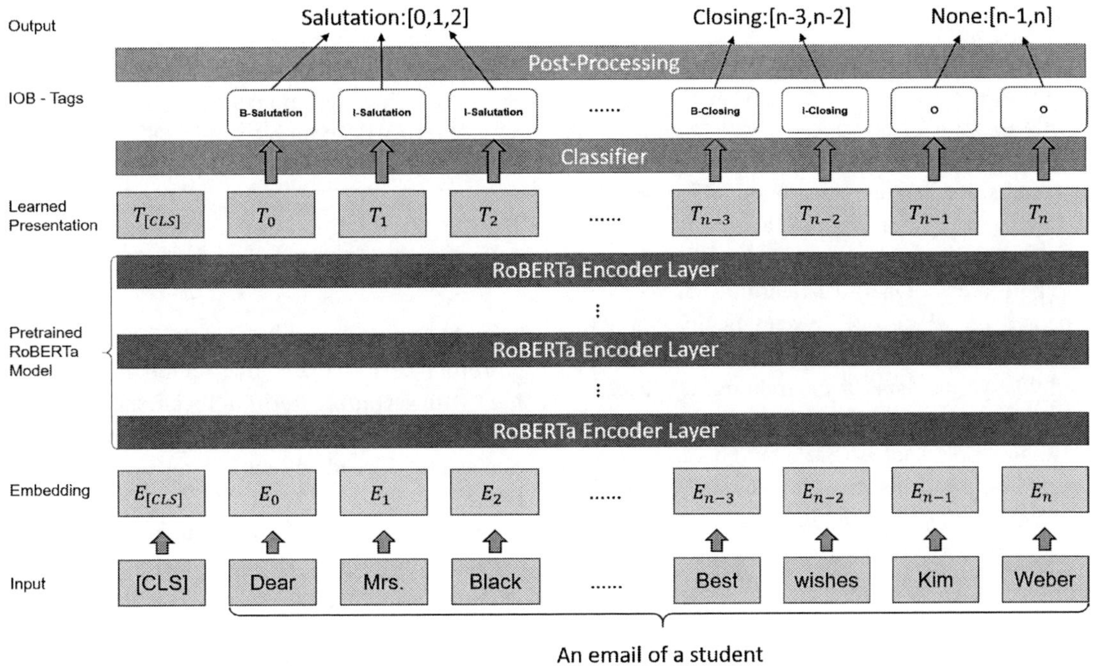

Figure 3: Adapted sequence labeling architecture from Ding et al. (2022).

Train	Test	F1	Acc.
Random Sentence Baseline		.06	.12
Sentence Order Baseline		.30	.42
All (CV)		**.89**	**.90**
All-reduced (CV)		.87	.89
Language school (CV)		.85	.88
Burger restaurant (CV)		.84	.88
Camping (CV)		**.88**	**.91**
Language school	Burger restaurant	.84	.87
Language school	Camping	.85	.87
Burger restaurant	Language school	.81	.83
Burger restaurant	Camping	.86	.87
Camping	Language school	.83	.84
Camping	Burger restaurant	.84	.84

Table 4: Segmentation results for two baselines and when training a generic or a prompt-based classifier (upper half) and for cross-prompt transfer (lower half).

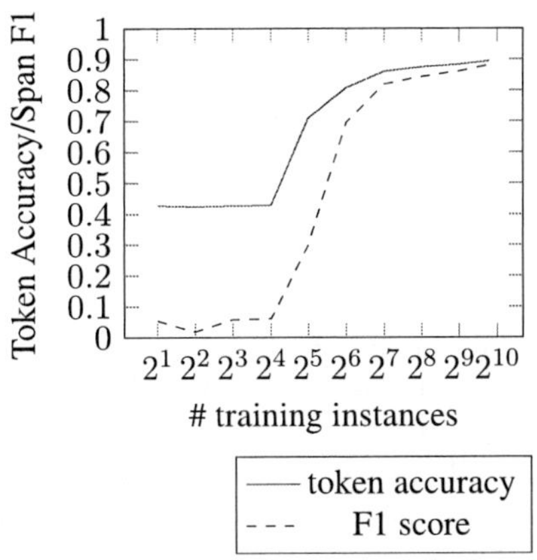

Figure 4: Learning curve experiment

lower than for the prompt-specific models, indicating that prompt-specific lexical material is certainly important. The criterion *salutation* can be best predicted in the cross-prompt segmentation, since it has a fixed form like "Dear xxx". *Subject line* can also be well predicted without context because it always spans over the first line of the email.

4.4 Experiment 3: The Influence of Training Data Sizes

In a practical application scenario when a teacher wants to train a model for a new prompt, it is important to know how much labeled data is required, since human annotation effort is often a crucial factor for creating a machine learning model.

Therefore, we perform learning curve experiments, in which we systematically vary the amount of training data. We use the **all condition** and 90% of the data for the training, while saving 10 % for testing.

Figure 4 plots labeled data on the x-axis vs segmentation performance (accuracy and F1) on the y-axis, showing that the algorithm is able to learn most of its performance from very few training instances. The curve flattens out in the end indicating that adding more training data will most likely not substantially improve performance any further.

4.5 Experiment 4: The Influence of Positional Information

Positional information is obviously important for the task as most elements typically appear at a certain position within the email. When students make errors in organizing their emails, i.e. when email elements do not appear in the expected location, one would expect a feedback that addresses this misplacement. It is thus important to correctly identify misplaced segments. As a worst-case scenario for emails in the wrong order, we therefore shuffle segments in emails randomly, i.e. we use gold standard information about email boundaries but randomly vary the order in which the elements appear. We use these scrambled emails in several ways. To assess the contribution of positional information in our original tagging models, we use scrambled test data (keeping the training data as is). To check how to make models more robust against misplacements, we train a model on scrambled training data, testing on both unchanged and scrambled test data.

Table 5 shows the results. We can observe a performance loss when using our normally trained model on scrambled test data (**scramble test**), indicating that the model indeed learns in part to rely on positional information and performs worse on test data that does not follow this convention. When also scrambling the training data, i.e. forcing the model to ignore positional information, scrambled test data can be handled with a similar performance to the baseline (compare **unscrambled** with **scramble both**), indicating that the data is somewhat redundant and that the same information can be learned without the positional information.

Setup	F1	Acc.
All (CV) - unscrambled	.89	.90
All (CV) - scramble test	.60	.78
All (CV) - scramble train	.85	.91
All (CV) - scramble both	.89	.92

Table 5: Segmentation results when training and/or testing on scramled data.

When comparing the performance on individual labels, we find that some labels, such as *subject line*, *salutation* and *closing* benefit more from positional information than others, i.e. for these labels there is a larger performance drop if positional information is missing.

4.6 Error Analysis

A confusion matrix between individual labels in the **all** condition (see Table 6) provides further information about the behavior of the algorithm. As can be seen in Table 6, most confusions occur between labeled segments and text segments without any label rather than between two labeled segments. This shows that assigning correct segment boundaries is sometimes difficult, resulting in segments without a counterpart with sufficient overlap. A comparison of the number of unmatched gold standard labels (1062) and unmatched predicted labels (277) shows that the algorithm tends to not assign a label rather than assign one.

When looking at the (substantially fewer) cases of confusion between two labels, most confusions unsurprisingly concern labels one would expect to be adjacent in an email, such as *matter of concern* and *information about the writer*. This corresponds to human annotation, as most overlapping annotations were found between these two labels. It often happens when the *information about the writer* is surrounded by *matter of concern* segments. Take the following sentences as an example: *I am interested to help you out over the summer holidays. I am 14 years old and my name is Kim Weber. I would like to earn some money in the summer holiday and i thought this is the right place to work in the summer holiday.* The first and

	Subject line	Salutation	Info. about writer	Matter of concern	Questions	Conclud. sent.	Closing	None
Subject line	917	1	0	0	0	0	0	3
Salutation	5	976	0	0	0	0	0	4
Info. about writer	0	2	751	15	1	0	0	63
Matter of concern	0	0	10	841	2	0	0	68
Questions	0	0	0	1	893	0	0	21
Conclud. sent.	0	0	0	0	0	640	2	43
Closing	0	0	0	0	0	11	537	75
None	5	10	245	297	185	162	108	N.A.

Table 6: Confusion matrix between gold standard (columns) and results in the *all* setting (rows)

the last sentence illustrate the *matter of concern*, whereas the sentence in-between was double annotated with both *matter of concern* and *information about the writer*.

5 Discussion & Practical Applications

With the developed technology, we envision two application scenarios. First, automatic segmentation could be used to provide formative feedback to students by showing them not only how their text was scored automatically, but also where the algorithm thought it had found the respective passages, pointing at the location where a revision could take place. According to CTML principles, this should reduce cognitive load and thus positively affect learning. Contiguity can be achieved by presenting feedback within the text rather than in the margins. By being able to highlight and assign colours to certain parts of the text, signaling can support the learners' understanding. Most importantly, the segmentation of the text can break a complex task down into smaller parts. Students can revise their text step-by-step rather than being faced with a lot of information at once. Especially when combined with evaluative feedback (automatic quality assessment) on the segment level, the reduction of cognitive load in the revision process may lead to higher feedback uptake and better learning outcomes. In addition, such formative feedback could also be enriched with automatic quality assessment similar to the study by Horbach et al. (2022). From an NLP perspective, the quality of automatic scoring, in turn, might also benefit from segmentation in that only relevant parts of the email would be fed into the scoring algorithm.

Second, segmentation could be the basis for the generation of various activity types useful for teaching students how to write an email. In particular, such activities could be set up with the texts written by the learners themselves. These could be identification tasks (*Please indicate where the* Matter of Concern *is in this email.*), reordering tasks (*Please bring these email segments into the right order.*), gap-filling tasks (*Which part is missing here?*) and many more. When combined with an automated model for judging the quality of the segments, further activity types may become possible such as judgment tasks (*Which texts have a suitable concluding sentence?*) or comparison tasks (*Which salutation is more appropriate in terms of register?*). A crucial advantage of generating such activities from automatically segmented texts is that arbitrary emails could be integrated into language-learning tasks, including emails the learners themselves have written.

6 Conclusion

We showed in this study that the individual segments of a formal email can be predicted with high accuracy, making segmentation a suitable instrument to give feedback in an EFL context. We have outlined ways how segmentation could be used to generate language learning tasks and - together with automatic scoring - could be used to generate formative feedback for language learners. We will explore these directions further in future work.

7 Acknowledgements

This work was partially conducted at "CATALPA - Center of Advanced Technology for Assisted Learning and Predictive Analytics" of the FernUniversität in Hagen, Germany, and partially within the KI-Starter project "Explaining AI Predictions of Semantic Relationships" funded by the Ministry of Culture and Science, Nordrhein-Westfalen, Germany.

References

Robert L Brennan and Dale J Prediger. 1981. Coefficient kappa: Some uses, misuses, and alternatives. *Educational and psychological measurement*, 41(3):687–699.

Christian Burkhart, Andreas Lachner, and Matthias Nückles. 2021. Using spatial contiguity and signaling to optimize visual feedback on students' written explanations. *Journal of Educational Psychology*, 113(5):998.

RC Clark and RE Mayer. 2011. Applying the segmenting and pretraining principles: Managing complexity by breaking a lesson into parts e-learning and the science of instruction.

Yuning Ding, Marie Bexte, and Andrea Horbach. 2022. Don't drop the topic - the role of the prompt in argument identification in student writing. In *Proceedings of the 17th Workshop on Innovative Use of NLP for Building Educational Applications (BEA 2022)*, pages 124–133, Seattle, Washington. Association for Computational Linguistics.

Thomas Eckes. 2011. Introduction to many-facet rasch measurement. *Franfurt am Main: Peter Lang*.

Chris Fournier. 2013. Evaluating text segmentation using boundary edit distance. In *Proceedings of the 51st Annual Meeting of the Association for Computational Linguistics (Volume 1: Long Papers)*, pages 1702–1712.

Kenji Hirohata, Naoaki Okazaki, Sophia Ananiadou, and Mitsuru Ishizuka. 2008. Identifying sections in scientific abstracts using conditional random fields. In *Proceedings of the Third International Joint Conference on Natural Language Processing: Volume-I*.

Andrea Horbach, Ronja Laarmann-Quante, Lucas Liebenow, Thorben Jansen, Stefan Keller, Jennifer Meyer, Torsten Zesch, and Johanna Fleckenstein. 2022. Bringing automatic scoring into the classroom–measuring the impact of automated analytic feedback on student writing performance. In *Swedish Language Technology Conference and NLP4CALL*, pages 72–83.

Ken Hyland. 2019. *Second language writing*. Cambridge university press.

Stefan D Keller, Ruth Trüb, Emily Raubach, Jennifer Meyer, Thorben Jansen, and Johanna Fleckenstein. 2023. Designing and validating an assessment rubric for writing emails in english as a foreign language. *Research in Subject-matter Teaching and Learning (RISTAL)*, 6(1):16–48.

Yinhan Liu, Myle Ott, Naman Goyal, Jingfei Du, Mandar Joshi, Danqi Chen, Omer Levy, Mike Lewis, Luke Zettlemoyer, and Veselin Stoyanov. 2019. Roberta: A robustly optimized bert pretraining approach.

Paul Kei Matsuda. 2003. Process and post-process: A discursive history. *Journal of second language writing*, 12(1):65–83.

Richard E Mayer. 2001. *Multimedia learning*. Cambridge University Press.

Richard E Mayer and Roxana Moreno. 2003. Nine ways to reduce cognitive load in multimedia learning. *Educational psychologist*, 38(1):43–52.

Yoko Mizuta and Nigel Collier. 2004. Zone identification in biology articles as a basis for information extraction. In *Proceedings of the International Joint Workshop on Natural Language Processing in Biomedicine and its Applications (NLPBA/BioNLP)*, pages 29–35.

Huy Nguyen and Diane Litman. 2018. Argument mining for improving the automated scoring of persuasive essays. In *Proceedings of the AAAI Conference on Artificial Intelligence*, volume 32.

Michael Noetel, Shantell Griffith, Oscar Delaney, Taren Sanders, Philip Parker, Borja del Pozo Cruz, and Chris Lonsdale. 2021. Video improves learning in higher education: A systematic review. *Review of educational research*, 91(2):204–236.

Nils Reiter. 2015. Towards annotating narrative segments. In *Proceedings of the 9th SIGHUM Workshop on Language Technology for Cultural Heritage, Social Sciences, and Humanities (LaTeCH)*, pages 34–38.

Günter Daniel Rey, Maik Beege, Steve Nebel, Maria Wirzberger, Tobias H Schmitt, and Sascha Schneider. 2019. A meta-analysis of the segmenting effect. *Educational Psychology Review*, 31:389–419.

Juliane Richter, Katharina Scheiter, and Alexander Eitel. 2016. Signaling text-picture relations in multimedia learning: A comprehensive meta-analysis. *Educational Research Review*, 17:19–36.

Noah L Schroeder and Ada T Cenkci. 2018. Spatial contiguity and spatial split-attention effects in multimedia learning environments: A meta-analysis. *Educational Psychology Review*, 30:679–701.

Henning Wachsmuth, Khalid Al Khatib, and Benno Stein. 2016. Using argument mining to assess the argumentation quality of essays. In *Proceedings of COLING 2016, the 26th international conference on Computational Linguistics: Technical papers*, pages 1680–1691.

Ramon Ziai and Detmar Meurers. 2014. Focus annotation in reading comprehension data. In *Proceedings of LAW VIII-The 8th Linguistic Annotation Workshop*, pages 159–168.

Speech Technology to Support Phonics Learning for Kindergarten Children at Risk of Dyslexia

Stine Fuglsang Engmose
University College Absalon
Trekroner Forskerpark 4
DK-4000 Roskilde, Denmark
stfe@pha.dk

Peter Juel Henrichsen
Danish Language Counsil
Adelgade 119B
DK-5400 Bogense, Denmark
pjh@dsn.dk

Abstract

We present the AiRO learning environment for kindergarten children at risk of developing dyslexia. The AiRO frontend, easy to use for pupils down to 5 years old, introduces each spelling task with pictural and auditive cues. AiRO responds to spelling attempts with phonetic renderings (synthetic voice). Below, we introduce the didactic and technical principles behind AiRO before presenting our first experiment with 49 kindergarten pupils. Our subjects were pre- and post-tested on reading an spelling. After four weeks of AiRO-based training the experimental group significantly out-performed the control group, suggesting that a new CALL-based pedagogical approach to prevent dyslexia for some children may be within reach.

1 Background

An early, but influential study[1] found that 12% of adult Danes had reading difficulties inhibiting their professional life. Dyslexia is a well-described cause of reading difficulties but until recently, dyslexia was studied only superficially in the Danish education system, leaving teachers little prepared to engage proactively (Pihl and Jensen, 2017). It is problematic if difficulties in reading are not met with appropriate support because adults with poor reading and writing skills are strongly overrepresented among those who have low-paid jobs and short educations (Rosdahl et al., 2013). Among dyslectic 25/26-year-olds, only 69% completed secondary school, compared to 81% among peers (Egmont, 2018). However, early intervention can lessen the problem significantly. Vellutino and Scanlon (2002) report that special training programs for pupils from the age of 7 years reduced the proportion of bad readers from 9% to 1.5%. Effective intervention should be based on intensive, sustained, and individually tailored courses focused on the relations between letters and sounds (Elbro and Petersen, 2004; Elbro, 2021). A solid grip of phonics is a necessary precondition to solid reading and spelling skills (Ehri, 2005; National Reading Panel, 2000; Share, 1995). Early intervention, more than anything else, holds a strong potential for societal and personal gains with dyslexia (Gellert et al., 2018). "We believe that CALL might hold a potential as a supplement to teacher's instruction in a didactic programme of early intervention. As will be clear in the following, our approach concerns a specific CALL setup with a pronounced focus on the writing situation. More specifically, we have developed a didactic tool for use in classrooms, exploiting a very close stimulus-response cycle from student

[1] Elbro et al (1995). Similar figures have been reported from other Western countries.

Stine Fuglsang Engmose and Peter Juel Henrichsen. Speech Technology to Support Phonics Learning for Kindergarten Children at Risk of Dyslexia. *Proceedings of the 12th Workshop on Natural Language Processing for Computer Assisted Language Learning (NLP4CALL 2023).* Linköping Electronic Conference Proceedings 197: 63–70.

production ("spelling") to system response ("correction" or "confirmation") with a level of granularity down to the individual letter/phone combination. To our knowledge, no other interactive training tool on the market for children at risk of dyslexia (such as Gissel & Andersen, 2021, Messer & Nash, 2018, and Solheim et al., 2018) use the same level of granularity."

2 Introduction to AiRO

The project AiRO[2], that we present results from in this paper, seeks to meet some of these societal and personal challenges. We expect that kindergarten children at risk of dyslexia can benefit from an early intervention characterized by a learning environment with positive interaction and corrective feedback. More specifically, a child with poor command of phonics will benefit from a quick and simple response (affirming or correcting) to their spelling attempt. A dedicated teacher can of course provide ideal feedback, but teachers' attention is limited in a classroom with more than 20 kindergarten children. AiRO is developed as an interactive learning tool to supplement ordinary teacher lead instruction.

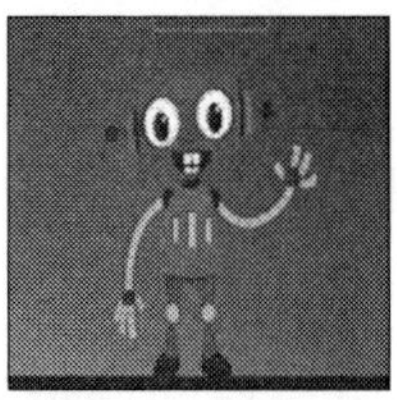

Figure 1. AiRObot greets the kindergarten children at the AiRO frontpage

[2] AiRO ≈ CALL-based pedagogical approach for children at risk of dyslexia (In Danish **A**daptiv **i**t-baseret støtte til børn i **R**isiko for **O**rdblindhed

2.1 AiRObot - your classroom assistant

Seen from the kindergartener's point of view, AiRO is a friendly robot (see the AiRObot in figure 1) presenting manageable spelling tasks, beginning from simple one-letter words and continuing slowly but steadily (depending on the pupil's profile and performance) with ever more demanding words.

AiRO is intended for use in classrooms or small groups. Individual pupils or a small group can use AiRO while the rest of the class are following the regular education. When using AiRO in school, headphones are mandatory; the application is however also available to the pupils at home.

In the following sections, we present AiRO's underlying didactive, linguistic, and computational principles. We also report on our recent experiments with pupils in the Danish pre-primary school (49 subjects). Finally we discuss some future perspectives.

3 Linguistic principles and technical design

To develop spelling and reading skills children must among others acquire and be able to use phonics rules. This is the objective of the CALL-based pedagogical approach for children at risk of dyslexia, AiRO.

Looking at the research of phonics instruction as an early intervention, Danish professor in reading sums up generations of research (Elbro, 2021) in the following headings. For phonics instruction to be helpful for children at risk of dyslexia it should be characterized by being:

- Systematic, e.g. introducing letter-sound-connections that are stable and frequent before connections that are less stable or rare
- Direct, e.g. instruction where words are chosen, in such a manner that the letter-sound-connections introduced can be practiced

- Applied, using phonics for reading and spelling words with support and feedback
- Intensive and extensive, small groups of 3-4 students or 1 on 1, daily 30 min. of practice, lots of time spend on the students practicing
- Motivating, making the progress of the student visible to the student and providing lots of task variation to deal with the students slow progress
- At the students instructional level, and progressing slowly

The CALL-based pedagogical approach is designed to create a learning situation with the above characteristics.

In AiRO the user are presented to 3 new and 3 earlier practiced target words at each level. At the initial level, target words are short (1-2 letters) with V, CV and VC structure (e.g. "å" *stream*, "is" *ice cream*) and straightforward pronunciation (see how target words are presented in figure 2). Only letters E, I, L, S, Å are used, and only the most basic letter-to-sound rules are in play. In general, rules trained at one level carry over to the next so that easier rules are practiced before more difficult ones. A total of 20 letter-to-sound rules are covered. The entire course comprises 16 levels, first focusing on the vowels and fricatives, then gradually introducing the plosives. The purpose is to create a learning situation that systematically and directly introduces the user to phonics applied in spelling with abundant opportunity for the user to practice at the appropriate level of instruction and progression.

Figure 2. How target words are presented in AiRO

The target words are accompanied with a picture, and the pronunciation of the specific word. To ensure that the child practices the intended word and also, has the possibility to access the pronunciation an unlimited number of times, a play bottom is provided.

The user responds by spelling the target word as best they can, letter by letter. For each keystroke, AiRO responds with an auditive rendering of the word-so-far (pronounced by a synthetic voice). Each letter entered by the user is immediately analyzed for correctness, response time, and other metrics. A sound file (synthetic speech) is generated in response, returned to the frontend and played without delay. In order to stimulate the learning process, the system responses must of course support the correct use of letter-sound-correspondances and discourage wrong ones. Later in the development of spelling it must support correct spellings and discourage spelling errors, in other words, be effective cues of promotion and inhibition and thus provide a relevant feedback that supports and encourages the user to apply their knowledge of letter-sound-connections when spelling. A speech generation algorithm was therefore designed with a close look to orthographic, phonetic and didactic theory. The algorithm, called Aspera[3] (Articulated Spelling Response Algorithm), is presented in some detail below.

With the word completed, an encouraging greeting is given, and a new word presented. The process is spiced up with a little game logic (points and praise). The purpose is to visualize the progress of the student.

3.1 A challenging phonetics

Among the European languages, Danish is often considered to be the most vowel-rich. Approximately 39 phonetic symbols are needed

[3]The name Aspera is inspired by the proverb *per Aspera ad Astra*, "through hardships to the stars"

to represent the distinctive vowel sounds (compared to ≈18 for Swedish and ≈20 for Norwegian). This unusual diversity has to do with two historical developments, (*i*) early influence from Low German replaced the Scandinavian rolled [r] by the German velar, thereby introducing several new phonetic vowels, (*ii*) the tonal system (still preserved in Swedish and Norwegian) was replaced in Danish by the 'stød'-feature, also adding to the inventory of vowels (Jespersen, 1897-99, 478; Brink and Lund, 1975, I §§8-26, II §36). Even with the extra alphabetic letters Æ Ø Å, Danish orthography still has only 9 vowel letters for 39 vowel sounds. Not surprisingly, the Danish graphemes are heavily overloaded with phonetic renderings. Some examples are given in table 1.

For these reasons, among others, Danish letter-to-sound rules are unusually hard to master (for humans and NLP-applications alike). This is not good news for children at risk of developing dyslexia who often have difficulties with the so called 'phonological attention'. AiRO's didactic design pays special attention, therefore, to the vowel-related intricacies.

"rejsefeber" [rAJs0fe:!bC]
E → [A][0][e:!][C]
"trestjernet" [trzsdjaR!n0D]
E → [z][a][0]
"tempererede"[tEmp0rz:!CD0]
E → [E][0][z:!][C][0]

Table 1. Frequent phonetic renderings of letter E.[4]

[4]Word translations: *three starred; travel fever; tempered.* Phonetic forms are shown in brackets. [:] is prolongation, [!] is stød (cf. the full SAMPA table at www.dsn.dk). SAMPA is IPA compatible but more keyboard friendly.

3.2 The well-formed syllable - and beyond

The Danish syllabic structure is governed by principles of phonology restricting the scope and location of the individual language sounds, very similar to the other Germanic languages (e.g. English; cf. Grønnum, 1998, chap.13). These are typical examples:

- The nasal [N] occurs only post-vocalically, as in "ping" [peN] *ping;* "vinge" [veN0] *wing*; "ting" [teN!] *thing*
- [h] occurs only syllable-initially, as in "hø" [hø:!] *hay*; "påhit" [pÅhid] *whim*
- Plosives [p][t][k] weaken to [b][d][g] in all positions except syllable-initially: "tip" [tib] *hint*; "skat" [sgad] *treasure*; "stærk" [sdaRg] *strong*

Certain sound combinations never occur in Danish syllables, and this fact makes them particularly suitable in the inhibitory function mentioned above. For instance, if the pupil targets the word "gnaven" (*grumpy*) by producing the letters 'N' - 'G' - 'A', the system can respond by uttering the 'impossible' syllable [Na], signalling the anomaly long before the word is completed. The 'unnatural' sound thus becomes an effective stimulus utilising the language knowledge that the child already possesses. In order to fully exploit the didactic potential of 'forbidden sounds', our speech synthesizer must of course be phonetically complete, in the sense of being able to pronounce any phone combination accurately, including those never occurring in Danish words. We call this capability **hyper-articulation**. At this time, there is no hyper-articulating speech synthesis for Danish on the market, so the AiRO project has had to develop its own voice, HYPERDAN, based on the principle of diphone resynthesis (a technology particularly suited to hyper-articulation; Henrichsen 2004).

3.3 Progressive response

Each spelling session begins with AiRO selecting a fresh target word *T* with the phonetic form *P* (say "sofa" pronounced [so:fa]). *T* is presented to the pupil (with picture and sound). The pupil begins spelling (by typing 'S'), and AiRO responds with the corresponding sound ([s]).

Input	Auditive response
"S"	[s]
"O"	[so:]
"F"	[so:f]
"A"	[so:fa]

Table 2: Illustration of progressive response

In flawless sessions (such as in table 2) the spoken feedback progresses continuously, in the sense that each speech production repeats and extends the preceding one until *P* is met. The feedback thus provides continuous confirmation that the speller remains on the right track. This didactive approach we term **progressive response**. [5]

How are the proper input-response patterns to be computed in order to support progressive response? In the simplest case where *T* and *P* are of identical length (i.e. consists of the same number of symbols), each letter maps to a single phone (as in "s-o-f-a"). For $|T|<|P|$ (*T* shorter than *P*) some of the letters extend the spoken response by more than a single phone (e.g. "t-a-x-i" [t-A-gs-i] *taxi*). However, for $|T|>|P|$ the mapping is less straight-forward (e.g. "ch-au-ff-ø-r" [S-o-f-ø-R!] *driver*) as some of the letters do not correspond to phonetic increments in any simple way, putting the progressive response at risk. Our solution is to allow the inclusion of sub-phones in Aspera's output. Aspera may thus choose to reconstrue the phonetic form of a target word (say "hvidt" [vid] *white*) as a string of sub-phones ([v_1-v_2-i-d_1-d_2]) ensuring that *T* and *P* can still be aligned, maintaining the progressive response.

Consequently, the synthetic voice must be able to accurately pronounce sub-phones (e.g. the first and second half of phone [v] represented by [v_1-v_2]). The AiRO synthesis was developed with special attention to this aspect of hyper-articulation.

3.4 Polarised feedback

What happens, or should happen, when the child makes a spelling error? Consider a target word *T* consisting of letters t_1-t_2-t_3-..-t_n and an intermediate input sequence *Þ* deviating from *T*, e.g. $Þ = t_1$-t_2-$þ$- (where $þ \neq t_3$). The spoken feedback for *Þ* must then be clearly distinct from the feedback for t_1-t_2-t_3- to provide an inhibiting effect. Here, for once, the complex Danish word-to-sound rules come in handy. Due to linguistic factors hinted at above, almost every string of letters has more than one phonologically acceptable pronunciation (if any at all). [6] A nonsense word "hog" could thus be faithfully pronounced in Danish as [hCg], [håg], [håW], [ho:!], [hOW] etc. Aspera exploits this ambiguity by always maximizing the phonetic distance between responses for correct and incorrect input (of course within the limits of phonological well-formedness). We term this principle **polarized feedback**. The phonetic distance is calculated based on the acoustic features of the individual phones. We will not pursue the details here; a journal article presenting the Aspera algorithm in formal detail is in preparation.

In case the input does not map to any phonologically acceptable pronunciation at all (say, having no vowels), Aspera's strategy is trivial: the input string then maps to the signature pronunciation of each letter (e.g. [e] for letter E; [gs] for letter X). This will necessarily produce an odd-sounding response – an inhibiting cue by nature.

5 Observe that the intermediate phonetic feedback (such as [so:f] in the example above) may not correspond to any known word. Even when the given (intermediate) input accidentally matches an existing Danish word T_X (e.g. 'SO' [so:!] *sow*), the phonetic feedback will not in general match T_X's pronunciation (compare [so:] and [so:!]).

6 This fact is a real challenge when developing Danish artificial voices, as experienced in trains, cars, call centers, home assistants, etc. where delusive pronunciations are commonplace.

4 Kindergarteners testing AiRO

AiRO was tested for the first time by kindergarteners in the Danish primary school during November 2021. Fifty kindergarteners were selected from 9 kindergarten classes. Kindergarten pupils are between 5 and 6 years old. In Danish kindergarten classrooms children are taught linguistic awareness, phonics, and reading and spelling of simple words (Juul and Elbro, 2005).

4.1 Design

We designed this testing as an effect study with an experimental group (*n*=26) and a business as usual control group (*n*=24), following Bryman (2016).

From each kindergarten classroom we selected 4-6 subjects based on their (low) scores in the national screening test (Sprogvurdering: BUVM, 2019). Parental consent was acquired for each participating subject. The reading professional at the schools helped us evenly distribute subjects with mild and severe spelling difficulties in the two conditions of the study.

Before and after the intervention the 49 subjects' spelling and reading skills were evaluated with customized versions of screening tests developed in Engmose (2019). These test focuses on phonics applied in spelling and reading. Each subject's attention to language sounds and knowledge of letters was also assessed with standardized tests from Language Assessment 3-6 (BVUM, 2019).

4.2 Description of the intervention

Before the intervention the participating teachers and reading professionals were given a two-hour introductory course. They were introduced to the design of the study, the purpose of the intervention, and how they should instruct and assist the pupils during the intervention.

Only subjects in the experimental group had access to AiRO, while the control group received ordinary instruction. The experimental group worked with AiRO during four weeks, four days a week, 10-15 minutes each time.

The intervention in the experimental group began with an individual introduction to AiRO and a guided practice of the first two levels. This was done by the teachers. The kindergarteners worked unattended[7] for the remaining levels (3-16). The participating subjects could ask questions to the teacher at all times. Due to too much noise in some of the kindergarten classrooms some teachers ended up separating the children working with AiRO from the remaining classroom e.g. in a nearby smaller room.

4.3 Descriptive statistics

For both spelling and reading we compared the control and the experimental group at pre- and posttest. Table 3 and 4 show descriptive statistics for both groups (experimental and control) at pre and posttest. For each measure the number of items (#items) and minimal and maximal score values (min-max) of the scale are listed. The descriptive statistics are the number of participants (N), mean performance (M), standard deviation (SD) and range of performance (Range). Notice, that scores are calculated as how far they are from correct, meaning that lower scores are better.

Measure (#items;min-max)	**M (SD)**	**Range**	**N**
AiRO group			
Spelling (10;0-28)	18 (9)	41-3	23
Reading (12;0-72)	53 (9)	64-31	26
Control group			
Spelling (10;0-28)	16 (7)	29-5	20
Reading (12;0-72)	45 (18)	72-4	22

[7] Most of the pupils found it difficult to log on to their personalized AiRO-homepage and needed help for this step throughout.

Table 3: Descriptive statistics from pretest

Measure (#items,min-max)	**M (SD)**	**Range**	**N**
AiRO group			
Spelling (10;0-28)	11(7)	25-1	21
Reading (12;0-72)	25 (14)	43-1	15
Control group			
Spelling (10;0-28)	12 (9)	36-0	16
Reading (12;0-72)	40 (20)	68-6	10

Table 4: Descriptive statistics from posttest

Notice in table 3 and 4 that not all 49 subjects were actually fully tested. This was due to corona-related challenges. These missing data affects the generalizability of our analysis as reported in section 4.4.

4.4 Results

For both spelling and reading we compared the control and the experimental group at the beginning and at the end of the experiment. We used paired t-test (two-tailed). In the experimental group these analyses showed significantly strengthened spelling, $t(20) = 5.127$, $p < .001$, $d = 1.12$, and reading, $t(14) = 7.566$, $p < .001$, $d = 1.95$. For the control group reading was also significantly strengthened, $t(9) = 4.312$, $p = .002$, $d = 1.36$, but spelling was not, $t(14) = 1.977$, $p = .068$, $d = 0.51$.

We used the two-way mixed ANOVA to determine whether there is an interaction effect between time of testing (pre- and posttest) and group (experimental and control). For reading we found a significant interaction effect between the two groups and time, $F(1, 23) = 8.552$, $p = .008$, partial $n^2 = .271$. This interaction was due to more progress in the experimental group than in the control group. For reading, the experimental group thus significantly out-performed the control group which received ordinary class teaching during the intervention period. For spelling the pattern was similar, but there was not a significant interaction effect between the two groups and time, $F(1, 34) = 0.980$, $p = .329$, partial $n^2 = .028$.

5 Conclusion

As mentioned before most Danish teachers have received very little formal education about dyslexia in young children. This is one of the barriers to providing the needed support for students at risk of dyslexia or students with dyslexia in primary school. In Denmark, every second adult dyslectic report that they have never received individual offers from the education system, such as one-on-one teaching, special courses (in or outside class) or indeed personalized help of any sort (Mejding et al., 2017; Egmont 2018).

The CALL-based pedagogical approach in AiRO is a starting point for exploring new ways to support the early and later stages of reading and spelling acquisition for struggling readers.

Given the promising results from our first small experiment with kindergarten children at risk of dyslexia, we feel encouraged to develop AiRO further. We are currently making preparations for a new and updated AiRO-tool (AiRO2), capable of screening its users while servicing them, providing the teacher with status reports on the performance of the class as a whole and of the individual pupils.

Acknowledgments

We would like to express our special gratitude to all the participating teachers, reading professionals, and pupils from Sydfalster Skole and Susåskolen, Taastrup Realskole, Holmegaard-skolen, Arenaskolen, and Fladsåskolen. The AiRO project was funded by the Danish Ministry of Research (Innovationsfonden).

References

Brink, L. and Lund, J. (1975) *Dansk Rigsmål*. Part I and II. København: Gyldendals Forlag.

Bryman, A. (2016). *Social research methods*. Oxford University Press.

BUVM (2021). https://www.uvm.dk/statistik/grundskolen/elever/skolestart [visited 05.01.22]

BUVM (2019). https://emu.dk/sites/default/files/2020-09/GSK_FællesMål_Børnehaveklassen.pdf [visited 05.01.22]

BVUM (2019). Vejledning til Sprogvurdering 3-6 https://www.sprogvurdering.dk/ [visited 05.01.22]

Elbro, C., Møller, S., and Nielsen, E.M. (1995). Functional reading difficulties in Denmark. A study of adult reading of common texts. *Reading and Writing*, 7, 257-276.

Egmont Fonden (2018). *Survey og registeranalyse - børn og unge med ordblindhed rapport.* København: Egmont Fonden.

Ehri, L.C. (2005). Learning to Read Words: Theory, Findings, and Issues. *Scientific Studies of Reading, 9*(2): 188-167.

Elbro, C. and Petersen, D. K. (2004). Long-term effects of phoneme awareness and letter name training. An intervention study with children at risk of dyslexia. *Journal of Educational Psychology*, 96(4), 660-670.

Egmont Fonden (2018). *Survey og registeranalyse - børn og unge med ordblindhed rapport.* København: Egmont Fonden.

Engmose, S.F. (2019). *IT-støttet børnestavning: studier af børnestavnings rolle i den tidlige skriftsproglige udvikling*. Ph.D. thesisCopenhagen: Københavns Universitet, Det Humanistiske Fakultet.

Gellert, A.S., Poulsen, M. and Elbro, C. (2018). Ordblindhed. *Samfundsøkonomen*, (1), 22-24.

Gissel, S.T., and Andersen, S.C. (2021). A cluster-randomized trial measuring the effects of a digital learning tool supporting decoding and reading for meaning in grade 2. *J Comput Assist Learn*, 37, 287– 304.

Grønnum, N. (1998) *Fonetik og Fonologi*. København: Akademisk Forlag.

Henrichsen, P.J. (2004). The Twisted Tongue: Tools for Teaching Danish Pronunciation Using a Synthetic Voice. *Copenhagen studies in language*, 30, 95-111

Jespersen, O. (1897-99) *Fonetik*. København: Det Schubotheske Forlag.

Juul, H. and Elbro, C. (2005). *Sproglige færdigheder ved starten af børnehaveklassen. Rapport om en undersøgelse gennemført for Undervisningsministeriet efteråret 2004.* København: Center for Læseforskning.

Mejding, J., Neubert, K. and Larsen, R. (2017). *En international undersøgelse om læsekompetence i 3. og 4. klasse.* Rapport. PIRLS 2016.

Messer, D., and Nash, G. (2018). An evaluation of the effectiveness of a computer-assisted reading intervention. *Journal of Research in Reading*, 41(1), 140-158.

National Reading Panel (2000). *Teaching children to read: An evidence-based assessment of the scientific research literature on reading and its implications for reading instruction*. Washington DC: The National Institute of Child Health and Human Development.

Pihl, M.D. and Jensen, T. (2017). *Færre læreruddannede i folkeskolen*. Danmarks Lærerforenings hjemmeside: https://www.dlf.org/nyheder/2017/marts/ae-raadet-hver-10-laereransatte-har-ikke-en-uddannelse [visit 05.01.22]

Rosdahl, A., Fridberg, T., Jakobsen, V., and Jørgensen, M. (2013). *Færdigheder i læsning, regning og problemløsning med it i Danmark*. København: SFI.

Share, D.L. (1995). Phonological Recoding and Self-teaching: sine qua non of Reading Acquisition. *Cognition*, *55*(2): 151-218.

Solheim, O. J., Frijters, J. C., Lundetræ, K., and Uppstad, P. H. (2018). Effectiveness of an early reading intervention in a semi-transparent orthography: A group randomised controlled trial. *Learning and Instruction*, 58, 65-79.

Vellutino, F.R. and Scanlon, D.M. (2002). The Interactive Strategies approach to reading intervention. *Contemporary Educational Psychology*, 27(4), 573-635.

On the Relevance and Learner Dependence of Co-text Complexity for Exercise Difficulty

Tanja Heck
Universität Tübingen / Germany
tanja.heck@
uni-tuebingen.de

Detmar Meurers
Universität Tübingen / Germany
detmar.meurers@
uni-tuebingen.de

Abstract

Adaptive exercise sequencing in Intelligent Language Tutoring Systems (ILTS) aims to select exercises for individual learners that match their abilities. For exercises practicing forms in isolation, it may be sufficient for sequencing to consider the form being practiced. But when exercises embed the forms in a sentence or bigger language context, little is known about how the nature of this co-text influences learners in completing the exercises.

To fill the gap, based on data from two large field studies conducted with an English ILTS in German secondary schools, we analyze the impact of co-text complexity on learner performance for different exercise types and learners at different proficiency levels. The results show that co-text complexity is an important predictor for a learner's performance on practice exercises, especially for gap filling and Jumbled Sentences exercises, and particularly for learners at higher proficiency levels.

1 Introduction

Exercise difficulty, which constitutes the probability of a learner answering the exercise correctly, plays an important role in intelligent tutoring systems. Macro-adaptive systems in particular rely on it to select exercises at the learner's proficiency level. Assigning a global difficulty score to an exercise, however, fails to consider the many facets of factors contributing to exercise difficulty and the varied learner profiles instantiating them (Beinborn, 2016). Approaches like Multidimensional Item Response Theory (Park et al., 2019) and Knowledge Tracing (Liu et al., 2021b) address this issue by tracking individual skills instead of a single, accumulated one. Yet they usually focus on the skills the learner is supposed to acquire through the exercises. More stable skills such as a learner's language affinity or their general language proficiency are therefore often neglected in these approaches. Such skills might not be relevant in mechanical drill exercises that practice the linguistic forms of the learning target in isolation (Wong and Van Patten, 2003). However, contextualized exercises, which practice linguistic constructions in the broader context of a coherent text, require learners to understand the clues provided by this co-text in order to give the correct answer (Walz, 1989). Yet understanding of how form-specific clues relate to general linguistic properties is still lacking. Approaches aligning a text's linguistic complexity with a learner's general language proficiency have so far been limited to the domain of readability assessment (Chen and Meurers, 2019). In order to apply it to adaptive exercise selection, the relationship between an exercise's co-text complexity and the learner's language proficiency level must have an impact on the learner's performance on an exercise. If the relevance of a relationship between these two factors can be established, it constitutes a valuable indicator to determine initial parameter settings while the system lacks learner data for more individualized adaptation.

Approaches trying to determine difficulty based on exercise parameters, thus allowing to calibrate exercise difficulty without available learner performance data in order to solve the cold start problem, have indeed found that general language parameters influence exercise difficulty (Pandarova et al., 2019). However, these approaches focus on a specific exercise type each. Since different exercise types elicit different processing of the linguistic co-material and target different skills (Grellet, 1981, p. 5), the relevance of individual linguistic parameters can be expected to vary from one exercise type to the other.

The cold-start problem is not only an issue with

Tanja Heck and Detmar Meurers. On the relevance and learner dependence of co-text complexity for exercise difficulty. *Proceedings of the 12th Workshop on Natural Language Processing for Computer Assisted Language Learning (NLP4CALL 2023)*. Linköping Electronic Conference Proceedings 197: 71–84.

new exercises, but also with learners interacting with the system for the first time or starting to practice a new learning target. If the learner has already completed other lessons, overall performance data might be used to determine initial exercise difficulty. Performance metrics for one particular learning target might, however, not be indicative of performance on another learning target. If the learner is new to the system, determining the appropriate exercise difficulty level becomes a matter of randomness. Many systems rely on user questionnaires asking about the proficiency level and in addition offer placement tests (Vesselinov and Grego, 2016). While specifically testing a learner's proficiency in the learning targets of the particular learning unit would provide the most representative picture of a learner's knowledge state, this could turn the first contact with the system into a frustrating experience for low-proficient learners. In addition, linguistic co-text material of exercises always contains linguistic constructions other than the learning targets. In order to process the semantic context of the exercises, learners need to have passive knowledge of of these constructions. Since text readability is traditionally linked to general language proficiency (Chen and Meurers, 2019), a measure reflecting this learner characteristic in relation to the complexity of the exercises' linguistic co-material might be more suitable to determine the optimal initial exercise difficulty. C-tests constitute a popular method of providing such a measure (Drackert and Timukova, 2020).

In this paper, we establish the groundwork to overcome the shortcomings of previous work on exercise difficulty calibration in terms of narrow exercise type coverage and learner-dependence of global exercise parameters. We determine for a range of different exercise types whether the global parameter of co-text complexity impacts learners' performance on the exercise. This will inform macro-adaptive algorithms as to which exercises warrant adaptive assignment with respect to co-text complexity. In addition, we analyze the relevance of the learner's proficiency to this parameter in order to determine whether co-text complexity has a similar impact on exercise difficulty for all learners.

The rest of the paper is structured as follows: Section 2 presents work on exercise difficulty calibration in the domain of language learning. Section 3 describes the dataset used for the evaluations. Section 4 presents the analyses and their results before discussing their implications for adaptive exercise selection. Section 5 concludes with a summary, including a discussion of some limitations of the approach and directions for future research.

2 Related Work

Macro-adaptive systems aim to provide personalized learning experiences by selecting exercises matching a learner's abilities (Slavuj et al., 2017). This has been tackled by a variety of approaches including the proportion of correct answers, Item Response Theory (IRT), Elo rating, and learner and expert ratings (Wauters et al., 2012). Human rating based approaches are subjective in nature and require human effort. Data based approaches are more objective, yet they rely on large amounts of learner answers in order to provide reliable difficulty estimates. Aiming to overcome this shortcoming, multiple strategies have been explored to determine exercise difficulty based on a range of exercise parameters instead. Hartig et al. (2012) point out that the relevant parameters vary depending on the skill targeted by the exercise so that the set of parameters needs to be determined individually for any domain. For language exercises, most work so far has focused on Cloze exercises with a particular emphasis on C-tests. In an early approach, Wilson (1994) used co-text readability as a single determining feature of exercise difficulty, acknowledging the need to yet establish its correlation with exercise difficulty. Others have identified a range of linguistic features on the word, sentence, and text levels that impact exercise difficulty (e.g. Galasso, 2018; Beinborn et al., 2014; McCarthy et al., 2021; Settles et al., 2020; Brown, 1989). The effect of exercise format parameters such as gap size, deletion pattern and deletion frequency on exercise difficulty varied across studies (Sigott, 1995; Lee et al., 2019; Kamimoto, 1993). Abraham and Chapelle (1992) explored different input types and found dropdown selection to be easier than text input. A number of Single Choice (SC) reading comprehension exercises applied machine learning and statistical approaches generating predictors of exercise difficulty from the text, the question, and answer options (Liu et al., 2021a; Huang et al., 2017; Loukina et al., 2016). While Holzknecht et al. (2021)

found that such exercises were more difficult when the correct option was in the last position, studies on SC exercises in other domains found exercises with the correct option in the first or last position (Attali and Bar-Hillel, 2003), or next to the most attractive distractor (Shin et al., 2020) to be harder. Also not focusing on language exercises, Swanson et al. (2006) explored the number of distractors, and Kubinger and Gottschall (2007) the number of correct options as indicators of exercise difficulty. Since language exercises are often automatically generated, their complexity is sometimes already determined and controlled for at generation time (Kurdi et al., 2020). In this line of work, Pilán et al. (2017) only considered the co-text complexity of their SC exercises for vocabulary practice. Generating the same type of exercises, Susanti et al. (2017) in addition used semantic similarity between the correct option and the distractors, as well as the word-level complexities of the distractors. In their comparisons of syntactically, paradigmatically and not related distractors, Hoshino (2013) found that syntactically related ones were the most difficult distractors, yet only in exercises that require semantic parsing of the co-text. Very little research has focused on grammar exercises. A noticeable exception constitutes the approach by Pandarova et al. (2019), which examines the effect on exercise difficulty of various linguistic properties on the gap, item, and text levels of Fill-in-the-Blanks (FiB) exercises to practice tenses.

Almost all of these analyses targeting difficulty parameters of language exercises use co-text complexity as one of the influencing features. However, they all consider only a single exercise type. In order to fill this gap and establish whether the results of such narrowly focused studies can be generalized to other exercise types, we present an evaluation of the impact of co-text complexity on exercise difficulty for seven exercise types.

Using a feature to predict static exercise difficulty only makes sense if the impact of the feature is similar for all learners. To the best of our knowledge, none of the approaches to exercise difficulty calibration have looked into learner dependence of the features impacting exercise difficulty. We therefore evaluate whether co-text complexity can be used as a static exercise complexity feature or whether it needs to be considered dynamically based on learner characteristics.

3 Data

The evaluations are based on data obtained in the context of the Interact4School (I4S) (Parrisius et al., 2022a,b) and the Digbindiff[1] projects. Both studies collected data from 7th grade learners of English in German secondary schools who worked with the Intelligent Language Tutoring System (ILTS) FeedBook over the course of one school year. The system offers practice exercises with intelligent feedback provided to the learners as they work on the exercises. The two versions of the FeedBook used in the studies differ slightly from one another. While the focus in the I4S study was on motivational aspects in a task based setting, the Didi project looked into user-adaptive exercise sequencing.

The exercises in the I4S version of the FeedBook are organized into task-based cycles that each contain multiple linguistically and pedagogically motivated learning targets. The Didi study, on the other hand, groups exercises only according to learning targets. In order to use a common terminology for both projects, we use *chapter* to denote cycles of I4S and learning targets of Didi, and *learning target* when referring to the learning targets of both system versions.

In addition to the submissions of learners to the practice exercises, both studies also collected performance data on C-tests. These were conducted once at the beginning and once at the end of the studies, thus framing the practice exercises. The C-tests used at both test timepoints and in both studies are identical and consist of six parts. Of the 1,360 learners consenting to participate in the studies, 1,102 completed the first and 774 the second C-test. 553 learners completed both C-tests.

The practice exercise types in the systems include FiB, Short Answer (SA), SC, Jumbled Sentences (JS), Mark-the-Words (MtW), Categorization, and Memory exercises. The 201 exercises in the I4S study – excluding listening exercises – attempted by at least one learner were submitted by a mean of 136.13 learners ($\sigma = 112.58$). They are grouped into four chapters and 9 learning targets and contain a total of 1,140 actionable elements. An actionable element can be the blank of a FiB or SC exercise, a sentence of a JS exercise, a clickable chunk in a MtW exercise, an element to sort in a Categorization exercise, a Memory pair, or an answer to a SA exercise. In the Didi study, a mean

[1] http://digbindiff.de

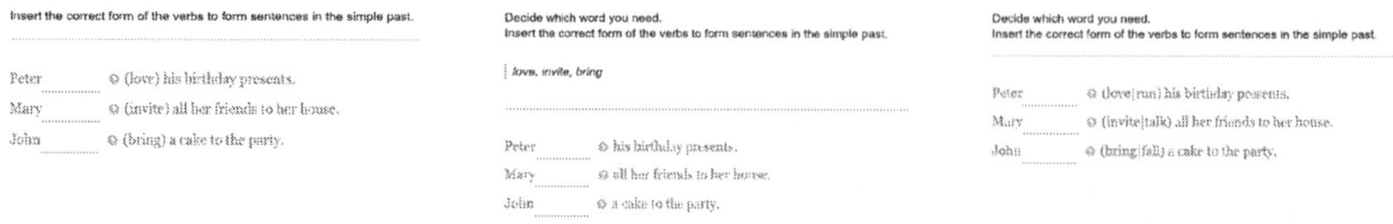

(a) Lemma in parentheses

(b) Lemmas as bag of words

(c) Distractor lemma in parentheses

Figure 1: Codings of FiB exercises

of 29.19 learners ($\sigma = 46.00$) attempted each of the 470 exercises with overall 2,003 actionable elements. These numbers differ considerably from those of the I4S study as the macro-adaptive focus of the Didi study resulted in a more varied practice environment adapted to the individual learner. The exercises are grouped into 4 chapters and learning targets. There is no overlap of learners or practice exercises between the two studies.

All data on exercises and learner submissions is stored in a PostgreSQL[2] database and managed through Hibernate[3].

4 Evaluation

We conducted a range of experiments to determine the relevance and learner dependence of co-text complexity for macro-adaptivity. For these analyses, the data was extracted from the databases with utility scripts written in Java which use the Hibernate setup to access the data. For further processing, the extracted learner submission and exercise data was stored in CSV files. Apart from the correctness of each learner's answers to the actionable elements of exercises, meta-information including the associated learning target, the exercise type, the length of the actionable elements, and exercise type specific information was extracted such as the number of chunks for JS or the number of distractors for SC exercises.

In addition to the metadata extracted from the databases, we determined IRT difficulty scores and co-text complexity scores for all exercises. IRT difficulty values b were determined for all actionable elements based on the Rasch model of the `TAM` package for R. Since the datasets of the two studies constitute discrete sets with no overlaps in learners or exercises, we determined the difficulty values independently for each dataset. For performance reasons, the data in addition needed to be split by learning targets. In order to determine co-text complexity of the exercises in the dataset, we extracted the text material from all exercises. This includes prompts as well as all actionable elements and surrounding co-text, but not instructions or any support texts. We approximated co-text complexity for all extracted texts through a number of different readability formulas. In lack of gold standard values for text complexity, we operationalized it as the mean value of normalized[4] readability scores obtained from various readability formulas. Although IRT scores were estimated separately for the learning targets, we used the joint dataset for the readability score determination as text complexity should be independent of exercises and learners.

Since we assumed that the effect of co-text complexity might only be relevant to some learning targets and to some exercise types, we extracted subsets of exercises for isolated analyses. Each combination of exercise type and learning target resulted in a distinct subset of exercises. In addition, FiB exercises support two possible codings, as illustrated in Figure 1: (1) Specifying the required lemma in parentheses behind the blank (1a) results in mechanical drill exercises. (2) Giving the lemmas as bags of words for the entire exercise (1b) or providing an additional distractor lemma in parentheses (1c) requires top-down skills in the form of parsing the co-text (Nagao, 2002) in order to successfully answer the exercise. Considering that co-text complexity might be less relevant in exercises where correct processing of the text is not essential (Hoshino, 2013), we extracted the co-text sensitive exercises into an additional subset. Some data might not be representative due to the low number of submissions for an exercise. A further subset of core exercises therefore is based

[2] http://postgresql.org

[3] http://hibernate.org

[4] We used the `StandardScaler` of the Python scikit-learn package for scaling of the readability scores of each formula, and the `MinMaxScaler` of the same library to scale the mean readability scores into the range [0,1].

on the number of learner submissions for the exercises. It encompasses all exercises which were submitted by at least 50% of all learners in the respective study. The next three subsets control for exercise difficulty. They consist of exercise items with similar IRT difficulties in the low, intermediate, and high difficulty ranges. Since IRT scores were determined for individual actionable elements instead of for entire exercises, these subsets contain actionable elements as items. In order to maximize the number of items per subset while minimizing the range of difficulty scores, in the intermediate difficulty subset we only included exercises that deviate from the median value in no more than 1%. For the low and high difficulty subsets, we used the same number of exercise items with the lowest and highest difficulty scores respectively. The last three subsets, created in a similar manner based on the scores of the first C-test, control for learner proficiency. They contain only the submission data for exercises attempted by the learners associated with the respective proficiency group.

After thus pre-processing the raw database data into a format independent of the ILTS and enriched with meta-information, we implemented the analyses in Python and R.

4.1 Relationship between C-test and practice performance

C-tests are widely used to assess general language proficiency and have been established to reliably and validly do so (Klein-Braley, 1996). However, more recent critical evaluations show mixed results, ranging from high (e.g. Lei, 2008; Rasoli, 2021) to very low (e.g. Farhady and Jamali, 2006; Mashad, 2008) validity for English. These discrepancies might stem from differences in the participants as Mashad (2008) found C-tests to only be reliable for certain proficiency groups. In order to determine the suitability of determining general language proficiency through C-tests for our target group, we determined the distributions of the C-test scores based on histogram plots. Although Daller and Phelan (2006) point out that C-tests are not necessarily normally distributed, we expect similar distributions for all C-test parts. As a reference point, we determined the overall distribution of C-test scores for both C-tests of the dataset, which was found to have a curved shape. Figure 2 shows that out of the six parts of each C-test, only the second, third and fourth parts reflect this form while the other three parts have monotonically increasing distributions. The meta information available for the C-tests confirms that these parts do indeed not provide representative data: The first part constitutes an example item. The last two parts were attempted by only a small number of learners who managed to complete them within the given time frame, thus presumably being more proficient than the slower learners. In the subsequent evaluations, we therefore only used the results of the second to fourth parts.

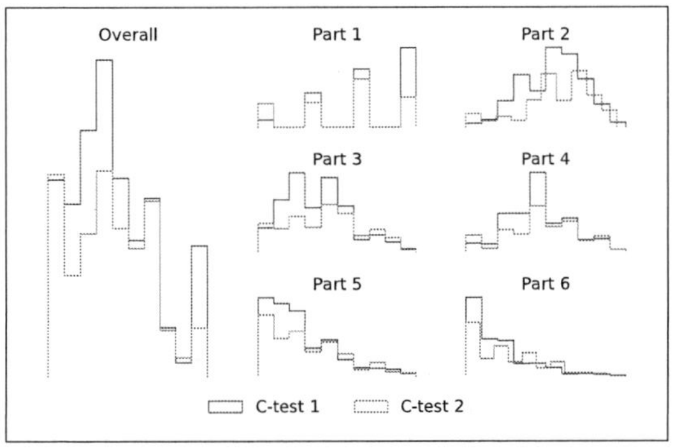

Figure 2: Distributions of C-test scores

The tests can only be indicative of varying performance on exercises if performance on the C-tests is varied across learners. In order to verify that our dataset covers learners of diverse proficiency levels, we determined the range of accuracies obtained on the C-tests. The values are similar for both C-tests with minimum scores of .00 and the highest observed accuracy at .62. When excluding the learners who did not correctly answer any item ($acc = .00$), the lowest score amounts to .01. The study participants thus indeed comprise learners of very low English proficiency who nevertheless made an effort to complete the C-tests. The dataset therefore covers learners with overall English language proficiencies ranging from very weak to moderately strong.

Since we aim to match text complexity to learner proficiency, the scores obtained for both parameters should be equally distributed across exercise texts and learners. We therefore compared the histograms representing the distribution of the text readability scores with that of the overall C-test scores per C-test. Figure 3 illustrates that the curve-shaped distribution of the C-test scores, even more pronounced when excluding the invalid

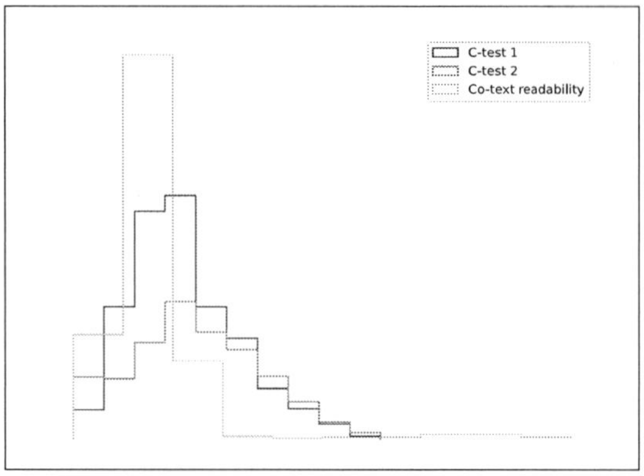

Figure 3: Distributions of C-test and readability scores

parts, is reflected in the histogram for text readability scores. Our dataset thus represents learners and exercises whose global language proficiency, operationalized as C-test scores, and co-text complexity, operationalized as text readability scores, respectively, have compatible distributions.

After establishing the validity of the C-tests in themselves as well as the possibility to map the scores to co-text complexity, we can effectively use them to operationalize a learner's general language proficiency. This learner characteristic can only impact exercise difficulty if there is any relationship between the operationalizations of both. In order to determine whether this is the case for our dataset, we calculated Pearson's correlation ρ between the learners' performance on the C-tests and that on practice exercises. C-test performance was defined as the accuracy on all items of the valid C-tests. Practice performance was defined as the accuracy on the actionable elements of all practice exercises. In addition to global correlation, we also looked at the correlations within the subsets representing combinations of exercise types and learning targets. This allowed us to determine whether C-test performance impacts exercise difficulty for only certain exercise types or learning targets. Table 1 gives an overview of the results. For the first C-test, the Pearson correlation reveals only a weak relationship between C-test accuracy and practice accuracy ($\rho = .28$). It does not increase when only considering core exercises ($\rho = .28$), and only marginally for co-text sensitive exercises ($\rho = .29$). This suggests that the data for the overall exercise pool reflects the picture of the subset most representative of our target group and that general language proficiency is not more relevant for exercises that require processing of the text material. When controlling for exercise difficulty, the relationship is even less pronounced with a weak correlation of $\rho = .27$ for intermediate-difficulty exercises and no relationship for low- ($\rho = .18$) and high-difficulty exercises ($\rho = .15$). When looking at the different learning targets and exercise types separately, correlations are higher for a number of sub-groups covering almost all exercise types and learning targets. The highest – although weak – correlation ($\rho = .47$) is for FiB exercises on *Simple past vs. Present perfect*. The gap filling exercise types FiB and SC, as well as the occasional JS exercise type, have the highest correlations for a number of learning targets. Of these, there is no pattern indicating that any learning target generally has higher correlations between C-test and practice performance than others.

Exercise set	ρ_{c1}	ρ_{c2}
All	.2811	.4070
Core	.2821	.3641
Co-text sensitive	.2887	.3882
Low difficulty	.1773	.2356
Intermediate difficulty	.2674	.2763
High difficulty	.1536	.2465
FiB – *Simple past vs. Pres. perf.*	.4688	.3890
SC – *Conditionals*	.4101	.4392

Table 1: Pearson's correlations of C-test 1 (ρ_{c1}) and C-test 2 (ρ_{c2}) with practice performance

Interestingly, the scores of the second C-test correlate much better with the learners' practice performance, although the relationship is still weak ($\rho = .41$). When looking at the subsets, the pattern is similar to that with the first C-test: Core exercises ($\rho = .36$) and co-text sensitive exercises ($\rho = .38$) have comparable correlations. Correlations for low- ($\rho = .24$) and high-difficulty exercises ($\rho = .25$) are considerably lower again and exercises of intermediate difficulty correlate slightly better with the C-test scores ($\rho = .28$) than the other two subsets, although much less relative to the overall exercise set than for the first C-test. The highest ranked combination of exercise type and learning target of the first C-test again shows a weak correlation ($\rho = .39$), and is only surpassed by one other combination. The correlation between performance on this C-test and practice performance is highest for SC exercises on *Conditionals* ($\rho = .44$). The patterns for specific exercise types and learning targets are similar to those for the first C-test. Since correlations are higher with the second than with the first C-test for all learning targets, the temporal proximity of the test to the practice session does not seem to be the cause of this observation.

In order to better compare the significance of the two C-tests with respect to their predictive power for practice performance, we generated a partial dependence plot based on an AdaBoost classifier trained to predict whether an actionable element is answered correctly depending on the C-test scores. As the probability increases, the colouring turns from purple to green. For the plot given in Figure 4, the colour changes progressively on the vertical axis representing the second C-test, but not on the horizontal axis representing the first C-test. This illustrates that while for the second C-test, the probability of a learner answering an element correctly increases with higher test scores, this is not the case for the first C-test.

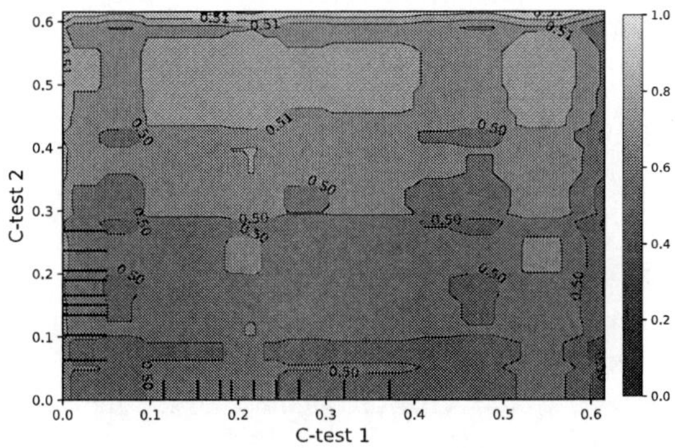

Figure 4: Partial dependence plot for the C-tests when predicting the correctness of a learner's answer

The approach to match co-text complexity to a learner's global language proficiency in order to improve the learner's performance on practice exercises requires valid indicators of learner proficiency from which to calculate the match. As a learner's general language proficiency may change during their involvement with the system, the validity of the initially elicited proficiency score might decrease over time. In order to determine whether this is the case for our learner population, we trained an AdaBoost classifier[5] individually for each of the four chapters to predict a learner's performance on an exercise from the C-test scores and co-text complexity. Since the chapter index represents the exercises' relative practice timepoint, the development of the feature importances of the two C-tests relative to each other over the sequence of succeeding chapters can give insights into whether recency of a C-test influences the predictive power of general language proficiency. While the classifier's feature rankings – outlined in Table 2 for the entire dataset – indicate varying priority of one of the two C-tests over the other, a C-test's importance does not monotonically increase with its temporal proximity to the practice unit. This is similar for all data subsets as illustrated in Figure 5, which displays the difference in feature importances between the first and second C-test depending on the chapter. Monotonically decreasing lines would indicate that the first C-test loses importance with later chapters while the second C-test's importance increases. However, this is not the case for any of the subsets. The test timepoint therefore does not seem to play a substantial role in the predictive power of C-tests.

	c1	**c2**	**c1-c2**	**Relative impact**
Chapter 1	.16	.12	.04	$1 > 2$
Chapter 2	.04	.10	-.06	$2 > 1$
Chapter 3	.02	.08	-.06	$2 > 1$
Chapter 4	.14	.10	.04	$1 > 2$

Table 2: Feature importances of the first (c1) and second (c2) C-tests

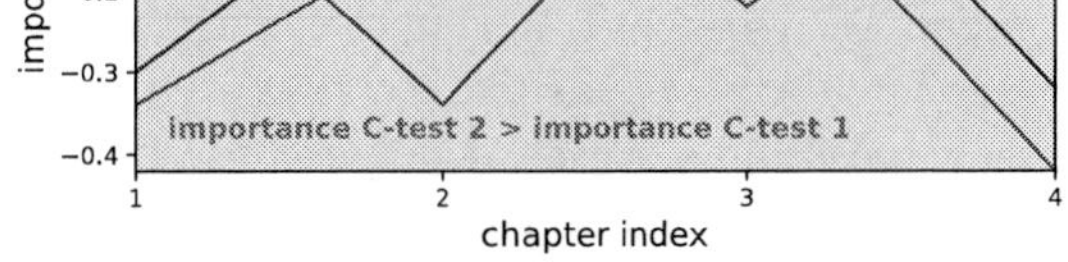

Figure 5: Importance of the C-test scores relative to each other over succeeding chapters

When looking at the development of the learners' C-test scores from one test timepoint to the

[5]The classification was based on the `scikit-learn` (https://scikit-learn.org) implementation for Python.

other, the scatter plot given in Figure 6 reveals that for a considerable number of learners, represented in the shaded area underneath the first bisector, the scores do not show the expected increase, but decrease over time. This also results in an only moderate correlation ($\rho = .5260$) between the two tests. Considering the previous findings that the scores of the second C-test correlate better with practice performance than those of the first C-test, this could indicate that C-tests taken during a learner's first interaction with the system are not entirely representative of their general language proficiency, possibly due to the novelty of the system and the test setup. A tentative conclusion assumes that C-tests do not lose validity over time, at least not within the course of a school year, but that tests are more representative if learners are already familiar with the test platform.

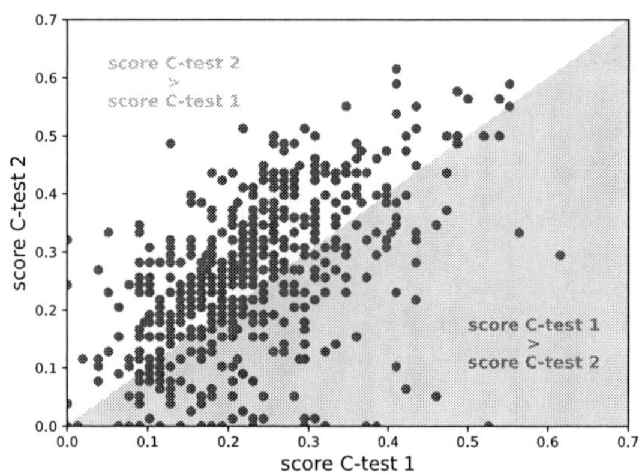

Figure 6: Development of C-test scores between test timepoints

Overall, these results indicate that C-test scores have no or only weak linear relationships with performance on exercises. Although correlations are generally higher for FiB exercises, this is not the case for the co-text sensitive exercises even though they constitute a subset of FiB exercises. Especially for low- and high-difficulty exercises, the relationship of general language proficiency with practice performance, if there is one, does not seem to be linear. C-tests are, however, more predictive of a learner's performance on practice exercises when taken after a period of familiarization with the system.

4.2 Linear relationship between co-text complexity and exercise difficulty

If exercise difficulty increases linearly with increasing co-text complexity, there should be a positive correlation between these two variables. We therefore determined Pearson's correlation between the readability scores and the IRT difficulty scores. Since there might not be a global relationship for all exercise types and learning targets, we calculated correlations for the various subsets in addition to the correlation for the entire dataset.

Exercise set	ρ	**Sample size**
All	.0991	3,104
I4S	.0076	1,101
Didi	.1381	2,003
Future Tenses	-.0094	127
Modals	.7270	34
FiB	.0022	1,849
JS	.3337	444
FiB – *Simple past vs. Present perfect*	-.0231	241
SC – *Conditionals*	.8291	8
Core	.0024	131
Co-text sensitive	.0804	208

Table 3: Pearson's correlation ρ of text readability with exercise difficulty

The results, summarized in Table 3, show that there is no linear relationship between co-text readability and exercise difficulty either for all exercises ($|\rho| = .10$) or for those of the individual I4S ($|\rho| = .01$) and Didi ($\rho = .14$) studies. The values vary considerably between learning targets ($|\rho| = .01$ for *Future Tenses* to $|\rho| = .73$ for *Modals*) and exercise types ($|\rho| = .00$ for FiB to $|\rho| = .33$ for JS). For the subsets comprising combinations of learning targets and exercise types, this variance is equally high ($|\rho| = .02$ for FiB exercises on *Simple past vs. Present perfect* to $|\rho| = .83$ for SC exercises on *Conditionals*[6]). There is no relationship for the subsets containing only core exercises ($|\rho| = .00$) or only co-text sensitive exercises ($|\rho| = .08$). Interestingly, some correlations are negative, suggesting that exercises are more difficult when co-text complexity is lower. While this might be due to insufficiently large sample sizes, it could also indicate

[6]We excluded those combinations with sample sizes of 2, although sample sizes may be too small in most other cases as well (4 - 385) to yield reliable results.

that exercise creators try to compensate some difficulty features with others in order to create exercises of overall approximately similar difficulties. The results, while not entirely conclusive due to data sparseness considering the multitude of parameters influencing exercise difficulty, indicate that co-text complexity does not have the same effect on exercise difficulty for all learning targets and exercise types. There is no overall linear relationship between these two parameters.

For the subsets controlling for exercise difficulty, the difficulty values differ only marginally by definition. We therefore determined the mean as well as the minimum and maximum readability scores within these subsets and compared them between the sets. Following the logic that higher readability scores result in higher exercise difficulties, these metrics should then be lowest for the subset of low-difficulty exercises and highest for the subset of high-difficulty exercises. However, the boxplots in Figure 7 illustrate that readability scores are very similar for all three subsets, with values ranging from .0000 to .4632 ($\mu = .1390$), from .0172 to .3841 ($\mu = .1503$), and from .0074 to 1.0 ($\mu = .1776$) for low-, intermediate-, and high-difficulty items respectively. It should be noted, though, that very high readability scores appear only with high-difficulty exercises, which could indicate that such high text complexities might indeed have an influence on overall exercise difficulty.

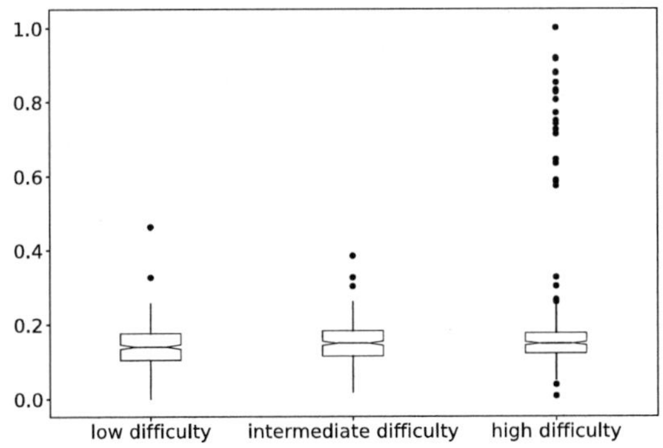

Figure 7: Boxplots of readability score distributions for difficulty controlled subsets

4.3 Non-linear relationships between co-text complexity and exercise difficulty

In order to capture non-linear relationships between co-text complexity and exercise difficulty, we trained various classifiers to predict whether a learner answers an actionable element correctly. The classifiers include a Decision Tree, a Random Forest, and an AdaBoost classifier from the Python `scikit-learn`[7] library, which all provide predictor rankings. As baseline model, we used only simple exercise features such as the exercise type, the number of tokens in the target answer, and the number of other targets in the exercise. We then analyzed a range of model variants for various subsets of the data and with different combinations of additional features targeting IRT difficulty, text readability, and C-test scores. While IRT difficulty scores can be expected to be the most indicative exercise parameter in terms of practice performance, this feature is unknown for new exercises. We therefore analyzed models both with and without the IRT difficulty predictor. All features were encoded as Integer values; not applicable features received the value *zero*. We determined precision, recall, and F1 scores as performance metrics for all model variants in order to evaluate whether adding certain features improves model performance. Precision, recall and F1 scores are comparable for all three classifiers, although the AdaBoost classifier slightly outperforms the others in most experiment settings. For the entire dataset, precision and recall are almost always identical and mirror the F1 scores. We therefore report only F1 scores of the AdaBoost classifier, which are summarized in Table 4. The baseline model already achieves a high F1 score of .72 which increases to .76 when adding the IRT difficulty predictor. When only using text complexity as additional feature, there is almost no increase in performance ($F1 = .72$) as compared to the baseline model. Adding the C-test scores to any of the experiment settings results in a slight increase in F1 scores. Although the best performing model ($F1 = .77$) incorporates all predictors, multiple models with a reduced feature set perform nearly as well. They all include the IRT difficulties as well as C-test scores. The two C-tests result in comparable model performances. The model using all features except for IRT difficulty achieves a F1 score of .73, which constitutes the best performance without IRT difficulties. Adding text complexity as a feature to the best performing models has a small positive effect on performance. F1 scores are gen-

[7]https://scikit-learn.org

Predictors / Set of exercises	base-line	+b	+co-text	+b+c1	+co-text +b+c1	+b+c2	+co-text +b+c2	+co-text +c1+c2	all	μ	σ
All	.7238	.7599	.7247	.7655	.7661	.7653	.7664	.7251	.7669	.7515	.0203
Core	.7510	.7612	.7508	.7709	.7784	.7779	.7751	.7630	.7798	.7676	.0115
Co-text sens.	.7070	.7393	.7108	.7431	.7407	.7491	.7505	.7108	.7516	.7337	.0186
$b_{intermediate}$	.7374	.7458	.7408	.7437	.7404	.7429	.7420	.7424	.7437	.7421	.0024
b_{low}	.9450	.9450	.9450	.9467	.9467	.9470	.9470	.9470	.9469	.9463	.0009
b_{high}	.8553	.8538	.8553	.8516	.8516	.8524	.8524	.8545	.8487	.8528	.0021
FiB	.7227	.7750	.7214	.7760	.7755	.7775	.7777	.7197	.7767	.7580	.0276
MtW	.6585	.6711	.6656	.6985	.6913	.7064	.7082	.7146	.7093	.6915	.0211
JS	.8350	.8549	.8362	.8531	.8538	.8587	.8527	.8343	.8549	.8482	.0099
SC	.7760	.7820	.7760	.7844	.7830	.7848	.7855	.7741	.7855	.7813	.0046
SA	.7277	.7652	.7256	.7562	.7546	.7578	.7620	.7361	.7657	.7501	.0159
Memory	.9535	.9535	.9535	.9535	.9535	.9535	.9535	.9581	.9628	.9550	.0033
Categorization	.6949	.6949	.6949	.7190	.7190	.6949	.6979	.7160	.7009	.7036	.0110

Table 4: Classifier performance

erally slightly higher for the subsets of core exercises ($\mu_{F1} = .77, \sigma_{F1} = .01$) and exercises of intermediate difficulty ($\mu_{F1} = .74, \sigma_{F1} = .00$), and marginally lower for co-text sensitive exercises ($\mu_{F1} = .73, \sigma_{F1} = .02$). For high-difficulty exercises, they are considerably higher ($\mu_{F1} = .85, \sigma_{F1} = .00$) and even more so for low-difficulty exercises ($\mu_{F1} = .95, \sigma_{F1} = .00$). The standard deviations show that there are almost no differences in F1 scores between the model variants of exercise sets with controlled difficulty, which highlights the high relevance of the IRT difficulty feature once again.

In addition, we analyzed the feature importances provided by the classifiers, which allow to estimate the relevance of the individual features to the models' predictions. While model performance metrics indicate that co-text complexity has only little impact on a learner's performance on exercises, the feature rankings, illustrated in the heatmaps in Figure 8, show that this parameter holds substantial predictive power. Not surprisingly, exercise difficulty is the overall most predictive feature. It is, however, followed by co-text complexity in most models integrating this feature and ranked highest in models not including IRT difficulty. The feature rankings for the analyzed features – IRT difficulty, text readability and C-test scores – are similar for all subsets of exercises in terms of relative rankings, although absolute values vary. Differences in the rankings concern mostly the simple exercise features and are quite pronounced between the different exercise types. However, co-text complexity also features greater importance for FiB, and most particularly co-text sensitive exercises, SC, and JS exercises compared to the other exercise types. This on the one hand supports the findings of Section 4.2 in terms of exercise types for which co-text plays a role, and on the other hand reveals that it is particularly relevant with co-text sensitive exercises after all. In addition, the relevance of C-test scores varies considerably from one exercise type to the other. According to the predictor rankings, general language proficiency is highly relevant – even more relevant than IRT difficulty – with Memory and Categorization exercises, and less so with JS, SC, SA, MtW, and particularly FiB exercises.

Overall, the classification experiments reveal that co-text complexity does have predictive power with respect to a learner's performance on an exercise.

4.4 Learner dependence of co-text complexity predictiveness

By comparing the performance of classifiers for the subsets of controlled learner proficiency using co-text complexity as a single predictor, we aimed to determine whether co-text complexity is a learner dependent or independent parameter. If the predictive power of co-text complexity varies with the learners' proficiency levels, we expect performance to differ between the subsets. The results indeed show differences in model performance, which is best for high learner proficiency ($F1 = .7755$) and lowest for low proficiency ($F1 = .6627$). Co-text complexity is therefore a good predictor of practice performance for high-proficiency learners, but less so for low-proficiency learners. This could indicate that less proficient learners do not process an exercise's co-text, either because they do not attempt to do so or

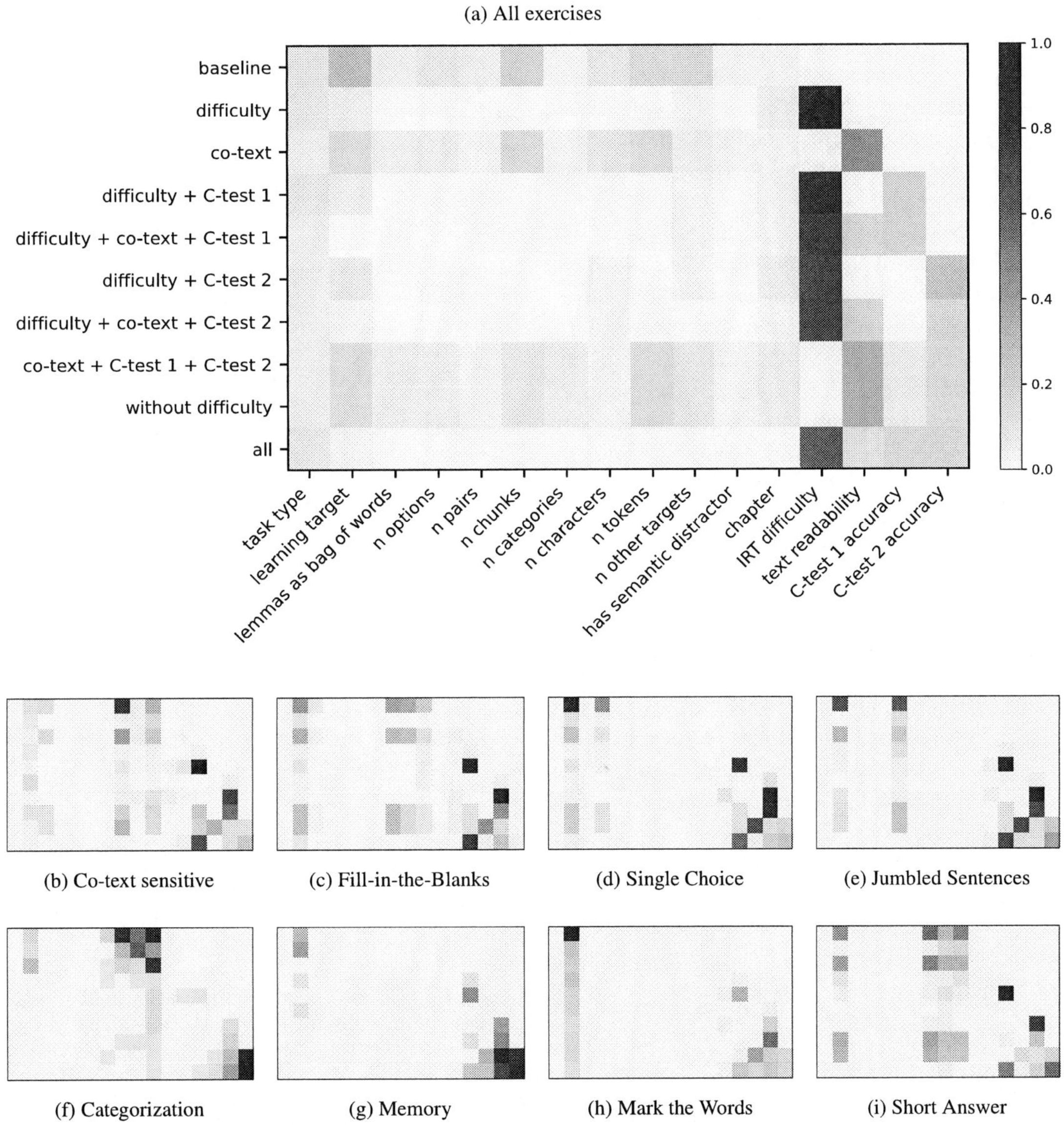

Figure 8: Feature importances

because even the easier texts are too challenging for them, so that this parameter has less impact on their practice performance. Co-text complexity thus seems to be a learner dependent parameter which holds more predictive power the higher the learner's proficiency.

5 Conclusion

We presented an extensive evaluation of the relevance of co-text complexity to exercise difficulty and its dependence on an individual learner's global language proficiency. The analyses cover seven exercise types that differ in the relevance of understanding the co-text in order to successfully answer them. We showed that while there is generally no linear relationship between co-text complexity and a learner's performance on the exercise, statistical models can capture the predictive power of this parameter in combination with other exercise and learner specific features. This is especially true for exercises going beyond mechanical drills, where the co-text provides guidance to successfully answer the exercise. However, its predictive power varies with a learner's proficiency. More proficient learners seem to make use of top-down skills, while less proficient learners use more local clues to solve grammar exercises. Co-text complexity should therefore be considered as a dynamic parameter in adaptive exercise selection in conjunction with a learner's general language proficiency.

We also acknowledge some limitations to our evaluations. Although the C-test scores cover a considerable range, our learners might still constitute a more homogeneous group than in other ILTS where learners do not follow the same curriculum and workbook. Similarly, since the exercises were created from manually composed texts, they do not represent the variability found in authentic texts, especially concerning higher complexities. In addition, readability formulas constitute easy-to-use measures of linguistic complexity thanks to their numerical output scores. However, they do not cover the entire spectrum of linguistic properties relevant to complexity which can be considered in more sophisticated approaches. These should also differentiate between different scopes of the features since for some exercises it might be sufficient to consider the linguistic constructs in the sentence of the actionable element instead of in the entire exercise's co-text.

Future work will need to determine the threshold defining high general language proficiency so that co-text complexity can be considered exclusively for those learners for whom it does make a difference.

References

Roberta G. Abraham and Carol A. Chapelle. 1992. The Meaning of Cloze Test Scores: An Item Difficulty Perspective. *Modern Language Journal*, 76(4):468–479.

Yigal Attali and Maya Bar-Hillel. 2003. Guess Where: The Position of Correct Answers in Multiple-Choice Test Items as a Psychometric Variable. *Journal of Educational Measurement*, 40:109–128.

Lisa Beinborn. 2016. *Predicting and Manipulating the Difficulty of Text-Completion Exercises for Language Learning*. Ph.D. thesis, Technische Universität Darmstadt.

Lisa Beinborn, Torsten Zesch, and Iryna Gurevych. 2014. Predicting the Difficulty of Language Proficiency Tests. *Transactions of the Association for Computational Linguistics*, 2:517–530.

James Dean Brown. 1989. Cloze item difficulty. *JALT journal*, 11(1):46–67.

Xiaobin Chen and Detmar Meurers. 2019. Linking text readability and learner proficiency using linguistic complexity feature vector distance. *Computer Assisted Language Learning*, 32(4):418–447.

Helmut Daller and David Phelan. 2006. The C-test and TOEIC ® as measures of students' progress in intensive short courses in EFL. *Zeitschrift für Interkulturellen Fremdsprachenunterricht*, 13(2):101–119.

Anastasia Drackert and Anna Timukova. 2020. What does the analysis of C-test gaps tell us about the construct of a C-test? A comparison of foreign and heritage language learners' performance. *Language Testing*, 37(1):107–132.

Hossein Farhady and Ferdos Jamali. 2006. Varieties of C-test as measures of general language proficiency. In Hossein Farhady, editor, *Twenty-five years of living with applied linguistics: collection of articles*, pages 287–302. Rahnama Press.

Sabrina Galasso. 2018. Automated C-test difficulty prediction: Integrating lexical, sentence, and text features in a multi-lingual perspective. Master's thesis, University of Tübingen, Tübingen.

Françoise Grellet. 1981. *Developing Reading Skills: A Practical Guide to Reading Comprehension Exercises*. Cambridge Language Teaching Library. Cambridge University Press, New York.

Johannes Hartig, Andreas Frey, Gúnter Nold, and Eckhard Klieme. 2012. An Application of Explanatory Item Response Modeling for Model-Based Proficiency Scaling. *Educational and Psychological Measurement*, 72(4):665–686.

Franz Holzknecht, Gareth McCray, Kathrin Eberharter, Benjamin Kremmel, Matthias Zehentner, Richard Spiby, and Jamie Dunlea. 2021. The effect of response order on candidate viewing behaviour and item difficulty in a multiple-choice listening test. *Language Testing*, 38(1):41–61.

Yuko Hoshino. 2013. Relationship between types of distractor and difficulty of multiple-choice vocabulary tests in sentential context. *Language Testing in Asia*, 3:16.

Zhenya Huang, Qi Liu, Enhong Chen, Hongke Zhao, Mingyong Gao, Si Wei, Yu Su, and Guoping Hu. 2017. Question Difficulty Prediction for READING Problems in Standard Tests. In *AAAI Conference on Artificial Intelligence*.

Tadamitsu Kamimoto. 1993. Tailoring the Test to Fit the Students : Improvement of the C-Test through Classical Item Analysis. *Language Laboratory*, 30:47–61.

Christine Klein-Braley. 1996. *Towards a theory of C-Test processing*, pages 23–94. R. Grotjahn, Rüdiger.

Klaus D. Kubinger and Christian H. Gottschall. 2007. Item difficulty of multiple choice tests dependant on different item response formats - An experiment in fundamental research on psychological assessment. *Psychology Science*, 49.

Ghader Kurdi, Jared Leo, Bijan Parsia, Uli Sattler, and Salam Al-Emari. 2020. A systematic review of automatic question generation for educational purposes. *International Journal of Artificial Intelligence in Education*, 30(1):121–204.

Ji-Ung Lee, Erik Schwan, and Christian Meyer. 2019. Manipulating the Difficulty of C-Tests. In *Proceedings of the 57th Annual Meeting of the Association for Computational Linguistics*, pages 360–370.

Lei Lei. 2008. Validation of the C-Test amongst Chinese ESL Learners. *Journal of Asia TEFL*, pages 117–140.

Qi Liu, Zhenya Huang, Yu Yin, Enhong Chen, Hui Xiong, Yu Su, and Guoping Hu. 2021a. EKT: Exercise-Aware Knowledge Tracing for Student Performance Prediction. *IEEE Transactions on Knowledge and Data Engineering*, 33(1):100–115.

Qi Liu, Shuanghong Shen, Zhenya Huang, Enhong Chen, and Yonghe Zheng. 2021b. A Survey of Knowledge Tracing. *Computing Research Repository*, abs/2105.15106.

Anastassia Loukina, Su-Youn Yoon, Jennifer Sakano, Youhua Wei, and Kathy Sheehan. 2016. Textual complexity as a predictor of difficulty of listening items in language proficiency tests. In *Proceedings of COLING 2016, the 26th International Conference on Computational Linguistics: Technical Papers*, pages 3245–3253, Osaka, Japan. The COLING 2016 Organizing Committee.

Iran Mashad. 2008. Another look at the C-Test: A validation study with Iranian EFL learners. *The Asian EFL Journal*, 10(1):154.

Arya D. McCarthy, Kevin P. Yancey, Geoffrey T. LaFlair, Jesse Egbert, Manqian Liao, and Burr Settles. 2021. Jump-Starting Item Parameters for Adaptive Language Tests. In *Proceedings of the 2021 Conference on Empirical Methods in Natural Language Processing*, pages 883–899, Online and Punta Cana, Dominican Republic. Association for Computational Linguistics.

Hirotaka Nagao. 2002. Using Top-Down Skills to Increase Reading Comprehension. Unpublished Report, ERIC Number ED475744.

Irina Pandarova, Torben Schmidt, Johannes Hartig, Ahcene Boubekki, Roger Jones, and Ulf Brefeld. 2019. Predicting the Difficulty of Exercise Items for Dynamic Difficulty Adaptation in Adaptive Language Tutoring. *International Journal of Artificial Intelligence in Education*.

Jung Yeon Park, Frederik Cornillie, Han L. J. van der Maas, and Wim Van Den Noortgate. 2019. A Multidimensional IRT Approach for Dynamically Monitoring Ability Growth in Computerized Practice Environments. *Frontiers in Psychology*, 10.

Cora Parrisius, Ines Pieronczyk, Carolyn Blume, Katharina Wendebourg, Diana Pili-Moss, Mirjam Assmann, Sabine Beilharz, Stephen Bodnar, Leona Colling, Heiko Holz, et al. 2022a. Using an Intelligent Tutoring System within a Task-Based Learning Approach in English as a Foreign Language Classes to Foster Motivation and Learning Outcome (Interact4School): Pre-registration of the Study Design.

Cora Parrisius, Katharina Wendebourg, Sven Rieger, Ines Loll, Diana Pili-Moss, Leona Colling, Carolyn Blume, Ines Pieronczyk, Heiko Holz, Stephen Bodnar, et al. 2022b. Effective Features of Feedback in an Intelligent Tutoring System-A Randomized Controlled Field Trial (Pre-Registration).

Ildikó Pilán, Elena Volodina, and Lars Borin. 2017. Candidate sentence selection for language learning exercises: From a comprehensive framework to an empirical evaluation. *Traitement Automatique des Langues*, 57.

Mohammad Kabir Rasoli. 2021. Validation of C-test Among Afghan Students of English as a foreign Language. *International Journal of Language Testing*, 11(2):109–121.

Burr Settles, Geoffrey T. LaFlair, and Masato Hagiwara. 2020. Machine Learning-Driven Language Assessment. *Transactions of the Association for Computational Linguistics*, 8:247–263.

Jinnie Shin, Okan Bulut, and Mark J. Gierl. 2020. The Effect of the Most-Attractive-Distractor Location on Multiple-Choice Item Difficulty. *Journal of Experimental Education*, 88(4):643–659.

Günther Sigott. 1995. The C-Test: Some Factors of Difficulty. *Aaa-arbeiten Aus Anglistik Und Amerikanistik*, 20(1):43–53.

Vanja Slavuj, Ana Meštrović, and Božidar Kovačić. 2017. Adaptivity in educational systems for language learning: a review. *Computer Assisted Language Learning*, 30(1-2):64–90.

Yunik Susanti, Takenobu Tokunaga, Hitoshi Nishikawa, and Hiroyuki Obari. 2017. Controlling item difficulty for automatic vocabulary question generation. *Research and Practice in Technology Enhanced Learning*, 12.

David Swanson, Kathleen Holtzman, Krista Allbee, and Brian Clauser. 2006. Psychometric Characteristics and Response Times for Content-Parallel Extended-Matching and One-Best-Answer Items in Relation to Number of Options. *Academic Medicine*, 81:52–5.

Roumen Vesselinov and John Grego. 2016. The Babbel efficacy study. Babbel White Paper.

Joel Walz. 1989. Context and Contextualized Language Practice in Foreign Language Teaching. *Modern Language Journal*, 73(2):160–168.

Kelly Wauters, Piet Desmet, and Wim Van Den Noortgate. 2012. Item difficulty estimation: An auspicious collaboration between data and judgment. *Computers & Education*, 58(4):1183–1193.

Eve Wilson. 1994. A User-Adaptive Interface for Computer Assisted Language Learning. In *Proceedings of ED-MEDIA 84–World Conference on Educational Multimedia and Hypermedia*.

Wynne Wong and Bill Van Patten. 2003. The Evidence is IN: Drills are OUT. *Foreign Language Annals*, 36(3):403–423.

Manual and Automatic Identification of Similar Arguments in EFL Learner Essays

Ahmed Mousa[1], Ronja Laarmann-Quante[2] and Andrea Horbach[3,4]
[1]University of Duisburg-Essen, Germany,
[2]Ruhr University Bochum, Faculty of Philology, Department of Linguistics, Germany,
[3]CATALPA, FernUniversität in Hagen, Germany,
[4]Universität Hildesheim, Germany

Abstract

Argument mining typically focuses on identifying argumentative units such as *claim, position, evidence* etc. in texts. In an educational setting, e.g. when teachers grade students' essays, they may in addition benefit from information about the content of the arguments being used. We thus present a pilot study on the identification of similar arguments in a set of essays written by English-as-a-foreign-language (EFL) students. In a manual annotation study, we show that human annotators are able to assign sentences to a set of 26 reference arguments with a rather high agreement of $\kappa > .70$. In a set of experiments based on (a) unsupervised clustering and (b) supervised machine learning, we find that both approaches perform rather poorly on this task, but can be moderately improved by using a set of six meta classes instead of the more fine-grained argument distinction.

1 Introduction

Argumentative essays are frequently written as part of foreign language instruction. A common natural language processing (NLP) task on these kinds of texts is argument mining, the task of automatically detecting argumentative units in texts (Lawrence and Reed, 2020). In argument mining, arguments are typically categorized according to their function, such as *claim, position, evidence* etc., but most argument mining approaches do not offer methods to categorize the content covered by a particular argument.

From an educational perspective, however, knowing which sub-topics of a certain prompt are addressed where in the essay could be beneficial both for summative and formative feedback. For example, while grading an essay, teachers could benefit from knowing how many different arguments or how many pro and con arguments occur and how they are distributed in the text. The automatic identification of arguments also allows for an easier comparison of the content of different essays. Students could receive such information as feedback. Figure 1 shows an example of an argumentative essay and how the information could be highlighted in the text.

This paper presents a pilot study on the automatic identification of similar arguments in texts of EFL students. We want to find out (a) how well human annotators agree when detecting similar arguments and (b) what performance on this task can be achieved with an automatic model and whether a supervised approached with limited training data or an unsupervised clustering approach works better. To do so, we conduct an annotation study in which we first determine a set of reference arguments found in the essays. By 'reference argument' we mean a statement that summarizes in one sentence the core of an argument found in one or more essays.

We then use these reference arguments to annotate a subset of the dataset for computing inter-annotator agreement and to be used as gold standard for evaluating automatic models. In our experiments, we compare variants of k-means clustering using different seed sets and vectorization methods. We evaluate them according to their ability to place gold segments with the same cluster ID in the same cluster and unrelated segments in different clusters and compare them with a supervised Machine Learning (ML) approach. We either distinguish between fine-grained arguments or merge different arguments into meta-classes such as *Pro*, *Contra* or *Irrelevant*.

Thus, our paper contributes to the research on similar argument identification in two ways. Firstly, we provide manual annotations of similar arguments for a set of EFL learner texts. We

Ahmed Mousa, Ronja Laarmann-Quante and Andrea Horbach. Manual and Automatic Identification of Similar Arguments in EFL Learner Essays. *Proceedings of the 12th Workshop on Natural Language Processing for Computer Assisted Language Learning (NLP4CALL 2023)*. Linköping Electronic Conference Proceedings 197: 85–93.

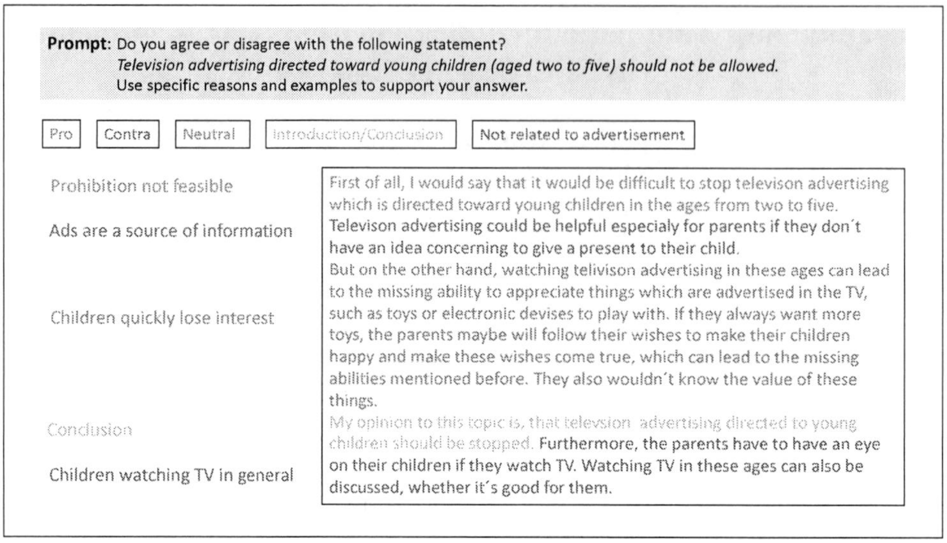

Figure 1: Example of an essay annotated with argumentative units and argument summaries.

make our annotated dataset available under https://github.com/andreahorbach/ArgumentClustering. Secondly, we provide a number of baselines results for automating the task based on different methods and for different levels of granularity.

2 Related Work

2.1 Argument Identification

Argument mining usually deals with identifying certain argument types based on their function in the text (Wachsmuth et al., 2016; Nguyen and Litman, 2018; Ding et al., 2022). While most such approaches work in a supervised way, Persing and Ng (2020) use an unsupervised approach to bootstrap argumentative units of different types based on a seed set obtained from applying simple heuristics. Our approach is related to argument mining but has the major difference that the goal is to classify any identified segment based on its content. In educational contexts, even when scoring argumentative essays, argumentative content is rarely explicitly focused on. In datasets such as the ASAP essay dataset[1] argumentative essays are either scored holistically or according to categories such as overall content, organization fluency etc. The content of individual arguments, however, is only rarely explicitly addressed. Horbach et al. (2017), for example, conduct experiments on German essays based on an annotation scheme indicating the presence or absence of certain arguments regarding a topic, but they do not mark the exact location in the text.

[1] https://www.kaggle.com/competitions/asap-aes/overview

2.2 Text Clustering

In the educational domain, clustering techniques have been employed to support automatic scoring of learner answers with the basic idea that answers appearing in the same cluster likely convey the same content and can therefore be graded together. Proposed approaches rely on surface representations (Horbach et al., 2014), semantic representation such as LSA (Zehner et al., 2016) or a combination thereof (Basu et al., 2013).

In essay scoring, clustering techniques have been used on the text level, such as Chen et al. (2010), who clustered an essay corpus into the number of different scores found in the data. On a more fine-grained level, and probably the closest to our study, Chang et al. (2021) annotate and cluster sentences in Finnish student essays based on their argumentative content. Besides clustering, they use an information retrieval approach but no supervised machine learning like we do.

3 Dataset and Manual Annotations

3.1 MEWS Dataset

We conduct our experiments on the MEWS dataset (Measuring Writing at Secondary Level; Keller, 2016). It consists of English essays written by 10th grade students in Germany and Switzerland who learn English as a foreign language. The

Method	# segments	Avg. # tokens
Sentences	38,715	18.79
W/ Connectives	37,505	19.27

Table 1: Average number and length of segments per essay for each segmentation method.

dataset contains four individual writing prompts, two for independent and two for integrated essays. In this paper, we focus on one of the two independent argumentative writing prompts, in which the learners are supposed to state whether they agree or disagree with a statement and to provide reasons for their answer. The prompt is: *Television advertising directed toward young children (age 2 to 5) should not be allowed.* In total, the dataset contains 2,382 essays in response to this prompt.

3.2 Argumentative Units

We consider different options to automatically segment the essays into units that can be clustered or labeled as different arguments. First, we looked into splitting at paragraph boundaries but as many learners did not arrange their texts into multiple paragraphs this approach turned out to be not feasible. Second, we consider **sentences**, which are an obvious linguistic unit and easy to extract. The potential shortcoming is that a sentence may contain more than one argument or an argument may stretch over multiple sentences. As an alternative, we split the texts using a comprehensive list of 215 **discourse connectives** such as *furthermore, on the other hand, in conclusion* as separators. In this segmentation variant, we only split at sentence boundaries when the next sentence starts with such a connective to indicate that a new argument is following. We decided not to split at discourse connectives within a sentence because we found that it too often leads to uninterpretable text snippets.

Table 1 shows the average number and length of segments found by either variant. We see that the two variants do not differ much numerically from each other. Upon manual inspection, we found that they indeed produced very similar results. Part of the reason may be that the learners do not use discourse connectives consistently. For the sake of simplicity, we therefore decided to use sentences as units, although in future work a proper argumentative unit detection based on gold standard segmentation might be a better alternative.

3.3 Annotation of Gold Standard Arguments

To create a gold standard, we used a two-step process.

Step 1: Determining the Number of Reference Arguments First, we determined how many different arguments there are in the dataset. To do this in a time-efficient manner, one annotator looked at a number of essays and compiled a list of found arguments and the corresponding sentences in an iterative process until no new arguments were detected in four subsequent essays. This happened after a total of 14 essays. There were no specific guidelines for this step. Then, a second annotator looked at the same set of essays and independently collected all different arguments that he found, i.e. he did not see which arguments annotator 1 had collected before. Together with two additional adjudicators, a final set of 26 **reference arguments** was compiled. Each reference argument consists of a short summary of the core content of the argument (produced by the annotators) and a set of sentences from the essays that correspond to this argument. See Table 2 for some examples.

There are some 'special' types of reference arguments worth mentioning: *Introduction* and *Conclusion* refer to all introductory or concluding sentences of an essay, which do not contain arguments per se, *Non-English* refers to all sentences written in a different language (e.g. when students copied material from the German instructions) and *Irrelevant*, which refers to sentences that are meta-comments or do not refer to the prompt e.g. *Sorry for not writing anything*. Furthermore, we added one additional category called *New Arguments* to account for arguments not detected before.

Step 2: Annotating Arguments in Text In the next step, the same two annotators were given the list of reference arguments that were compiled in step 1 and annotated a set of 235 sentences from new essays with the reference arguments they correspond to. We aimed at a set of sentences that would cover all reference arguments. To approximate this, we automatically clustered all sentences from the essays as described in Section 4.1 (with the reference arguments as centroids and tf-idf vectorization) and picked five random sentences from each cluster for the manual annotation. The annotators agreed in 169 out of 235 annotated sentences, reaching an inter-annotator

Argument summary	Corresponding sentences from the essays
Advertisements can have positive effects on children's behavior.	Advertisement for children does not have to be a bad thing, it can be used to influence them so that their behaviour will have a positive effekt on society and nature.
	But that argument is quite small since the children might want something for the outdoor fun like a new special ball and so they want to play outside and stop sitting in front of the TV and that can´t be bad at all.
It does not really matter because young children normally do not watch TV that often or shouldn't be allowed to.	I also remember me having fun to go outside and not having to worry about an television advertisement
	Also one has to add that young children aged two to five normally do not watch TV that often. Therefore it does not really matter
	there seems to be no need for a prohibition of especially this type of advertisements since most of the children aged 2 to 5 are allowed to watch television
Young children are easily manipulated by advertisements.	The advertisment has an influence on the Children and in this age they don't know when they are under an influence
	Chlidren form the age of two to five have not been able to develop their own charcter jet, that makes them an easy target for advertisement
	Because they are so easy to influence and probably believe the things that are said, even though they are not true.

Table 2: Examples of manually identified arguments and corresponding sentences from the essays. We refer to these as reference arguments.

agreement of Cohen's $\kappa = 0.718$. After the annotators were shown where they disagreed, one annotator corrected six obvious errors, raising the inter-annotator agreement to 0.732. This rather high agreement value shows that despite the large number of reference arguments and the overall diverse texts (resulting from an independent rather than integrated writing prompt), arguments in student essays can be clustered consistently – with the limitation that only one prompt was analyzed in this study.

The major sources of disagreements (24 and 20 cases, respectively) were that one annotator tended to assign arguments to the *New Argument* or *Irrelevant* category, respectively, while the other annotator would assign them to one of the existing reference arguments. We chose the annotations of the annotator who preferred to assign the arguments to the existing reference arguments as the final gold standard for our evaluation.

The most frequently occurring arguments/categories are *Irrelevant* (11.5%), *Children shouldn't watch TV in general* (8.1%) and *Children are easily manipulated by advertisements.* (8.1%). Two arguments were found only once, namely *Children may adopt undesired behavior from advertisements* and *Children want to be treated like adults*.

4 Argument Identification Experiments

4.1 Experimental Setup

In our experiments, we compare several instantiations of k-means clustering with supervised machine learning.

Clustering algorithm The basic k-means algorithm (Arthur and Vassilvitskii, 2006) iteratively assigns elements to be clustered to the closest instance from a set of centroids. These centroids are often randomly chosen in the first iteration, later the centroid of each cluster from the previous round is used until the cluster assignment is stable. We choose the number of clusters k to be 26, i.e. the number of reference arguments we manually identified as described in Section 3.3.

One obvious parameter in the setup of k-means clustering is the choice of a suitable **distance metric** between items operationalized by the vectorization method to be combined with cosine similarity. We use four different methods. Cosine similarity between **tf-idf weighted ngram** features is a baseline relying on surface features. We compare it with three embedding-based methods, also using cosine similarity. First we average word vectors using pretrained word embeddings from Word2Vec (Mikolov et al., 2013) or FastText (Joulin et al., 2016) to create sentence vectors. Second, we make use of Sentence-BERT (SBERT, Reimers and Gurevych, 2019) to create an embedding vector per sentence.[2]

A second parametrization of k-means concerns the initialization of seed centroids. We either use random sentences as seeds (**random seeds**) or use our manually annotated reference arguments as centroids (**gold centroids**) by averaging over sentence vectors for all sentences identified for a reference argument as described in Section 3.3. We assume that our gold centroids are already optimal in a sense that they represent the individual arguments in the essays, therefore we stop after one round of clustering in the **gold centroids** setup. In the **random seeds** setup, we iterate as usual until the clustering is stable, i.e. until cluster assignments do not change anymore.[3]

Supervised approach As an alternative, we explore a supervised machine learning approach using logistic regression with different feature setups: tf-idf weighted n-grams or SBERT vectors. We perform 10-fold cross validation on the manually annotated gold-standard sentences from Section 3.3 with cluster ID as the target label. That means, in each iteration, we train on about 212 sentences, which is a rather small number of instances given the 26 target classes.

Evaluation Metrics As we do not have a fully annotated gold-standard cluster assignment for every sentence in the dataset, we rely on the subset of human annotations described in Section 3.3, meaning that most established cluster evaluation techniques (Amigó et al., 2009) are not applicable to our evaluation setup in a straightforward manner. Furthermore, we cannot easily say which cluster represents which reference argument (i.e. which gold-standard label) in order to report instance-based accuracy. Therefore we adapt pair-counting cluster evaluation methods (Halkidi et al., 2001) that use only the annotated subset of sentences in the clusters. From this annotated subset, we form pairs of sentences which belong either into the same cluster or into different clusters according to the gold standard. We thus evaluate for every clustering what percentage of same-cluster pairs was indeed clustered into the same cluster and how many different-cluster pairs ended up in different clusters, as well as using the established Jaccard coefficient J:

$$J = \frac{SS}{SS + SD + DS} \qquad (1)$$

where SS ('same-same') is the number of pairs that belong into one cluster according to the gold standard and are assigned to the same cluster by the algorithm, SD ('same-different') is the number of pairs that are in the same gold cluster but ended up in different clusters in the algorithm and DS ('different-same') the opposite case. The Jaccard coefficient thus ranges from 0 to 1 with 1 being the best possible value. In addition, we report precision and recall, which refer to 'same'-pairs as the positive class, and overall accuracy. One has to be aware that for the pairwise evaluation, accuracy is overall high due to the high number of DD ('different-different') pairs.

4.2 Experiment 1 - Fine-Grained Argument Distinction

Comparison of Clustering Algorithms and Vectorization Methods In a first set of experiments, we compare the different vectorizing approaches for the two variants (gold centroids vs. random seeds) of k-means. The results are shown in Table 3.

We observe that, against our initial expectations, there is no clear advantage of using gold centroids over random seeds. In terms of accuracy and Jaccard, the gold centroids work slightly better than random seeds when tf-idf or FastText is used for vectorization but overall, the differences are rather small. When comparing the different vectorization methods, SBERT and Word2Vec outperform the other two methods for most evaluation metrics. The overall best clustering result is achieved with k-means with random seeds using SBERT, but only reaching a Jaccard index of .115.

We cannot directly compare the (unlabeled) clusters to the gold standard but we can compare the distribution of cluster size. For each clustering setup, we order clusters by size in descending order and plot the cluster size. A horizontal line would mean that all clusters have the same size. A steeply falling line which then becomes flat would mean that there are few clusters with many instances and many clusters with only few instances

[2] We use the following pre-trained models: https://drive.google.com/file/d/0B7XkCwpI5KDYNlNUTTlSS21pQmM/edit?usp=sharing (Word2Vec), https://dl.fbaipublicfiles.com/fasttext/vectors-crawl/cc.en.300.bin.gz (FastText), all-mpnet-base-v2 from https://www.sbert.net/docs/pretrained_models.html (SBERT).

[3] We also tried a mix of both, i.e. starting with gold seeds and then iterating until the cluster assignments are stable. However, since the results were overall worse than for the gold centroids setup, we will not report them in detail for space reasons.

	Vectorization	SS	DD	DS	SD	Acc.	Prec.	Rec.	Jaccard
k-means	tf-idf	240	20,497	3,260	979	.830	.197	.069	.054
	SBERT	246	22,846	911	973	.925	.202	.213	.115
	Word2Vec	258	22,102	1,655	961	.895	.212	.135	.090
	FastText	202	20,793	2,964	1,017	.841	.166	.064	.048
gold centroids	tf-idf	185	22,730	1,027	1,034	.917	.152	.153	.082
	SBERT	200	22,893	864	1,019	.925	.164	.188	.096
	Word2Vec	244	22,243	1,514	975	.900	.200	.139	.089
	FastText	181	22,201	1,556	1,038	.896	.148	.104	.065
supervised ML	tf-idf	812	9,239	14,518	407	.402	.666	.053	.052
	SBERT	589	19,148	4,609	630	.790	.483	.113	.101

Table 3: Results of Experiment 1: Fine-grained argument distinction. Comparison of different clustering techniques and supervised machine learning.

	Vectorization	SS	DD	DS	SD	Acc.	Prec.	Rec.	Jaccard
k-means	tf-idf	2,803	10,571	8,410	3,192	.536	.468	.250	.195
	SBERT	1,393	16,209	2,772	4,602	.705	.233	.335	.159
	Word2Vec	2,047	12,813	6,168	3,948	.595	.342	.299	.168
	FastText	2,108	12,993	5,988	3,887	.605	.352	.260	.176
gold centroids	tf-idf	2,276	14,851	4,130	3,719	.686	.380	.355	.22
	SBERT	2,010	15,559	3,422	3,985	.703	.335	.370	.21
	Word2Vec	2,267	14,237	4,744	3,728	.661	.378	.323	.21
	FastText	2,302	14,339	4,642	3,693	.666	.384	.332	.22
supervised ML	tf-idf	3,311	10,065	8,916	2,684	.536	.552	. 271	.222
	SBERT	3,241	12,489	6,492	2,754	.630	.541	.333	.260

Table 4: Results of Experiment 2: Distinction of broader argument classes: Comparison of different clustering techniques and supervised machine learning.

(like a zipf curve). Figure 2 shows the results for the random seeds setup in comparison with the gold standard. We see that in the gold standard (solid red line), most clusters have roughly the same size. For clusters with tf-idf and FastText vectorization, however, we see that there are a few very dominating clusters with many instances. Overall, the SBERT curve looks most similar to the gold standard.

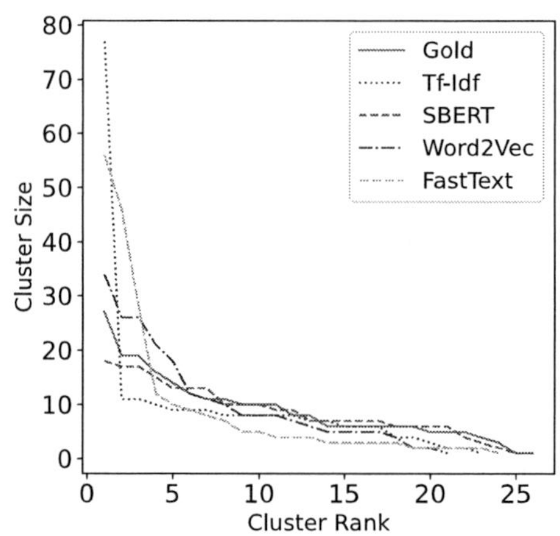

Figure 2: Cluster sizes of the gold standard clusters and the clusters produced by k-means with random seeds and different vectorization methods.

Comparison with Supervised ML The results of the supervised ML experiments based on pairwise evaluation is shown in the lower part of Table 3. As in the unsupervised clustering setup, we see that SBERT features outperform tf-idf based features in terms of accuracy and Jaccard index. Overall, with a maximum Jaccard index of .10, the performance of the supervised ML approach is lower than the best unsupervised clustering setup. This is probably due to the limited amount of labeled training data and the high number of classes.

When we look at the number of correctly assigned instances, we achieve a classification accuracy of .31 (SBERT) and .23 (tf-idf), respectively. What is particularly striking about the results is that SBERT assigns sentences only to 10 out of the 26 reference arguments (tf-idf: 8 out of 26). Unsurprisingly, most sentences are assigned the labels that occurred most frequently in the manually annotated training data.

Class	# Ref. Args.
Pro	9
Contra	9
Neutral	4
Irrelevant	2
Intro	1
Conclusion	1

Table 5: Distribution of reference arguments over the merged classes.

4.3 Experiment 2 - Distinction of Broader Argument Classes

In the previous experiment, we found that the results for distinguishing between individual arguments were rather unsatisfactory. Especially for the supervised ML approach, this may be due to the imbalance of a high number of classes and rather few training instances. Therefore, we conduct a second set of experiments in which we merge the 26 reference arguments into six meta-classes: *Pro*, *Contra*, *Neutral*, *Irrelevant*, *Introduction*, *Conclusion*. Table 5 shows how many reference arguments fall into which class. We see that there are as many different pro arguments as contra arguments in our set of manually identified arguments.

We repeat our experiments on these broader argument classes, i.e. setting *k* to 6 in the clustering experiments. The results are shown in Table 4. We see that compared to the fine-grained argument distinction, the overall accuracy drops in the pairwise evaluation setup because of the smaller number of different-different pairs. In terms of precision, recall and Jaccard index, we see that the clustering works better in the merged classes setup than in the fine-grained setup. Furthermore, the differences between the different vectorization methods are again rather small but unlike in the fine-grained setup we see a slight advantage of using gold centroids over random seeds.

The supervised machine learning approach again performs worse than the unsupervised clustering, but only in terms of accuracy. With SBERT features, the supervised ML approach reaches a Jaccard index of .26, outperforming both the tf-idf features as well as the unsupervised clustering. When looking at instance-based classification accuracy of the supervised ML approach, we get an accuracy of .46 for tf-idf based features and .53 for SBERT features. However, the overall accuracy is misleading. Figure 3 shows the distribution of

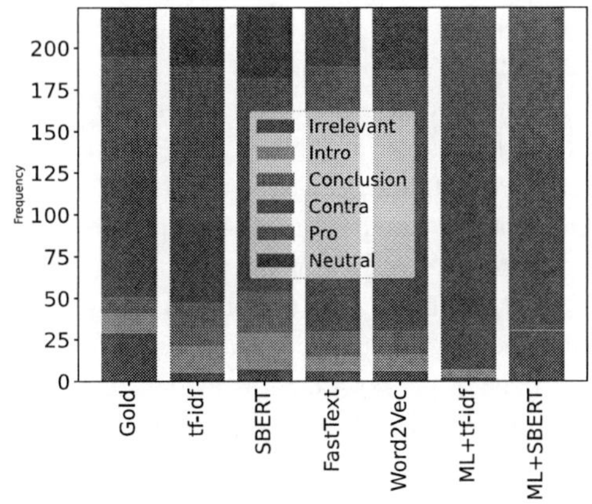

Figure 3: Distribution of argument classes in the gold standard (left), and in the outcome of the clustering and machine learning experiments.

classes in the gold standard (leftmost bar) and in the two ML setups (two rightmost bars). We see that with SBERT features, the algorithm never assigns sentences to the *Conclusion* or *Neutral* class and hardly any to *Introduction*. With tf-idf features, almost 60% of the sentences are assigned to the *Contra* class, which does not reflect the distribution in the gold standard at all.

For comparison, the four bars in the middle show the distribution resulting from the unsupervised clustering with gold centroids. We assigned the labels to the clusters by propagating the majority label of the annotated sentences to the whole cluster.[4] We see that their distributions are much closer to the gold standard but underestimate the number of *Irrelevant* arguments and overestimate the number of *Conclusion* sentences.

5 Discussion and Implications for Practice

Our experiments clearly show that fine-grained argument distinction is rather hard to perform – both with unsupervised clustering and supervised machine learning with rather limited training data (about 200 sentences – probably still more than one could expect in a natural classroom situation).

In an ideal teaching scenario, all sentences from a set of student essays would be clustered automatically, without manual annotation effort. In our study, we used k-means as clustering algorithm, and found that cluster assignment based on

[4]Such a procedure was not feasible in the fine-grained setting due to the large number of classes.

random seeds works as well as explicitly setting gold centroids, which implies that no manual intervention would be required at this step. However, for k-means it is required to set the expected number of outcome clusters. This, in turn, requires that the number of different arguments that can occur is known. Our approach from Experiment 2, i.e. merging the arguments into six broad meta-classes, would overcome this issue in that these classes do not depend on the essay topic. We found that reducing the number of classes also improves the performance. However, highlighting these classes in an essay would convey information about argumentation structure rather than about the content of the argumentation.

6 Conclusion and Outlook

We presented a pilot study for the automatic identification of similar arguments in students' EFL essays. In an annotation study, we found that human annotators are able to assign sentences to a set of reference arguments with a rather high agreement of $\kappa > .70$. Our machine learning experiments showed that for both supervised ML and unsupervised clustering the performance for distinguishing between a set of 26 different arguments was rather poor. In a second set of experiments based on broader argument classes, a better performance could be achieved at the cost of losing information about essay content. Our experiments were based on essays from a single prompt only. In future work, we want to extend both the manual annotation study as well as the ML experiments to a larger set of essays from different topics and prompts.

Acknowledgments

This work was partially conducted at "CATALPA - Center of Advanced Technology for Assisted Learning and Predictive Analytics" of the FernUniversität in Hagen, Germany.

References

Enrique Amigó, Julio Gonzalo, Javier Artiles, and Felisa Verdejo. 2009. A comparison of extrinsic clustering evaluation metrics based on formal constraints. *Information Retrieval*, 12:461–486.

David Arthur and Sergei Vassilvitskii. 2006. k-means++: The advantages of careful seeding. Technical report, Stanford.

Sumit Basu, Chuck Jacobs, and Lucy Vanderwende. 2013. Powergrading: a clustering approach to amplify human effort for short answer grading. *Transactions of the Association for Computational Linguistics*, 1:391–402.

Li-Hsin Chang, Iiro Rastas, Sampo Pyysalo, and Filip Ginter. 2021. Deep learning for sentence clustering in essay grading support. *arXiv preprint arXiv:2104.11556*.

Yen-Yu Chen, Chien-Liang Liu, Tao-Hsing Chang, and Chia-Hoang Lee. 2010. An unsupervised automated essay scoring system. *IEEE Intelligent systems*, 25(05):61–67.

Yuning Ding, Marie Bexte, and Andrea Horbach. 2022. Don't drop the topic - the role of the prompt in argument identification in student writing. In *Proceedings of the 17th Workshop on Innovative Use of NLP for Building Educational Applications (BEA 2022)*, pages 124–133, Seattle, Washington. Association for Computational Linguistics.

Maria Halkidi, Yannis Batistakis, and Michalis Vazirgiannis. 2001. On clustering validation techniques. *Journal of Intelligent Information Systems*, 17:107–145.

Andrea Horbach, Alexis Palmer, and Magdalena Wolska. 2014. Finding a tradeoff between accuracy and rater's workload in grading clustered short answers. In *Proceedings of the Ninth International Conference on Language Resources and Evaluation (LREC'14)*, pages 588–595.

Andrea Horbach, Dirk Scholten-Akoun, Yuning Ding, and Torsten Zesch. 2017. Fine-grained essay scoring of a complex writing task for native speakers. In *Proceedings of the 12th Workshop on Innovative Use of NLP for Building Educational Applications*, pages 357–366.

Armand Joulin, Edouard Grave, Piotr Bojanowski, and Tomas Mikolov. 2016. Bag of tricks for efficient text classification. *arXiv preprint arXiv:1607.01759*.

Stefan Keller. 2016. Measuring Writing at Secondary Level (MEWS). Eine binationale Studie. *Babylonia*, 3:46–48.

John Lawrence and Chris Reed. 2020. Argument mining: A survey. *Computational Linguistics*, 45(4):765–818.

Tomas Mikolov, Ilya Sutskever, Kai Chen, Greg S Corrado, and Jeff Dean. 2013. Distributed representations of words and phrases and their compositionality. In *Advances in Neural Information Processing Systems*, volume 26. Curran Associates, Inc.

Huy Nguyen and Diane Litman. 2018. Argument mining for improving the automated scoring of persuasive essays. In *Proceedings of the AAAI Conference on Artificial Intelligence*, volume 32.

Isaac Persing and Vincent Ng. 2020. Unsupervised argumentation mining in student essays. In *Proceedings of the Twelfth Language Resources and Evaluation Conference*, pages 6795–6803, Marseille, France. European Language Resources Association.

Nils Reimers and Iryna Gurevych. 2019. Sentence-bert: Sentence embeddings using siamese bert-networks. In *Proceedings of the 2019 Conference on Empirical Methods in Natural Language Processing*. Association for Computational Linguistics.

Henning Wachsmuth, Khalid Al Khatib, and Benno Stein. 2016. Using argument mining to assess the argumentation quality of essays. In *Proceedings of COLING 2016, the 26th international conference on Computational Linguistics: Technical papers*, pages 1680–1691.

Fabian Zehner, Christine Sälzer, and Frank Goldhammer. 2016. Automatic coding of short text responses via clustering in educational assessment. *Educational and Psychological Measurement*, 76(2):280–303.

DaLAJ-GED -
a dataset for Grammatical Error Detection tasks on Swedish

Elena Volodina[1], **Yousuf Ali Mohammad**[1],
Aleksandrs Berdicevskis[1], **Gerlof Bouma**[1], **Joey Öhman**[2]

[1]Språkbanken Text, Department of Swedish, Multilingualism, Language Technology,
University of Gothenburg, name.surname1.surname2@gu.se
[2]AI Sweden, name.surname1.surname2@ai.se

Abstract

DaLAJ-GED is a dataset for linguistic acceptability judgments for Swedish, covering five head classes: lexical, morphological, syntactical, orthographical and punctuation. DaLAJ-GED is an extension of DaLAJ.v1 dataset (Volodina et al., 2021a,b). Both DaLAJ datasets are based on the SweLL-gold corpus (Volodina et al., 2019) and its correction annotation categories.

DaLAJ-GED presented here contains 44,654 sentences, distributed (almost) equally between correct and incorrect ones and is primarily aimed at linguistic acceptability judgment task, but can also be used for other tasks related to grammatical error detection (GED) on a sentence level. DaLAJ-GED is included into the Swedish SuperLim 2.0 collection,[1] an extension of SuperLim (Adesam et al., 2020), a benchmark for Natural Language Understanding (NLU) tasks for Swedish.

This paper gives a concise overview of the dataset and presents a few benchmark results for the task of linguistic acceptability, i.e. binary classification of sentences as either correct or incorrect.

1 Introduction

The DaLAJ dataset has been inspired by the English CoLA dataset (Warstadt et al., 2019) and, like the CoLA dataset, is primarily aimed at linguistic acceptability judgments as a way to check the ability of models to distinguish correct language from incorrect. Other members of the CoLA-family are represented by, among others, RuCoLA for Russian (Mikhailov et al., 2022), NoCoLA for Norwegian (Samuel and Jentoft, 2023), ItaCoLA for Italian (Trotta et al., 2021), CLiMP for Chinese (Xiang et al., 2021) and a few others. Unlike most of the CoLA datasets that contain artificially constructed incorrect sentences, DaLAJ is based on originally written learner essays and learner errors in SweLL-gold corpus (Volodina et al., 2019). The DaLAJ approach as a way to create datasets for linguistic acceptability judgments has been introduced in Volodina et al. (2021a). A follow-up on this approach is presented in Samuel and Jentoft (2023) for Norwegian based on the ASK corpus (Tenfjord et al., 2006).

The Swedish DaLAJ – Dataset for Linguistic Acceptability Judgments – is a part of SuperLim, the Swedish equivalent of the English SuperGLUE (Wang et al., 2019) benchmark for NLU tasks.

2 Dataset description

The DaLAJ-GED dataset contains 44,654 sentences, of which 22,539 are incorrect sentences from the SweLL-gold corpus (Volodina et al., 2019) and 22,115 are correct ones from both SweLL-gold and Coctaill (Volodina et al., 2014) corpora (Table 1).

Split	Correct sent	Incorr. sent	Total sent	Total tokens
Train	17,472	18,109	35,581	603,625
Dev	2,424	2,278	4,702	77,251
Test	2,219	2,152	4,371	72,349
Total	**22,115**	**22,539**	**44,654**	**753,225**

Table 1: Sentence and token counts in DaLAJ-GED

[1]https://spraakbanken.gu.se/resurser/superlim

Elena Volodina, Yousuf Ali Mohammed, Aleksandrs Berdicevskis, Gerlof Bouma and Joey Öhman. DaLAJ-GED - a dataset for Grammatical Error Detection tasks on Swedish. *Proceedings of the 12th Workshop on Natural Language Processing for Computer Assisted Language Learning (NLP4CALL 2023)*. Linköping Electronic Conference Proceedings 197: 94–101.

Figure 1: Sample of a DaLAJ-GED sentence in the Huggingface repository for SuperLim.
Literal translation: 'Are they really most important [thing] in the life?'. Expected: *Är de verkligen **det** viktigaste i livet?* 'Are they really **the** most important [thing] in life?'

Column	Explanation/values	Example
Sentence		Är de verkligen viktigaste i livet?
Label	correct or incorrect	incorrect
Error span: start	character index, as counted from 0 in the sentence	16
Error span: stop	character index, as counted from 0 in the sentence; half-open range	16 (in this case, the range [16, 16] denotes an empty string)
Confusion pair: incorrect span	string representing the error token(s) or empty	
Confusion pair: correction	string representing the correct version	det
Error label	one or more error labels describing the same error segment. Values: Punctuation, Orthography, Lexical, Morphology, Syntax)	M
Education level	Nybörjare, Fortsättning , Avancerad ('Beginner', 'Intermediate', 'Advanced')	Fortsättning
L1	mother tongue(s), full names in Swedish	Polska ('Polish')
Data source	DaLAJ/SweLL or Coctaill	DaLAJ/SweLL gold

Table 2: DaLAJ-GED columns using the example from Figure 1

Each learner-written sentence is associated with the writer's mother tongue(s) and information about the level of the course at which the essay was written. Perhaps unsurprisingly, the number of fully correct sentences in the learner essays is lower than the number of sentences that contain some mistake. To compensate for this imbalance, we added correct sentences from the Coc-

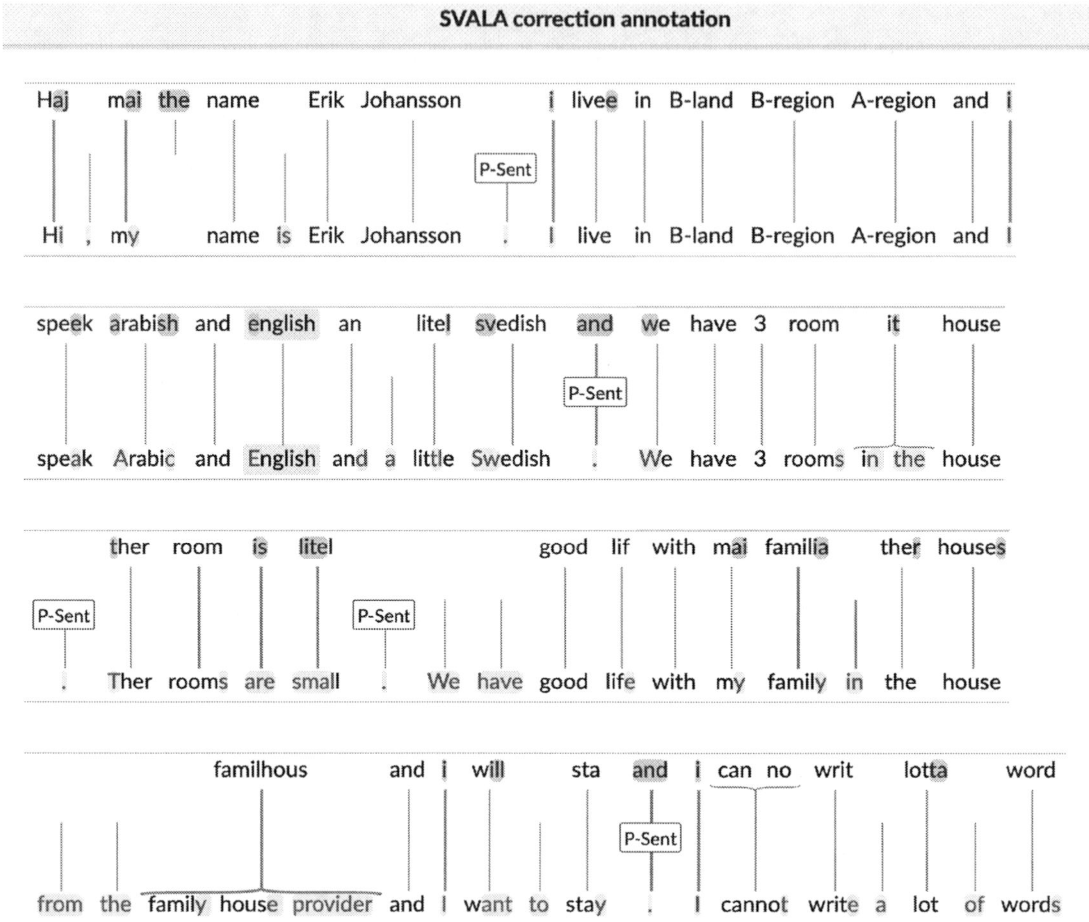

Figure 2: A mock-up translation of an original SweLL-gold sentence. Note the one-to-many (1-to-5) relation between the number of sentences in the original (the top row) and the number of sentences in the target version (the second row). Label `P-Sent` indicates a punctuation correction leading to a sentence split or merge.

taill corpus of coursebooks aimed at second language learners of Swedish (Volodina et al., 2014), keeping the same distribution over beginner-intermediate-advanced levels as among the incorrect sentences. For that, CEFR labels (CoE, 2001) used in Coctaill, have been grouped into (approximate) levels:

- beginner: A1-A2 levels;
- intermediate: B1-B2 levels;
- advanced: C1 level (C2 missing in Coctaill).

This version of DaLAJ is an official improved variant of the previously tested experimental version presented in Klezl et al. (2022).

DaLAJ-GED is distributed as part of SuperLim 2.0[2] in a `jsonl` format (primarily), but is also available in tab-separated `tsv` format. See Figure 1 and Table 2 for a description of items / columns in the `jsonl` / `tsv` representations. The example sentence *Är de verkligen viktigaste i livet?* can be literally translated as 'Are they really most important [thing] in life?' and is missing an obligarory definite article (determiner) *det*. A correct Swedish counterpart would be *Är de verkligen* ***det*** *viktigaste i livet?* 'Are they really **the** most important [thing] in life?'). The incorrect token is thus an empty string (i.e. the correct token *det* is omitted).

2.1 Source corpora

The **SweLL-gold corpus** (Volodina et al., 2019), used as a source of incorrect sentences, is an error-annotated corpus of learner Swedish. It contains

[2]https://github.com/spraakbanken/SuperLim-2

Current		Replacement suggestion
A-,B-,C-,D-	geoplats	Fafjällen, Undberget, Baraön, Lokomitt
A-,B-,C-,D-	hemland	Brasil, Spanien, Irak, Kina
A-,B-,C-,D-	institution	Volvodrömmen, Linsbiblioteket, Forkecentralen, Bungavård
A-,B-,C-,D-	land	Danmark, Mongoliet, Sudan, Peru
A-,B-,C-,D-	plats	Burocentrum, Andeplats, Storetorg, Bungafors
A-,B-,C-,D-	skola	Buroskola, Andeskola, Storeskola, Bungahjulet
A-,B-,C-,D-	region	Sydlunda, Undered, Hanskim, Bungalarna
A-,B-,C-,D-	stad	Oslo, Paris, Bagdad, Caracas
A-,B-,C-,D-	svensk-stad	Sydden, Norrebock, Rosaborg, Ögglestad
A-,B-,C-,D-	linjen	buss

Table 3: Pseudonymized strings and suggestion for their replacement

502 essays written by adult learners of Swedish at different levels of proficiency (beginner, intermediate, advanced) and representing 81 unique mother tongues in 117 unique combinations of 1-4 languages. The essays represent different topics and genres, some examples being "Describe your lodging", "My first love", "Discuss marriage and other lifestyles", book and film reviews, etc.[3] All essays have been first pseudonymized, then rewritten to represent correct language (i.e normalized) and finally differences between the original and normalized versions were annotated with correction labels (aka error labels).

The **COCTAILL corpus** (Volodina et al., 2014), used as a source of correct sentences for DaLAJ-GED, is a corpus of textbooks used for teaching Swedish to adult second language learners. Each chapter in each textbook is annotated with CEFR labels (A1, A2, B1, B2, C1). The labels are projected to all texts used in each particular chapter, and subsequently to all sentences used in those texts. Texts represent various topics and various genres, including narratives, dialogues, fact texts, instructions, etc.

2.2 Preparation steps

For DaLAJ, only 1-to-1 mappings between original and corrected sentences in SweLL-gold (Volodina et al., 2019) have been used, i.e. where segmentation at the sentence level was unambiguos. Cases like the one mocked in Figure 2 were excluded from DaLAJ. Sentences containing labels `X` (unintelligible string) and `Unid` (unidentified type of correction) were also excluded. Note that the sentences are presented in random order to prevent the possibility to restore original essays – which is a prerequisite for sharing the dataset openly.

To generate several one-error DaLAJ sentences from multi-error original SweLL sentences, we started from the normalized/corrected sentences and projected one error from the original sentences at a time. This means that every incorrect sentence taken from SweLL occurs as many times in DaLAJ as the number of errors it contains. Sometimes, the same token/segment could be described by a cluster of error tags, which were then projected as a group to the single error segment, e.g. *Jag i Stockholm borr* ('I in Stockholm leave'), where *leave* (correct version 'live') is both misspelled (label `O`) and has word order problem with the placement of a finite verb (label `S-FinV`). All resulting incorrect sentences therefore have exactly one error segment with one or more labels describing that error segment. As such, DaLAJ sentences are neither original, nor artificial, and are best described as hybrid ones.

In a post-processing step, we paid special attention to a class of errors called *consistency corrections* in the SweLL-gold annotation (label: `C`). This label was assigned when a correction was a follow-up of another correction. For example, when a sentence-initial mistake *I slutligen* 'In finally' is corrected to *Slutligen* 'Finally', the capitalization of *Slutligen* is in a sense a consequence of the correction of the erroneous preposition, and therefore it is marked as a consistency correction. In out-of-context sentences the `C` category is not self-explanatory. Therefore, we excluded in a few

[3]A summary of corpus characteristics is provided in the metadata file: `https://spraakbanken.github.io/swell-release-v1/Metadata-SweLL`

cases such sentences and replaced the C label with a label that describes the error more precisely in others. In case of *slutligen* $\rightarrow$ *Slutligen*, this is the label O-Cap (orthographical correction of capitalization).

Due to anonymization of the learner essays in SweLL, the dataset contains pseudonyms of the form *D-stad* 'D-city', *A-linje* 'A-line', etc. We suspect them to be disruptive for automatic tools. Before using the dataset for training and testing, we suggest, therefore, replacing those pseudonyms with more realistic-looking (sometimes nonsense) names like the ones suggested in Table 3.

The incorrect DaLAJ sentences are split into training, development and test sets, the proportion being approximately 80:10:10 of the whole number of sentences. The development and test sets were manually proofread to ensure the quality.

Finally, the incorrect sentences were complemented with correct ones from the COCTAILL corpus.

3 Tasks

DaLAJ-GED is prepared for several *sentence-level tasks*:

Linguistic Acceptability Judgments is the primary task (and the only official SuperLim task). Given a sentence, detect whether it contains any errors (incorrect) or not (correct), i.e. the task is to perform binary classification on a sentence level.

Grammatical Error Detection (GED) Given a sentence, detect which token(s) need to be corrected, and provide their start-and-end indices, e.g., the omission of det with indices [16-16) in the example in Table 2.

Multi-Class GED Given a sentence, classify what types of errors need to be corrected, by head classes (punctuation, orthography, lexical, morphology, syntax [POLMS]), e.g.
[16,16) $\rightarrow$ M (Morphological error).

Grammatical Error Correction (GEC) Given the incorrect sentence, rewrite it to obtain a correct version, e.g.

Är de verkligen viktigaste i livet?
$\rightarrow$
Är de verkligen **det** viktigaste i livet?

4 Acceptability judgments – official SuperLim benchmark

The SuperLim benchmark contains various datasets to evaluate the capability of language models. In this paper we present results for the task of acceptability judgments on the DaLAJ-GED dataset that were produced in the context of the SuperLim projekt.

Table 4 shows the results of the initial baseline models on DaLAJ-GED for the task of linguistic acceptability judgments. The horizontal line separates transformer models (Vaswani et al., 2017; Acheampong et al., 2021) from the more traditional machine learning systems and random baselines.

SuperLim by default uses Krippendorff's α coefficient (Krippendorff, 2004) as its metric for summarizing system performance on the different tasks. Krippendorff's α is a measure of agreement where 1 indicates a perfect score and 0 indicates that the system's predictions are at chance level. Clearly negative scores indicate systematic mispredictions. Krippendorff's α is given in Table 4 together with the standard accuracy metric for reasons of familiarity.

Part of the SuperLim benchmark is a leaderboard website,[4] which makes it possible to compare models and opens for an asynchronous competition focused on Swedish. The results for the baseline models presented here applied to a range of SuperLim tasks are included on this leaderboard. The website also contains a more detailed explanation for the choice of Krippendorff's α.

Each transformer model was fine-tuned as demonstrated in Devlin et al. (2019) on the training split with a binary classification learning objective, using Huggingface with early stopping and a coarse-grained hyperparameter tuning with respect to the development split. The hyperparameter space was inspired by RoBERTa (Liu et al., 2019), see Table 5, with the remaining hyperparameters left as the Huggingface default values. The results indicate that larger models typically perform better and that Swedish pre-trained models perform better than multilingual variants. Moreover, the transformer models significantly outperform traditional systems. A comparison of the α and Accuracy metrics shows that they mostly demonstrate the same picture here, albeit on a different scale. However, for the two worst perform-

[4] www.example.org (to be supplied)

Model	α	Acc
KBLab/megatron-bert-large-swedish-cased-165k	**0.753**	**0.877**
KBLab/bert-base-swedish-cased-new	**0.753**	0.876
AI-Nordics/bert-large-swedish-cased	0.745	0.872
KB/bert-base-swedish-cased	0.740	0.870
xlm-roberta-large	0.738	0.869
KBLab/megatron-bert-base-swedish-cased-600k	0.718	0.860
xlm-roberta-base	0.701	0.851
NbAiLab/nb-bert-base	0.644	0.822
SVM	0.518	0.758
Decision Tree	0.269	0.636
Random	0.007	0.503
Random Forest	-0.312	0.498
Majority label (`incorrect`)	-0.340	0.492

Table 4: SuperLim results for a selection of models on DaLAJ-GED task, reported in Krippendorff's alpha coefficient (Superlim's default measure) and accuracy.

Hyperparameter	Value(s)
Learning Rate	{1e-5, 2e-5, 3e-5, 4e-5}
Batch Size	{16, 32}
Warmup Ratio	0.06
Weight Decay	0.1
Max Epochs	10

Table 5: Hyperparameter configuration for fine-tuning transformer models

ing systems, we see very low α-scores, whereas Accuracy hovers around the .5 mark. This is because these models grossly overpredict one of the labels, a characteristic that is punished by α.

The results suggest that the dataset is of a size and quality that is sufficient for neural models. An interesting further comparison could be with human baselines, which is a potential future step.

Replicability Each pre-trained language model is publicly available on Huggingface, with the model names as presented here. The traditional baselines are implemented using the scikit-learn Python library (Pedregosa et al., 2011). Full source code and instructions for reproducing the results are made publicly available on GitHub.[5]

Pre-trained language models Below we provide additional details and references to a few of the most prominent language models in the results. In the official SuperLim benchmark, the best-performing model in terms of the average score is KBLab/megatron-bert-large-swedish-cased-165k.[6] This 340M parameter model is trained and published by KBLab[7] and was trained for 165K steps using a batch size of 8K. It was trained on about 70GB of textual data, consisting mostly of OSCAR (Suárez et al., 2019; Ortiz Suárez et al., 2020) and Swedish newspapers curated by the National Library of Sweden.

The second best model, AI-Nordics/bert-large-swedish-cased[8] is of the same size and trained for 600K steps with a batch size of 512. The training data is composed of various sources of internet data and sums to about 85GB.

Among the smaller pre-trained language models, KB/bert-base-swedish-cased[9] (Malmsten et al., 2020) is the greatest performing model, trained on 15-20GB text from a mix of data deposited at the National Library of Sweden and internet data. The model's pre-training consisted of two steps as presented in the original BERT article. First, it was trained 1M steps with a sequence length of 128 and batch size of 512, and then 100K steps with a sequence length of 512 and batch size of 128.

[5]https://github.com/JoeyOhman/SuperLim-2-Testing

[6]https://huggingface.co/KBLab/megatron-bert-large-swedish-cased-165k

[7]https://huggingface.co/KBLab

[8]https://huggingface.co/AI-Nordics/bert-large-swedish-cased

[9]https://huggingface.co/KB/bert-base-swedish-cased

5 Concluding remarks

The contributions of the DaLAJ-GED are twofold. First, efforts like DaLAJ, SuperLim and similar stimulate development of models and approaches to languages other than English, correcting the existing dominance of English in the NLP field (Søgaard, 2022). We expect an increased interest to Swedish NLP following the release of DaLAJ-GED and other SuperLim datasets. The dataset can also be used by researchers who do not have any specific interest in Swedish, but need a high-quality benchmark in order to evaluate transfer learning from another language (e.g. English).

Second, DaLAJ-GED supports the area of automatic method development for Swedish learner language, since it offers not only the data for testing models' general ability to differentiate between correct and incorrect language, but – additionally – offers tasks within second language learning domain for sentence-level grammatical error detection (GED), error classification and error correction (GEC).

DaLAJ-GED complements two other recently released SweLL-gold derivative datasets relevant for second language domain, namely, Swedish MultiGED dataset for error detection on a token level[10] (Volodina et al., 2023) and Swedish MuClaGED dataset for error classification on a token level (Moner and Volodina, 2022). Next steps would be to prepare datasets for feedback generation and for error correction in a larger context than a single sentence as well as in authentic context.

Acknowledgments

The work on the dataset and benchmarking was supported by the Vinnova project *Superlim 2.0*, through the grant 2021-04165. Work on the dataset was also partially funded by a grant from the Swedish Riksbankens Jubileumsfond (*SweLL - research infrastructure for Swedish as a second language*, dnr IN16-0464:1), and by *Nationella språkbanken* and *HUMINFRA*, both funded by the Swedish Research Council (2018-2024, contract 2017-00626; 2022-2024, contract 2021-00176) and their participating partner institutions.

[10]https://github.com/spraakbanken/multiged-2023

References

Francisca Adoma Acheampong, Henry Nunoo-Mensah, and Wenyu Chen. 2021. Transformer models for text-based emotion detection: a review of BERT-based approaches. *Artificial Intelligence Review*, pages 1–41.

Yvonne Adesam, Aleksandrs Berdicevskis, and Felix Morger. 2020. SwedishGLUE – towards a Swedish test set for evaluating Natural Language Understanding models. Research Reports from the Department of Swedish, GU-ISS-2020-04.

CoE. 2001. *Council of Europe. Common European framework of reference for languages: Learning, teaching, assessment.* Cambridge University Press.

Jacob Devlin, Ming-Wei Chang, Kenton Lee, and Kristina Toutanova. 2019. BERT: Pre-training of deep bidirectional transformers for language understanding. In *Proceedings of the 2019 Conference of the North American Chapter of the Association for Computational Linguistics: Human Language Technologies, Volume 1 (Long and Short Papers)*, pages 4171–4186, Minneapolis, Minnesota. Association for Computational Linguistics.

Julia Klezl, Yousuf Ali Mohammed, and Elena Volodina. 2022. Exploring Linguistic Acceptability in Swedish Learners' Language. In *Proceedings of the 11th Workshop on NLP for Computer Assisted Language Learning*, pages 84–94.

Klaus Krippendorff. 2004. Reliability in content analysis: Some common misconceptions and recommendations. *Human communication research*, 30(3):411–433.

Yinhan Liu, Myle Ott, Naman Goyal, Jingfei Du, Mandar Joshi, Danqi Chen, Omer Levy, Mike Lewis, Luke Zettlemoyer, and Veselin Stoyanov. 2019. Roberta: A robustly optimized bert pretraining approach. *arXiv preprint arXiv:1907.11692.*

Martin Malmsten, Love Börjeson, and Chris Haffenden. 2020. Playing with words at the national library of sweden – making a swedish bert.

Vladislav Mikhailov, Tatiana Shamardina, Max Ryabinin, Alena Pestova, Ivan Smurov, and Ekaterina Artemova. 2022. RuCoLA: Russian Corpus of Linguistic Acceptability. *arXiv preprint arXiv:2210.12814.*

Judith Casademont Moner and Elena Volodina. 2022. Swedish MuClaGED: A new dataset for Grammatical Error Detection in Swedish. In *Proceedings of the 11th Workshop on NLP for Computer Assisted Language Learning*, pages 36–45.

Pedro Javier Ortiz Suárez, Laurent Romary, and Benoît Sagot. 2020. A monolingual approach to contextualized word embeddings for mid-resource languages. In *Proceedings of the 58th Annual Meeting of the Association for Computational Linguistics*, pages

1703–1714, Online. Association for Computational Linguistics.

F. Pedregosa, G. Varoquaux, A. Gramfort, V. Michel, B. Thirion, O. Grisel, M. Blondel, P. Prettenhofer, R. Weiss, V. Dubourg, J. Vanderplas, A. Passos, D. Cournapeau, M. Brucher, M. Perrot, and E. Duchesnay. 2011. Scikit-learn: Machine learning in Python. *Journal of Machine Learning Research*, 12:2825–2830.

David Samuel and Matias Jentoft. 2023. NoCoLA: The Norwegian Corpus of Linguistic Acceptability. In *The 24rd Nordic Conference on Computational Linguistics*.

Anders Søgaard. 2022. Should We Ban English NLP for a Year? In *Proceedings of the 2022 Conference on Empirical Methods in Natural Language Processing*, pages 5254–5260.

Pedro Javier Ortiz Suárez, Benoît Sagot, and Laurent Romary. 2019. Asynchronous pipelines for processing huge corpora on medium to low resource infrastructures. Proceedings of the Workshop on Challenges in the Management of Large Corpora (CMLC-7) 2019. Cardiff, 22nd July 2019, pages 9–16, Mannheim. Leibniz-Institut für Deutsche Sprache.

Kari Tenfjord, Paul Meurer, and Knut Hofland. 2006. The ASK corpus–a language learner corpus of Norwegian as a second language.

Daniela Trotta, Raffaele Guarasci, Elisa Leonardelli, and Sara Tonelli. 2021. Monolingual and cross-lingual acceptability judgments with the Italian CoLA corpus. *arXiv preprint arXiv:2109.12053*.

Ashish Vaswani, Noam Shazeer, Niki Parmar, Jakob Uszkoreit, Llion Jones, Aidan N Gomez, Łukasz Kaiser, and Illia Polosukhin. 2017. Attention is all you need. *Advances in neural information processing systems*, 30.

Elena Volodina, Christopher Bryant, Andrew Caines, Orphée De Clercq, Jennifer-Carmen Frey, Elizaveta Ershova, Alexandr Rosen, and Olga Vinogradova. 2023. MultiGED-2023 shared task at NLP4CALL: Multilingual Grammatical Error Detection. In *Proceedings of the 12th Workshop on NLP for Computer Assisted Language Learning*.

Elena Volodina, Lena Granstedt, Arild Matsson, Beáta Megyesi, Ildikó Pilán, Julia Prentice, Dan Rosén, Lisa Rudebeck, Carl-Johan Schenström, Gunlög Sundberg, et al. 2019. The SweLL Language Learner Corpus: From Design to Annotation. *Northern European Journal of Language Technology*, 6:67–104.

Elena Volodina, Yousuf Ali Mohammed, and Julia Klezl. 2021a. DaLAJ–a dataset for linguistic acceptability judgments for Swedish. In *Proceedings of the 10th Workshop on NLP for Computer Assisted Language Learning*, pages 28–37.

Elena Volodina, Yousuf Ali Mohammed, and Julia Klezl. 2021b. DaLAJ-a dataset for linguistic acceptability judgments for Swedish: Format, baseline, sharing. *arXiv preprint arXiv:2105.06681*.

Elena Volodina, Ildikó Pilán, Stian Rødven Eide, and Hannes Heidarsson. 2014. You get what you annotate: a pedagogically annotated corpus of coursebooks for Swedish as a Second Language. In *Proceedings of the third workshop on NLP for computer-assisted language learning*, pages 128–144.

Alex Wang, Yada Pruksachatkun, Nikita Nangia, Amanpreet Singh, Julian Michael, Felix Hill, Omer Levy, and Samuel Bowman. 2019. Superglue: A stickier benchmark for general-purpose language understanding systems. *Advances in neural information processing systems*, 32.

Alex Warstadt, Amanpreet Singh, and Samuel R Bowman. 2019. Neural network acceptability judgments. *Transactions of the Association for Computational Linguistics*, 7:625–641.

Beilei Xiang, Changbing Yang, Yu Li, Alex Warstadt, and Katharina Kann. 2021. CLiMP: A benchmark for Chinese language model evaluation. *arXiv preprint arXiv:2101.11131*.

Automated Assessment of Task Completion in Spontaneous Speech for Finnish and Finland Swedish Language Learners

Ekaterina Voskoboinik, Yaroslav Getman, Ragheb Al-Ghezi,
Mikko Kurimo, Tamás Grósz
Department of Information and Communications Engineering
Aalto University, Finland
firstname.lastname@aalto.fi

Abstract

This study investigates the feasibility of automated content scoring for spontaneous spoken responses from Finnish and Finland Swedish learners. Our experiments reveal that pre-trained Transformer-based models outperform the tf-idf baseline in automatic task completion grading. Furthermore, we demonstrate that pre-fine-tuning these models to differentiate between responses to distinct prompts enhances subsequent task completion fine-tuning. We observe that task completion classifiers exhibit accelerated learning and produce predictions with stronger correlations to human grading when accounting for task differences. Additionally, we find that employing similarity learning, as opposed to conventional classification fine-tuning, further improves the results. It is especially helpful to learn not just the similarities between the responses in one score bin, but the exact differences between the average human scores responses received. Lastly, we demonstrate that models applied to both manual and ASR transcripts yield comparable correlations to human grading.

1 Introduction

The assessment of content is an important dimension of oral proficiency evaluation. It complements other areas like fluency, pronunciation, and the range and accuracy of grammar and vocabulary (Brown et al., 2005). This work examines the automatic evaluation of content by scoring task completion. A successful response should demonstrate both comprehension of the prompt and mastery in speech production, making task completion an important component of oral proficiency assessment.

The research in automated scoring of non-native English speech has shown that it is possible to automatically evaluate the content relevance of a response (Yoon and Lee, 2019). It was demonstrated that fine-tuning Transformer-based models is especially beneficial for this task (Wang et al., 2020).

The present study aims to evaluate the potential of BERT models (Devlin et al., 2019) for content scoring of non-native Finnish and Finland Swedish spontaneous speech. Additionally, we explore the effectiveness of fine-tuning BERT for task classification to enhance performance in subsequent fine-tuning for task completion. Given the multi-modal nature of our prompts, we find it challenging to map them to the same vector space as our responses for prompt awareness as in (Wang et al., 2021b). Consequently, we integrate task classification to inform the model about different tasks. Our choice to experiment with fine-tuning for an intermediate task is based on previous findings, which showcased improved robustness and effectiveness in the resulting target task model, particularly in low-resource scenarios (Phang et al., 2019). Our experiments reveal that this approach accelerates learning for task completion evaluation and leads to better correlations with human scores.

Due to the limited size and imbalance of our datasets, we further explore the use of similarity learning. We fine-tune BERT in a Siamese manner in two ways: first, to place responses that belong to the same task completion score bin closer together and those that belong to different score bins further away; second, to learn to position responses proportionately to the distance of their average task

Ekaterina Voskoboinik, Yaroslav Getman, Ragheb Al-Ghezi, Mikko Kurimo and Tamas Grosz. Automated Assessment of Task Completion in Spontaneous Speech for Finnish and Finland Swedish Language Learners. *Proceedings of the 12th Workshop on Natural Language Processing for Computer Assisted Language Learning (NLP4CALL 2023).* Linköping Electronic Conference Proceedings 197: 102–110.

completion scores. Our results indicate that treating response scores as continuous numbers instead of bin categories leads to better correlation with human scores.

2 Related Work

The progress of research in content scoring of spontaneous non-native speech was initially hindered by the quality of ASR systems. Early approaches (Xie et al., 2012; Chen, 2013) explored techniques developed for automatic essay scoring. Typically, a vector space model like tf-idf, LSA (Landauer et al., 1998), or PMI (Turney, 2001) would be trained on a set of pre-graded responses for each prompt. The tasks would be represented by vectors for every score category. The to-be-graded response is then mapped to the same vector space and compared to the score vectors. The similarities between response and score vectors were used as content features for holistic grade prediction. However, this approach had several drawbacks. It relied on a large number of pre-graded responses to build a reliable vector space and did not take word relations into account. It was shown in (Loukina et al., 2014) that for tasks like giving a summary of a prompt material, ROUGE (Lin, 2004) would outperform tf-idf similarity and needed fewer reference responses. And (Evanini et al., 2013) demonstrated that comparing responses and prompts is a viable option even though it was slightly outperformed by comparison to pre-graded responses.

The exploration of more context-aware vector representations, such as doc2vec, demonstrated a higher correlation to holistic scores compared to tf-idf based approaches (Tao et al., 2016). The work in (Yoon et al., 2018) continued the research started in (Evanini et al., 2013) by comparing tf-idf and averaged word2vec embeddings for computing similarities between responses and prompts. The pre-trained embeddings proved more advantageous than tf-idf.

More recently, it was demonstrated that neural and pre-trained approaches are highly effective in scoring content relevancy. In one study (Qian et al., 2018), the authors used an attention LSTM-RNN model to directly score the proficiency level of a response based on its transcript. They found that conditioning the model on task prompts led to even better performance. Similarly, the authors of (Yoon and Lee, 2019) compared a Siamese CNN model to a tf-idf based one and found that the former outperformed the latter when predicting holistic proficiency scores based on the similarity between responses and a set of key points generated by experts for each task. Taking things further, (Wang et al., 2020) trained multi-task Transformer-based models that were able to detect missing key points or the spans of present key points and predict how well each present key point was communicated in a response. These models outperformed human agreement on these tasks. The success of Transformer-based models was further supported by experiments in (Wang et al., 2021b), which showed that fine-tuning BERT and XLNet for holistic proficiency scoring using only ASR response transcripts already surpassed human agreement. Additionally, augmenting the models with prompt awareness led to even better results.

Inspired by these findings, this study explores the capabilities of pre-trained BERT models for scoring content appropriateness of Swedish and Finnish learners' oral responses.

3 Data

This study investigates content relevancy scoring using two corpora of non-native spontaneous speech: Finnish and Finland Swedish (Al-Ghezi et al., 2021, 2023). The Swedish data was collected from upper secondary school students, while the Finnish data contains responses from both upper secondary school students and university students. The datasets include responses to semi-structured and open-ended tasks, such as reacting to a text or a picture prompt or simulating a phone call by answering pre-recorded questions.

Originally, the recordings were rated by humans across the following dimensions: holistic level, pronunciation, fluency, accuracy, range, and task completion (Al-Ghezi et al., 2023). The raters were asked to either assign a score for each dimension or mark a dimension as ungradable (zero). In our experiments, we include only the recordings that received non-zero scores from all raters across all criteria. Additionally, one task from the Swedish dataset was excluded, as it contained only two responses.

This work is focused on automatically assessing task completion (TC) criterion as a measure of content relevancy. Task completion was rated on a scale of 1 to 3, where 1 indicates that the assignment was answered only partially with many significant gaps in the response, and 3 signifies that the test-taker fulfilled the assignment excellently with no significant gaps in the response. The responses that received multiple human assessments were assigned an average of those assessments. We used binning to convert the average scores back to discrete classes. The range of scores from 1 to 3 was divided into three equal intervals, and each score was labeled based on the interval it fell into. In this study, we explore both continuous and binned scores. The data described in this study will be published in The Language Bank of Finland (FIN-CLARIN) [1].

To establish a reference for human agreement, we compared the scores of all recordings assessed by at least two raters. We report the Spearman correlation coefficient and Quadratic Weighted Kappa between two random raters in Table 1. The measures suggest a fair level of agreement. These numbers indicate that assigning task completion scores can be a challenging task for human raters. The Swedish samples were evaluated by 18 human raters, with 101 samples rated by one rater, 1358 samples rated by two raters, 42 samples rated by three raters, and 39 recordings rated by five raters. The Finnish recordings were rated by 25 raters, with 302 samples rated by one person, 1790 samples rated by two people, and 24 samples rated by three raters.

	cor	**kappa**
Swedish	0.372	0.377
Finnish	0.298	0.340

Table 1: Spearman correlation coefficient (cor) and Quadratic Weighted Kappa (kappa) between two random raters for Swedish and Finnish data.

Table 2 describes the overall statistics of the corpora. However, these numbers vary from task to task. For instance, the duration of responses is highly task dependent. In the Swedish dataset, the task that elicits the longest answers has responses averaging 26.4 seconds, while the task with the shortest answers has responses averaging about 4.2 seconds. In the Finnish dataset, the task eliciting the shortest answers on average has responses of 3.2 tokens, and the task eliciting the longest answers has an average response length of 91 tokens. The distribution of scores varies between the tasks as well. In the Swedish data, the task with the highest-scored responses has an average score of 2.8, while the task with the lowest-scored responses has an average score of 1.5. In the Finnish data, the lowest average score for task completion in a task is 2.1, and the highest average score in a task is 2.9.

	Swedish	**Finnish**
# of samples	1540	2112
# of students	178	308
# of tasks	21	25
avg. TC score	2	2.6
total duration (h)	5.6	14.1
# of samples per task		
min.	30	6
max.	110	173
avg.	73.3	72.8
Response duration		
min. (s)	1.1	2
max. (s)	30.7	91
avg. (s)	13	24
Response length (words)		
min.	1	1
max.	49	228
avg.	9.4	31.6

Table 2: Dataset statistics.

The distribution of task completion scores is quite unbalanced. This problem is the most pronounced for the Finnish dataset: the average task completion score is 2.6, which indicates the prevalence of high-scoring responses. Moreover, there are five tasks with no responses in the lowest score bin. In total, 17 out of 29 tasks have less than 5% of responses with the lowest score bin. The distribution of scores in the datasets can be found in Table 3.

	1	**2**	**3**
Swedish	517	368	655
Finnish	134	339	1639

Table 3: Score bin distributions of Swedish and Finnish data.

[1] https://www.kielipankki.fi

4 Methods

4.1 Baselines

First, we evaluate the ability of out-of-the-box BERT and tf-idf-based vector spaces to represent the differences between high and low-scoring responses. We will use their performance as our baselines.

For training tf-idf models, we generated task documents from all the responses to each prompt and derived the inverse document frequency (idf) from them. Each response in the dataset was then mapped to a vector by weighing its word counts (tf) by the idf. To obtain response representations using BERT models, we applied mean pooling to the outputs of the final layer, since (Reimers and Gurevych, 2019) demonstrated that it produces better representations than other pooling strategies.

4.2 Task classification fine-tuning

In our first experiment, we fine-tuned the model to classify the recordings according to the tasks they were answering using Siamese fine-tuning. We opted for this approach due to its efficiency, as it enabled us to leverage the weights already learned by the model rather than requiring it to learn the weights for a classification head from scratch. The goal of this fine-tuning stage is to place the responses to the same prompt closer to each other and further away from the responses to other prompts. While we were not primarily interested in the model's performance for this problem, we focused on adjusting the final embeddings. We measured the changes in cosine distances between task centroids and in the properties of task clusters. To establish how well different categories of responses are represented in a vector space we use the Calinski-Harabasz score (Caliński and Harabasz, 1974). It measures the ratio of between-cluster dispersion to within-cluster dispersion. The score gets higher when data points are close to each other within the same cluster and are far from other clusters' centroids. In other words, the Calinski-Harabasz score measures the separation of vector classes in a space. We would like to have a high Calinski-Harabasz score when measuring the distance between responses belonging to different tasks.

We trained the models using positive and negative examples of responses to the same task. Each response in our dataset was paired with one positive example and five negative examples. The positive example was randomly selected, while negative examples were chosen based on their level of "hardness" (closest responses from other tasks were selected). Similarly to our BERT baseline, we embed a response in a vector space using mean pooling.

4.3 BERT with a classification head

To investigate the impact of pre-fine-tuning for task classification on subsequent task completion fine-tuning, we compared BERT models trained for task completion before and after task classification fine-tuning. We employed a linear classification head preceded by dropout. The head receives a vector obtained by mean-pooling, as this was the representation learned during task classification.

4.4 BERT Siamese

We further sought to experiment with similarity learning as an alternative to classic fine-tuning for our limited and imbalanced datasets, following previous findings of its potential benefits (Schroff et al., 2015). Our goal was to adjust the vector space so it would place higher scored responses further away from lower scored responses. For these means, we experiment using both score bins and average scores to learn similarities between the responses.

To learn response similarity using score bins, we generated pairs of samples from each response within a task. A pair received a label of 1 if both samples belonged to the same score bin and 0 if they originated from different bins. To train using average grades, we assigned the desired cosine distances in the range of 0-1 based on the differences between the samples' scores. For instance, a pair consisting of a sample with a score of 1 and a sample with a score of 3 would be assigned a cosine distance label of 1. On the other hand, a pair with samples having scores of 1 and 2 would receive a cosine distance label of 0.5.

5 Experiments and Results

5.1 Speech-to-text

For the experiments, we employed a 4-fold cross-validation strategy to evaluate our models. In this approach, each model was trained on three folds and evaluated on the remaining fold. The folds were designed by creating four non-overlapping student sets. Furthermore, we stratified the folds by tasks and holistic levels, ensuring that every task was represented in each split.

In this work, we used wav2vec 2.0 models (Baevski et al., 2020) to produce ASR transcripts for the responses. For L2 Finland Swedish, we used a monolingual Swedish model that was pretrained on 11.5K hours of unlabeled speech from the collections of the National Library of Sweden (Malmsten et al., 2022), such as local radio broadcasts and audiobooks, and fine-tuned on the Common Voice (Ardila et al., 2020) and the NST (Birkenes, 2020) corpora. For Finnish ASR experiments, we used a multilingual model pretrained on the Uralic (Finnish, Estonian, and Hungarian) subset of the European parliamentary session recordings collection called Voxpopuli (Wang et al., 2021a) and fine-tuned on a 100-hour subset of the Finnish colloquial speech dataset Lahjoita Puhetta (Donate Speech) (Moisio et al., 2022). The models were further fine-tuned on the target data with 4-fold cross-validation mentioned above. After aggregating the test set outputs produced by each of the 4 sub-systems, the total word and character error rates are 17.71% / 9.08% and 21.89% / 7.06% for the L2 Finland Swedish and the L2 Finnish data, respectively (Al-Ghezi et al., 2023).

5.2 Baselines

For tf-idf models, we utilized the TfidfVectorizer from the scikit-learn Python package (Pedregosa et al., 2011). As for BERT representations, we used FinBERT[2] trained by (Virtanen et al., 2019) for the Finnish part of the data and a BERT model trained by National Library of Sweden[3] for the Swedish part.

We evaluate the models using simple k-NN classifiers, where a response is assigned a score based on its similarity to reference vectors. We compare two approaches for selecting these reference vectors: either using bin centroids (CTR) or all historical responses to a task prompt (1-NN). In the first approach, each score bin in a task is represented by the mean embedding of its responses. A new response is then assigned a score based on its closest score bin vector. In the second approach, a test response is compared to all prior responses given to a prompt and assigned the score of the nearest one. Due to data imbalance, we opted for only one nearest neighbor in this experiment, as selecting more than one neighbor could prevent our system from recognizing underrepresented score intervals.

	Human		ASR	
	cor	kappa	cor	kappa
Swedish				
tf-idf CTR	0.381	0.360	0.392	0.373
tf-idf 1-NN	0.561	0.491	0.537	0.462
BERT CTR	0.451	0.439	0.445	0.431
BERT 1-NN	**0.580**	**0.524**	**0.560**	**0.500**
Finnish				
tf-idf CTR	0.213	0.242	0.253	0.275
tf-idf 1-NN	0.170	0.196	0.199	0.220
BERT CTR	**0.286**	**0.313**	**0.279**	**0.305**
BERT 1-NN	0.259	0.232	0.277	0.248

Table 4: Spearman correlation coefficient (cor) and Quadratic Weighted Kappa (kappa) of Baseline Models.

We assess performance by comparing the predicted scores with human scores using two metrics: the Spearman correlation coefficient between average human scores and predicted scores, and the Quadratic Weighted Kappa between binned average human scores and binned machine scores. The results can be found in Table 4. Here, we see that BERT models outperformed tf-idf models for both Swedish and Finnish. The strategy of assigning a score based on a single nearest neighbor proved to be more effective for Swedish, but it was less successful than using bin centroid vectors for Finnish. Finally, models applied to ASR transcripts demonstrated results comparable to those of human transcripts, with the correlations to human scores being only marginally lower for the best-performing approaches.

5.3 Task Classification

The models were trained with SentenceTransformers Python package (Reimers and Gurevych, 2019), using Contrastive loss (Chopra et al., 2005) with a margin of 0.5. To achieve vector spaces with similar properties in order to keep the models comparable in the subsequent experiments, the Swedish model was trained for 4 epochs, and the Finnish model was trained for 5 epochs. Each fold was trained with 50 warm-up steps for every new epoch. We used a batch size of 16. The prop-

[2]https://hf.co/TurkuNLP/bert-base-finnish-cased-v1

[3]https://hf.co/KBLab/bert-base-swedish-cased-new

	BC distance	Task cluster score
SWE	0.11	20
SWE ft	0.66	1676
FIN	0.18	58
FIN ft	0.66	1762

Table 5: Properties of out-of-the-box models vs the models fine-tuned (ft) for task classification. We report average cosine distances between bin centroids (BC) and Calinski-Harabasz score (Task cluster score).

erties of the resulting vector spaces are described in Table 5. The task cluster scores have significantly improved from 20 to 1676 for Swedish, and from 58 to 1762 for Finnish. The average cosine distance between the task centroids also went up from 0.11 to 0.66 for Swedish, and from 0.18 to 0.66 for Finnish.

5.4 Task completion with a classification head

For this experiment, we either trained the models described in the previous subsection or used the models explored as BERT baselines. We then finetuned the models with HuggingFace's Transformers library (Wolf et al., 2020), using dropout with 0.1 probability, a learning rate of 2e-5, and a batch size of 4. For the models initialized with a baseline BERT, we used 15 epochs for Swedish, and 9 epochs for Finnish. For the models that were pretrained with task classification, we used 3 epochs for Swedish and 4 epochs for Finnish. Here and in the next section the number of reported epochs indicates the epoch after which the performance stopped improving with more training. One can notice that pre-fine-tuning results in fewer epochs needed for further fine-tuning.

The results of fine-tuning BERT for task completion classification with (cls_task) and without (cls_no_task) task classification pre-fine-tuning showed strong favor for task classification pre-fine-tuning. The results can be found in Table 6.

5.5 Task completion Siamese

In this part, we continue to fine-tune the models trained on task classification problems. For learning score bin similarity we have applied Contrastive loss with 0.5 margin. For learning distances between average task completion, mean squared-error loss was employed as the objective function. We used a batch size of 16 and 50 warm-up steps for every fold in every new epoch. All

	Human		ASR	
	cor	kappa	cor	kappa
Swedish				
cls_no_task	0.530	0.507	0.507	0.486
cls_task	0.603	0.584	0.601	0.583
S_bins	0.656	0.617	0.658	0.611
S_cosine	**0.714**	**0.650**	**0.679**	**0.623**
Finnish				
cls_no_task	0.271	0.336	0.242	0.299
cls_task	0.295	0.325	0.286	0.308
S_bins	0.291	0.328	0.286	**0.357**
S_cosine	**0.390**	**0.365**	**0.368**	0.354

Table 6: Results of task completion fine-tuning. cls stands for BERT with classification head, task stands for task classification pre-finetuning, S is short for Siamese.

models were trained for 2 epochs. For task completion scoring, we used 1-NN approach.

In Table 6, we demonstrate that employing similarity learning further enhances the results of task completion scoring. It is particularly advantageous to organize the space not only by score bins of the responses but also by the distance proportional to the difference in task completion scores between the responses. Again, while the correlation to human scores is higher when using manual transcripts for the best-performing approach, the results for ASR transcripts are close.

For a more comprehensive understanding of the technical aspects involved in our experiments, we encourage interested readers to examine our scripts[4].

6 Discussion

In this work, we explore different approaches to content scoring of spontaneous spoken responses of non-native Finnish and Finland Swedish learners.

As was expected, pre-trained BERT models have shown to be more efficient for our data than tf-idf baseline since they already contain language knowledge. We demonstrate that training BERT models to separate responses to different tasks before fine-tuning directly for task completion brings similar benefits to prompt awareness. The models subsequently achieve higher correlations to human scores while requiring fewer training epochs. This improvement can likely be attributed to several

[4] https://github.com/katildakat/NLP4CALL_TC

factors. Firstly, in order to accurately score task completion, a model must comprehend the typical responses associated with a specific prompt. Secondly, the data utilized for task classification fine-tuning is the same data subsequently employed for task completion fine-tuning, thereby facilitating domain adaptation.

We have also shown that similarity learning was more helpful than fine-tuning with the classification head. We believe that it happens because we can translate our data into a larger labeled set this way. It was especially beneficial not to limit the similarities between responses to their score bins, but to organize the space in accordance with how different the scores are.

Additionally, we show the applicability of our approach not only for manual transcripts but for ASR transcripts as well. Although the results of ASR transcripts are generally slightly behind the manual transcripts, they are not far off. This is an important finding since using human transcripts is not feasible in real-life applications.

Finally, we should address the differences in performance between the Swedish and Finnish models. The predictions of Swedish models correlated better with human scores than those of Finnish models. We believe that there might be several reasons for this behavior. The first one is that inter-human agreement between the raters was lower for Finnish responses than for Swedish as reported in Table 1. The second reason is that the Finnish corpus is considerably more imbalanced than the Swedish one with most of the scores receiving the highest score. For many tasks, it is impossible or almost impossible to get a score of 1, so the models, in turn, favor higher score bins.

7 Conclusions

In conclusion, this study demonstrates the effectiveness of pre-trained Transformer-based models in automated content scoring for spontaneous spoken responses from non-native Finnish and Finland Swedish learners. Our findings show that pre-fine-tuning these models to differentiate between responses to distinct prompts significantly improves task completion fine-tuning, resulting in faster learning and stronger correlations to human grading. Additionally, we discovered that similarity learning, compared to traditional classification fine-tuning, further enhances the results. It is especially useful to learn not only the similarities within responses of the same score bin but also the exact differences between the average human scores received.

Importantly, our work highlights that the performance of models applied to both manual transcripts and ASR transcripts is comparable, suggesting the feasibility of using this approach in real-life scenarios. The ability to obtain similar results with ASR transcripts enables the potential deployment of automated scoring systems in various educational contexts without the need for manual transcription, increasing efficiency and reducing costs.

For future work, we would like to explore the applicability of similarity learning in text and audio Transformers for automatic scoring of other dimensions in our assessments.

Acknowledgments

This work has been funded by the Academy of Finland grant number 322625 "Digital support for training and assessing second language speaking". The computational resources were provided by Aalto ScienceIT.

References

Ragheb Al-Ghezi, Yaroslav Getman, Aku Rouhe, Raili Hildén, and Mikko Kurimo. 2021. Self-Supervised End-to-End ASR for Low Resource L2 Swedish. pages 1429–1433.

Ragheb Al-Ghezi, Yaroslav Getman, Ekaterina Voskoboinik, Mittul Singh, and Mikko Kurimo. 2023. Automatic Rating of Spontaneous Speech for Low-Resource Languages. In *2022 IEEE Spoken Language Technology Workshop (SLT)*, pages 339–345.

Rosana Ardila, Megan Branson, Kelly Davis, Michael Kohler, Josh Meyer, Michael Henretty, Reuben Morais, Lindsay Saunders, Francis Tyers, and Gregor Weber. 2020. Common Voice: A Massively-Multilingual Speech Corpus. In *Proceedings of the Twelfth Language Resources and Evaluation Conference*, pages 4218–4222, Marseille, France. European Language Resources Association.

Alexei Baevski, Henry Zhou, Abdelrahman Mohamed, and Michael Auli. 2020. wav2vec 2.0: A Framework for Self-Supervised Learning of Speech Representations.

M. B. Birkenes. 2020. NST Swedish Dictation (22 kHz). https://www.nb.no/sprakbanken/en/resource-catalogue/oai-nb-no-sbr-17/.

Annie Brown, Noriko Iwashita, and Tim McNamara. 2005. An examination of rater orientations and test-taker performance on English-for-academic-purposes speaking tasks. *ETS Research Report Series*, 2005(1):i–157.

Tadeusz Caliński and Jerzy Harabasz. 1974. A dendrite method for cluster analysis. *Communications in Statistics-theory and Methods*, 3(1):1–27.

Lei Chen. 2013. Applying Unsupervised Learning T Support Vector Space Model Based Speaking Assessment. In *Proceedings of the Eighth Workshop on Innovative Use of NLP for Building Educational Applications*, pages 58–62, Atlanta, Georgia. Association for Computational Linguistics.

S. Chopra, R. Hadsell, and Y. LeCun. 2005. Learning a similarity metric discriminatively, with application to face verification. In *2005 IEEE Computer Society Conference on Computer Vision and Pattern Recognition (CVPR'05)*, volume 1, pages 539–546 vol. 1.

Jacob Devlin, Ming-Wei Chang, Kenton Lee, and Kristina Toutanova. 2019. BERT: Pre-training of Deep Bidirectional Transformers for Language Understanding.

Keelan Evanini, Shasha Xie, and Klaus Zechner. 2013. Prompt-based Content Scoring for Automated Spoken Language Assessment. In *Proceedings of the Eighth Workshop on Innovative Use of NLP for Building Educational Applications*, pages 157–162, Atlanta, Georgia. Association for Computational Linguistics.

Thomas K Landauer, Peter W Foltz, and Darrell Laham. 1998. An introduction to latent semantic analysis. *Discourse processes*, 25(2-3):259–284.

Chin-Yew Lin. 2004. Rouge: A package for automatic evaluation of summaries. In *Text summarization branches out*, pages 74–81.

Anastassia Loukina, Klaus Zechner, and Lei Chen. 2014. Automatic evaluation of spoken summaries: the case of language assessment. In *Proceedings of the Ninth Workshop on Innovative Use of NLP for Building Educational Applications*, pages 68–78, Baltimore, Maryland. Association for Computational Linguistics.

Martin Malmsten, Chris Haffenden, and Love Börjeson. 2022. Hearing voices at the National Library – a speech corpus and acoustic model for the Swedish language. *arXiv preprint. arXiv:2205.03026*.

Anssi Moisio, Dejan Porjazovski, Aku Rouhe, Yaroslav Getman, Anja Virkkunen, Ragheb Al-Ghezi, Mietta Lennes, Tamás Grósz, Krister Lindén, and Mikko Kurimo. 2022. Lahjoita puhetta: a large-scale corpus of spoken Finnish with some benchmarks. *Language Resources and Evaluation*.

F. Pedregosa, G. Varoquaux, A. Gramfort, V. Michel, B. Thirion, O. Grisel, M. Blondel, P. Prettenhofer, R. Weiss, V. Dubourg, J. Vanderplas, A. Passos, D. Cournapeau, M. Brucher, M. Perrot, and E. Duchesnay. 2011. Scikit-learn: Machine Learning in Python. *Journal of Machine Learning Research*, 12:2825–2830.

Jason Phang, Thibault Févry, and Samuel R. Bowman. 2019. Sentence Encoders on STILTs: Supplementary Training on Intermediate Labeled-data Tasks.

Yao Qian, Rutuja Ubale, Matthew Mulholland, Keelan Evanini, and Xinhao Wang. 2018. A Prompt-Aware Neural Network Approach to Content-Based Scoring of Non-Native Spontaneous Speech. pages 979–986.

Nils Reimers and Iryna Gurevych. 2019. Sentence-BERT: Sentence Embeddings using Siamese BERT-Networks. In *Proceedings of the 2019 Conference on Empirical Methods in Natural Language Processing*. Association for Computational Linguistics.

Florian Schroff, Dmitry Kalenichenko, and James Philbin. 2015. FaceNet: A unified embedding for face recognition and clustering. In *2015 IEEE Conference on Computer Vision and Pattern Recognition (CVPR)*. IEEE.

Jidong Tao, Lei Chen, and Chong Min Lee. 2016. DNN Online with iVectors Acoustic Modeling and Doc2Vec Distributed Representations for Improving Automated Speech Scoring. In *Proc. Interspeech 2016*, pages 3117–3121.

Peter D Turney. 2001. Mining the web for synonyms: PMI-IR versus LSA on TOEFL. In *Machine Learning: ECML 2001: 12th European Conference on Machine Learning Freiburg, Germany, September 5–7, 2001 Proceedings 12*, pages 491–502. Springer.

Antti Virtanen, Jenna Kanerva, Rami Ilo, Jouni Luoma, Juhani Luotolahti, Tapio Salakoski, Filip Ginter, and Sampo Pyysalo. 2019. Multilingual is not enough: BERT for Finnish.

Changhan Wang, Morgane Riviere, Ann Lee, Anne Wu, Chaitanya Talnikar, Daniel Haziza, Mary Williamson, Juan Pino, and Emmanuel Dupoux. 2021a. VoxPopuli: A Large-Scale Multilingual Speech Corpus for Representation Learning, Semi-Supervised Learning and Interpretation. In *Proceedings of the 59th Annual Meeting of the Association for Computational Linguistics and the 11th International Joint Conference on Natural Language Processing*, volume 1, pages 993–1003. Association for Computational Linguistics.

Xinhao Wang, Keelan Evanini, Yao Qian, and Matthew Mulholland. 2021b. Automated Scoring of Spontaneous Speech from Young Learners of English Using Transformers. In *2021 IEEE Spoken Language Technology Workshop (SLT)*, pages 705–712.

Xinhao Wang, Klaus Zechner, and Christopher Hamill. 2020. Targeted Content Feedback in Spoken Language Learning and Assessment. In *INTERSPEECH*, pages 3850–3854.

Thomas Wolf, Lysandre Debut, Victor Sanh, Julien Chaumond, Clement Delangue, Anthony Moi, Pierric Cistac, Tim Rault, Rémi Louf, Morgan Funtowicz, Joe Davison, Sam Shleifer, Patrick von Platen, Clara Ma, Yacine Jernite, Julien Plu, Canwen Xu, Teven Le Scao, Sylvain Gugger, Mariama Drame, Quentin Lhoest, and Alexander M. Rush. 2020. Transformers: State-of-the-Art Natural Language Processing. In *Proceedings of the 2020 Conference on Empirical Methods in Natural Language Processing: System Demonstrations*, pages 38–45, Online. Association for Computational Linguistics.

Shasha Xie, Keelan Evanini, and Klaus Zechner. 2012. Exploring Content Features for Automated Speech Scoring. In *Proceedings of the 2012 Conference of the North American Chapter of the Association for Computational Linguistics: Human Language Technologies*, pages 103–111, Montréal, Canada. Association for Computational Linguistics.

Su-Youn Yoon and Chong Min Lee. 2019. Content modeling for automated oral proficiency scoring system. In *Proceedings of the Fourteenth Workshop on Innovative Use of NLP for Building Educational Applications*, pages 394–401, Florence, Italy. Association for Computational Linguistics.

Su-Youn Yoon, Anastassia Loukina, Chong Min Lee, Matthew Mulholland, Xinhao Wang, and Ikkyu Choi. 2018. Word-Embedding based Content Features for Automated Oral Proficiency Scoring. In *Proceedings of the Third Workshop on Semantic Deep Learning*, pages 12–22, Santa Fe, New Mexico. Association for Computational Linguistics.

Association for Computational Linguistics
209 N. Eighth Street
Stroudsburg, Pennsylvania 18360

ISBN 978-1-7138-9058-4

9 781713 890584

CURRAN ASSOCIATES INC.
proceedings.com